AF616795

# THE BIBLE AND THE TAROT

*BY CORINNE HELINE*

Seventh Printing, 1993

ISBN: 0-87516-443-9

DeVorss & Company, Publisher
P.O. Box 550
Marina del Rey, CA 90294

Printed in the United States of America

*Interpretation*

The interlaced triangles at the top of this diagram and the double triangle at its center symbolize the interaction of the three fold creative powers of God on the spiritual and on the material planes of being.

Deity expresses Itself as Will, Wisdom and Activity. In Christian terminology these three aspects of the triune God are known as the Father, Son and Holy Ghost.

In the mystical interpretation of the Hebrew alphabet is outlined the path of human evolution from clod to God.

Yod, the tenth letter of the Hebrew alphabet, represents the Divine creative power which is latent in all beings. It is for this reason that the letter Yod is found in some form within each and every one of the twenty-two Hebrew letters.

By the processes of spiritual evolution, man, made in the image and likeness of his Creator, is ultimately to attain to the state of Divine perfection. Such is the high and glorious destiny awaiting all humanity.

## ACKNOWLEDGMENTS

Grateful acknowledgment is hereby extended to Ann Barkhurst for her invaluable assistance in the compilation and edition of the material in this volume, and with special credit for her work on the Kabbalah.

The author is also deeply indebted to Gertrude Aye for her contribution in the chapter on the Correlations of the Sayings of Christ with the Tarot.

Also, to Elizabeth Hill, long-time faithful associate in all branches of the publishing activity of the Press, for the diagram and its interpretation which appears on the preceding page.

## CONTENTS

## PART I

*BASIC PRINCIPLES*

### Chapter I

LETTERS, NUMBERS, CIPHERS AND CODES . . . . . . . . 1
The Hebrew Letters as Cosmic Glyphs . . . . . . . . . . . . 5
The Vowels and the Seven Thunders . . . . . . . . . . . . 7
*Music and Color* . . . . . . . . . . . . . . . . . . . . . . . 7
The Physiological Interpretation of the Letters . . . . . . 10

### Chapter II

THE KABBALAH:
RELIGION FOR THE ASTRONOMER . . . . . . . . . . 14
A Vision of the Universe . . . . . . . . . . . . . . . . . . . . 14
The Ten Sephiroth . . . . . . . . . . . . . . . . . . . . . . . . 16
The Tree of Life . . . . . . . . . . . . . . . . . . . . . . . . . 18
*The Cosmic Christ Tree* . . . . . . . . . . . . . . . . . . 18
*The Tree as Caduceus* . . . . . . . . . . . . . . . . . . . 19
*The Tree as a Fountain* . . . . . . . . . . . . . . . . . . 20
*The Tree as the Temple of Solomon* . . . . . . . . . 22
*The Tree as the Fiery Chariot* . . . . . . . . . . . . . 25
*That Men May Find a Path* . . . . . . . . . . . . . . . 26

### Chapter III

THE SEVEN HOLY NAMES OF GOD
AND THE TETRAGRAMMATON . . . . . . . . . . . . . 31
The Seven Mighty Archangels Who Stand Before God . . . 36

### Chapter IV

THE LETTERS OF FLAME . . . . . . . . . . . . . . . . . . 40
Stars and the Alphabet . . . . . . . . . . . . . . . . . . . . . 40

The Masoretic Points . . . . . . . . . . . . . . . . . . . . . 42
The Rules of Philo Judeus . . . . . . . . . . . . . . . 47

## PART II

## *THE HEBREW ALPHABET*

A Series of Cosmic Glyphs

### Chapter V

THE FIRST SEPTENARY:
ALEPH THROUGH ZAIN . . . . . . . . . . . . . . . . . . 53
ALEPH . . . . . . . . . . . . . . . . . . . . . . . . . . . . . . . 53
BETH . . . . . . . . . . . . . . . . . . . . . . . . . . . . . . . . 56
GIMEL . . . . . . . . . . . . . . . . . . . . . . . . . . . . . . . 58
DALETH . . . . . . . . . . . . . . . . . . . . . . . . . . . . . . 61
HE . . . . . . . . . . . . . . . . . . . . . . . . . . . . . . . . . . 62
VAU . . . . . . . . . . . . . . . . . . . . . . . . . . . . . . . . . 64
ZAIN . . . . . . . . . . . . . . . . . . . . . . . . . . . . . . . . 66

### Chapter VI

THE SECOND SEPTENARY:
CHETH THROUGH NUN . . . . . . . . . . . . . . . . . . . 69
CHETH . . . . . . . . . . . . . . . . . . . . . . . . . . . . . . . 69
TETH . . . . . . . . . . . . . . . . . . . . . . . . . . . . . . . . 71
YOD . . . . . . . . . . . . . . . . . . . . . . . . . . . . . . . . . 77
KAPH . . . . . . . . . . . . . . . . . . . . . . . . . . . . . . . . 81
LAMED . . . . . . . . . . . . . . . . . . . . . . . . . . . . . . . 83
MEM . . . . . . . . . . . . . . . . . . . . . . . . . . . . . . . . . 85
NUN . . . . . . . . . . . . . . . . . . . . . . . . . . . . . . . . . 86

### Chapter VII

THE THIRD SEPTENARY:
SAMEKH THROUGH SCHIN . . . . . . . . . . . . . . 89
SAMEKH . . . . . . . . . . . . . . . . . . . . . . . . . . . . . . 89
AYIN . . . . . . . . . . . . . . . . . . . . . . . . . . . . . . . . 91

PHE . . . . . . . . . . . . . . . . . . . . . . . . . . . . 92
TZADDI . . . . . . . . . . . . . . . . . . . . . . . . . . 94
KOPH . . . . . . . . . . . . . . . . . . . . . . . . . . . 96
RESCH . . . . . . . . . . . . . . . . . . . . . . . . . . 101
SCHIN . . . . . . . . . . . . . . . . . . . . . . . . . . 102

Chapter VIII

THE TWENTY-SECOND LETTER: TAV OR TAU . . . . . 105
God Geometrizes . . . . . . . . . . . . . . . . . . . 105
The Point of Perfection . . . . . . . . . . . . . . . 114
The Superior Numbers . . . . . . . . . . . . . . . 115

Chapter IX

PARABLE OF THE LETTERS . . . . . . . . . . . . . . . 119

**PART III**

*A COMPARATIVE STUDY OF THE BIBLE AND THE TAROT*

Chapter X

TAROT ORIGINS . . . . . . . . . . . . . . . . . . . . . . 127

Chapter XI

THE FIRST SEPTENARY OF ARCANA . . . . . . . . . . . 132
ARCANE I: *The Magus* . . . . . . . . . . . . . . . . 132
ARCANE II: *The High Priestess* . . . . . . . . . . . 134
ARCANE III: *The Iris-Urania* . . . . . . . . . . . . 136
ARCANE IV: *The Cubic Stone* . . . . . . . . . . . . 138
ARCANE V: *The Master of the Arcanes* . . . . . . . . 140
ARCANE VI: *The Two Ways* . . . . . . . . . . . . . . 141
ARCANE VII: *The Chariot of Osiris* . . . . . . . . . . 142

Chapter XII

THE SECOND SEPTENARY OF ARCANA . . . . . . . . . . 145
ARCANE VIII: *The Balance and the Sword* . . . . . . 145
ARCANE IX: *The Veiled Lamp* . . . . . . . . . . . . . . . 148
ARCANE X: *The Sphinx* . . . . . . . . . . . . . . . . . . . 150
ARCANE XI: *The Maiden and the Lion* . . . . . . . . . 153
ARCANE XII: *The Sacrifice* . . . . . . . . . . . . . . . . 155
ARCANE XIII: *The Reaping Skeletons* . . . . . . . . . 157
ARCANE XIV: *The Two Urns* . . . . . . . . . . . . . . . 158

Chapter XIII

THE THIRD SEPTENARY OF ARCANA . . . . . . . . . . . . 161
ARCANE XV: *Typhon* . . . . . . . . . . . . . . . . . . . . 161
ARCANE XVI: *The Thunderstruck Tower* . . . . . . . . 163
ARCANE XVII: *The Star of the Magi* . . . . . . . . . 166
ARCANE XVIII: *The Twilight* . . . . . . . . . . . . . . 167
ARCANE XIX: *The Dazzling Light* . . . . . . . . . . . 168
ARCANE XX: *The Rising of the Dead* . . . . . . . . . 169
ARCANE XXI: *The Crown of the Magi* . . . . . . . . . 170

Chapter XIV

THE TWENTY-SECOND ARCANUM: THE FOOL . . . . . 173
ARCANE XXII: *The Fool* . . . . . . . . . . . . . . . . . . 173
Summary of Arcana . . . . . . . . . . . . . . . . . . . . . . 174

Chapter XV

SAYINGS OF CHRIST
CORRELATED WITH THE TAROT . . . . . . . . . . . 176

**PART IV**

*OUTLINE OF THE PATH*
*AS SYMBOLIZED IN THE HEBREW LETTERS,*
*THE 119TH PSALM AND THE TAROT*

## Chapter XVI

SONGS OF INITIATION
AND THEIR ALPHABETICAL KEYS . . . . . . . . . . . 185
Diagram: The Twenty-Two Hebrew Letters,
Numbers and Keywords . . . . . . . . . . . . . . . . . . 193
Resume: Numbers and Cycles . . . . . . . . . . . . . . . . . 195

## Chapter XVII

THE FIRST SEPTENARY,
ALEPH – ZAIN, VERSES 1 – 56 . . . . . . . . . . . . 197
ARCANE I: *Aleph* – A = 1, Verses 1 – 8 . . . . . . . . 197
Meditation for Aleph . . . . . . . . . . . . . . . . . 198
ARCANE II: *Beth* – B = 2,Verses 9 – 16 . . . . . . . 198
Meditation for Beth . . . . . . . . . . . . . . . . . . 200
ARCANE III: *Gimel* – G = 3, Verses 17 – 24 . . . . . 200
Meditation for Gimel . . . . . . . . . . . . . . . . . 201
ARCANE IV: *Daleth* – D = 4, Verses 25 – 32 . . . . . 202
Meditation for Daleth . . . . . . . . . . . . . . . . . 203
ARCANE V: *He* – E = 5, Verses 33 – 40 . . . . . . . . 203
Meditation for He . . . . . . . . . . . . . . . . . . . 205
ARCANE VI: *Vau* – U-V = 6, Verses 41 – 48 . . . . . 205
Meditation for Vau . . . . . . . . . . . . . . . . . . 207
ARCANE VII: *Zain* – Z = 7, Verses 49 – 56 . . . . . 208
Meditation for Zain . . . . . . . . . . . . . . . . . . 209

## Chapter XVIII

THE SECOND SEPTENARY,
CHETH – NUN, Verses 57 – 112 . . . . . . . . . . . . 211
ARCANE VIII: *Cheth* – C-H, H = 8, Verses 57 – 62 . 211
Meditation for Cheth . . . . . . . . . . . . . . . . . 213
ARCANE IX: *Teth* – T or TH = 9, Verses 63 – 72 . . 214
Meditation for Teth . . . . . . . . . . . . . . . . . . 215
ARCANE X: *Yod* – I, J or Y = 10, Verses 73 – 80 . . 217
Meditation for Yod . . . . . . . . . . . . . . . . . . 219
ARCANE XI: *Kaph* – K = 20, Verses 81 – 88 . . . . . 220
Meditation for Kaph . . . . . . . . . . . . . . . . . . 222
ARCANE XII: *Lamed* – L = 30, Verses 89 – 96 . . . 223
Meditation for Lamed . . . . . . . . . . . . . . . . . 225

ARCANE XIII: *Mem* – M = 40, Verses 97 – 104 . . . 226
Meditation for Mem . . . . . . . . . . . . . . . . . . . . 227
ARCANE XIV: *Nun* – N = 50, Verses 105 – 112 . . . 229
Meditation for Nun . . . . . . . . . . . . . . . . . . . . 232

Chapter XIX

THE THIRD SEPTENARY,
SAMEKH – SCHIN, VERSES 113 – 168 . . . . . . . . 233
ARCANE XV: *Samekh* – S = 60, Verses 113 – 120 . . 233
Meditation for Samekh . . . . . . . . . . . . . . . . . . 235
ARCANE XVI: *Ayin* – 0 = 70, Verses 121 – 128 . . . 237
Meditation for Ayin . . . . . . . . . . . . . . . . . . . . 239
ARCANE XVII: *Pe* – Pe = 80, Verses 129 – 136 . . . 241
Meditation for Pe . . . . . . . . . . . . . . . . . . . . . 243
ARCANE XVIII: *Tzaddi* – Tz = 90, Verses 137 – 144 245
Meditation for Tzaddi . . . . . . . . . . . . . . . . . . 248
ARCANE XIX: *Koph* – Q = 100, Verses 145 – 152 . . 249
Meditation for Koph . . . . . . . . . . . . . . . . . . . 250
*The Wedding Song of Wisdom* . . . . . . . . . . . . 250
ARCANE XX: *Resh* – R = 200, Verses 153-160 . . . . 253
Meditation for Resh . . . . . . . . . . . . . . . . . . . 256
ARCANE XXI: *Schin* – S = 300, Verses 161 – 168 . . 257
Meditation for Schin . . . . . . . . . . . . . . . . . . . 260

Chapter XX

THE TWENTY-SECOND LETTER,
TAU, VERSES 169 – 171 . . . . . . . . . . . . . . . . 261
ARCANE XXII: *Tau* – T = 400, Verses 169 – 176 . . 261
Meditation for Tau . . . . . . . . . . . . . . . . . . . . 263

# PART I

# BASIC PRINCIPLES

# PART I

## *BASIC PRINCIPLES*

## Chapter I

## LETTERS, NUMBERS, CIPHERS AND CODES

The letters of the Hebrew alphabet, twenty-two in number, are cosmic hieroglyphs of great spiritual significance and power.

Hebrews, Greeks, Romans–among others–used letters to indicate numbers, and therefore there are "kabbalistic" systems in all of these languages; but the Greek and Roman systems have not survived, and the Hebrew kabbalah alone has come down to modern times by way of Christian and Hebrew schools of esoteric Bible interpretation. Intricate ciphers have been created from the elements of letters and numbers in which to record mysteries for future generations. Three sets of symbols were chiefly used: *Gematria*, in which letters and numbers were interchanged and used as a cipher; *Notarikon*, similar to the Roman shorthand, in which initial or final letters of words in a sentence might be formed into a code word, or a sacred word or secret might be turned into a sentence; and *Temura*, by which hundreds of combinations and "permutations" of words, names and secret messages might be discovered in the Bible text through substitution. In this last category the "combinations of Tziruph" were especially popular from ancient times. These consisted of alphabetical ciphers in which one letter was substituted for another in about as many ways as there were letters in the alphabet. One of these ciphers, the atbash cipher, has been discovered worked into the Dead Sea Scrolls in at least one instance.

The word "kabbalah" is popularly used to designate all of these mystical codes and ciphers of esoteric Judaism by which occult mysteries are drawn from the text of the Hebrew-Christian Bible. "Kabbalah," however, is more than a mere secret code of letters and numbers. The term means "to receive" a "Secret Doctrine" or Teaching transmitted from Master to Disciple and also the mystical state of consciousness by which the mind of man is attuned to the Wisdom of God and becomes God-taught.

The Hebrew letters are used for numbers in this way: Aleph to Yod, the first ten letters, are written to signify the numbers 1 to 10. From Kaph, the eleventh letter, the numeration is by tens; instead of being written for the number 11, Kaph or K is written for 20. The letters follow in order from Kaph (K) to Koph or Quoph (Q), signifying the numbers from 20 to 100. The remaining three letters, like Quoph, are written for hundreds: R for 200, S for 300, and T for 400. The numeration is then taken by the five "Final" letters. These are the letters which have a different symbol when they fall at the end of a word. Beginning again with Kaph, K-final is 500, M-final is 600, N-final is 700, P-final is 800, and Tz-final is 900. For 1,000, throughout the Old Testament, a word is used which is read "Many," and which may also denote tribe or family. Sometimes Ayin (Oin) is ascribed to Zero.

The Greco-Egyptian mysteries of Thoth-Hermes were taken into the Hebrew kabbalah during the Greek Period, when Platonism and Pythagoreanism also were incorporated in a new form. So wide was this interchange that even the Druidic ciphers show Hebraic interactions as well as Greek, dating to a time when the Druids, like the Egyptians, were beginning to use the Greek letters in which to write their own language. Thus the various ciphers mingled, passed along from one Mystery School to another. Druid and Hebrew numerologies alike show Pythagorean influence because Pythagorean teachers had found their way to western Europe, including the British Isles, and Pythagoras himself was born and lived during the era when the Hebrews were gathering together their ancient documents in Babylon and in Jerusalem after the Exile. Pythagoras had, indeed, in his youth visited Mount Carmel, sacred to the memory of Elijah and his School of Prophets and it was at Babylon that he reached the crown and summit of wisdom, Iamblichus tells us. Abraham came from Ur of the Chaldees and was learned in the Babylonian wisdom; the Hebrews who were exiled in Babylon renewed their ancient knowledge and adopted anew the Aramaic spoken by their ancestors. Hence the Babylonian science and astral mysticism are discernible in both the Hebrew and Pythagorean systems, and Pythagorean teachers of the far west of Europe built a bridge which eventually united Christianity and Druidism. It is significant that Greek culture had taken roots in Gaul during and before the time that the Greek spirit of Athens was faltering and failing.

Pythagoras is credited with having discovered the correlation of numbers and musical vibrations and is called the creator of the modern musical scale. He taught that numbers are principles which have no age or beginning but have always existed as inherent powers of being in cosmic space. Numbers precede both tone and sound, which are *represented* by the written letters. Every one of the Hebrew letters has a numerical equivalent, and this is the basis of the system of Gematria in which numbers and letters are substituted to create a cipher concealing many profound meanings for the initiated. Similar principles have been applied to the English alphabet, based on the Arabic numbers from 1 to 10.

In this book, however, we confine our attention to the Hebrew alphabet and endeavor to show how it conceals and reveals certain ancient Mysteries which are otherwise lost to history. This is first intimated in the letter Kaph, which is the 11th of the 22 letters of the Hebrew alphabet, and in the Tarot by a maiden closing the mouth of a lion with her hand. In the zodiac Leo is the fifth sign and Virgo the sixth, their numbers 5 and 6 adding up to 11.

According to kabbalistic modes of interpretation, the number 22 amplifies, augments or completes the forces of 2 and 11, being the "double" of both of these numbers. It also amplifies and completes the forces of 1 (one). The numbers 11 and 22 are a summation of the influence of all the letters of the Hebrew alphabet considered as mystical powers.

Spiritually Virgo correlates with the feminine principle, Leo with the masculine. The feminine principle is termed "fallen," being dominated by the masculine on the physical plane; but in the alchemical processes of regeneration the feminine pole of spirit is brought into balance with the masculine, and equilibrium (11) is established, without and within.

The numbers 11 and 22 are, in a mystical sense, supernumeraries, for Ten (10) is the true basis of the Hebrew alphabet, and a profound mystery attaches to both numbers in the kabbalistic theosophy.

Tau, the Cross, is the last of the twenty-two letters of the Hebrew alphabet. The series terminates with the cross, Tau, not as a symbol of pain, tragedy and defeat but as an emblem of victory over limitation and the release of the spirit into new spheres of freedom. When the supreme Way-Shower carried the cross up Mount Calvary, a symbol of the incompleteness and duality of human consciousness, He was still abiding in the exalted state that had found expression in the words, "My yoke is easy and my burden is light."

The number 11 marks man's entrance into the new heaven and the new earth through the attainment of polarity or equilibrium, which is the consummation of the initiatory work upon the terrestrial planes. The number 22 marks the entrance into the realm of everlasting light and the state of celestial being. Eleven finishes all karmic causation and concludes all earthly pilgrimages. Twenty-two partakes of the waters of eternal life and self-conscious immortality. The Initiate henceforth returns into earth life only as a Brother of Compassion in times of human crisis to bring succor and release to souls in pain and bondage or to inaugurate and regulate new processes and set the keynote of new and higher evolutionary trends.

As the letter-numbers 11 and 22 convey the secret of the victory over the forces of materiality, so the Hebrew alphabet as a whole is constructed on a pattern which relates the 22 letters to the 7 planes of life in which man is evolving. The letters are grouped into three septenaries (3 x 7 = 21), with the 22nd standing alone. These septenaries embody all of the processes involved in the 3 steps or degrees leading to Initiation or self-mastery, which in Esoteric Masonry are designated as the Apprentice, the Fellowcraft and the Master of the Craft, and in Esoteric Christianity are designated the Neophyte, the Probationer and the Disciple. The symbol of both is the finished stone, which is a Cube that unfolds to become a Cross.

Again, the 22 letters are divided into groups of 3, 7 and 12. There are 3 mother letters, 7 doubles and 12 singles. The 3 mother letters are Aleph, Mem and Schin; the 7 doubles are Beth, Daleth, Kaph, Phe, Resh, Gimel and Tau; the 12 singles are He, Vau, Zain, Teth, Nun, Samekh, Ayin, Tsaddi, Heth, Yod, Quoph and Lamed.

When the letters are studied as numbers a further mystery unfolds, for the meaning of all things visible and invisible lies in Number. In the Bible, that most mystic of books, the numbers 1, 3, 7 and 12 occur repeatedly throughout, and considered from the numerological viewpoint the Bible mysteries are found to be based largely upon these numbers, which are ciphers of infinite and illimitable God-Power.

This arrangement of letters and numbers is an intimation of the profound cosmic significance of the Hebrew alphabet, both as a whole and in each one of its parts. It follows the numerical pattern of our immediate universe and the solar system in which our planet has its being.

## *THE HEBREW LETTERS AS COSMIC GLYPHS*

It is well and truly said that man's first Bible was the starry heavens. There we behold the twelve glorious zodiacal Hierarchies which surround the solar system to which Earth belongs. The planets and other bodies of this system are receiving centers through which forces emanating from the zodiacal Hierarchies are focused and do ordered work, as shown in the laws of evolution and the great world cycles in which civilizations rise and fall. The twelve celestial Hierarchies pour their powers upon and through the planets of our solar system to guide, strengthen and illumine the living beings thereon and are part of the forces we know as the Forces of Destiny.

The Sun, which is central to the planets, is the principal focus for the powers poured out by the zodiacal Hierarchies. It symbolizes the Holy Trinity relative to our system—Father, Son and Holy Ghost—that vast threefold Power of the cosmos which is reflected in the human being as Will, Wisdom and Activity principles of the Virgin Spirit or essential man; the trinity of force symbolically described as Fire, Water and Air (to which Earth is added to form the Quaternary). These are cosmic principles which fructify, nourish and sustain all things and which are aroused to a specialized action in the work of Initiation.

The threefold Power, or Solar Logos, correlates with the 3 mother letters of the Hebrew alphabet: Aleph (Fire), Mem (Water) and Schin (Air). In the same way the 12 constellations of the zodiac correlate with the 12 single letters, and the 7 planets with 7 double letters.

In terms of the planet Earth the 22 letters and their grouping into 3 mothers, 7 doubles, 12 singles and 3 septenaries, with final Tau omitted, embody the sevenfold mystery of the evolution of life, form and consciousness. Each letter, moreover, in and of itself, contains a sevenfold meaning, and in the following pages we shall touch briefly upon these.

Our primary aim is to provide a useful key-book for the biblical student and teacher. Since we confine our discussion to universally applicable principles, this key-book can serve equally well any creed or cult which accepts the Bible as the Book of Light – that Book which, in the words of the illumined seer, Max Heindel, was given to man "by the Recording Angels, who gave to each and all exactly what they need for their development. They are above mistakes, and if we seek the *light* we shall find it there."

The sevenfold meaning of the Hebrew letters include the numerological, the astrological, the physiological, the initiatory and the cosmic and their relation to tone and to color.

## *THE VOWELS AND THE SEVEN THUNDERS*

### *Music and Color*

Since the relationships of the Hebrew letters with sound and color are the least understood, we may say by way of introduction that the 3 mother letters (Aleph, Mem, Schin) represent the dominant, sub-dominant and tonic, or the 1-3-5 intervals of the diatonic scale. These three power ciphers signify also the three fundamental colors of the spectrum: blue, yellow and red (or in the kabbalistic reading, blue, green and red, with white given as a fourth color). The three basic colors symbolize the threefold being of spirit, mind and body; or spirit, soul and body. The 12 single letters correlate with the 12 tones of the chromatic scale, each of which is associated with a distinctive color. The 7 doubles correlate with the 7 tones of the scale and the 7 colors of the rainbow or color spectrum as commonly recognized; the 8th note of the scale completing one octave and beginning the next. Musicians are often very sensitive to the color emanations of music.

The Zohar states, "Darkness is a black fire, strong in color. There is a red fire, strong in visibility, a yellow fire, strong in shape, and a white fire, which includes all. Darkness is the strongest fire." The last refers to the heat waves which are not visible as light.

Again the Zohar states, "And I will look upon it (the rainbow) that I may remember the everlasting covenant: This means that God's desire is constantly for the bow and that he who is not visible therein will not enter into the presence of his Master. The inner meaning of the words, And I will look upon it, is to be found in the words, And set a mark upon the forehead (Ezekiel ix,4), so as to be clearly visible ..." This is assuredly so, but the rainbow that appears in the sky has a profound mystical significance.

"Do not expect the Messiah until the rainbow appears decked out in resplendant colors which will illumine the world... At present the bow appears in dull colors...but at that time it will appear in its full panoply of colors as a bride does for her husband."

And again, "The three colors are displayed in all who issue from the side of holiness.... And if you ponder the mystery of grades, you will find how the colors radiate to all sides until they enter through those twenty-seven mystic channels which are the sides of the door that stop up the abyss. All this is known to the adepts in mystic lore."

These passages, among others in the Zohar, attest to the clairvoyance of the sages who guarded the Secret Doctrine of Israel. "The three colors are displayed in all who issue from the side of holiness." These words show that the auric colors of angels and human beings had been observed and understood by the mystics of Israel.

Yet again the Zohar states "The firmament with its enclosed square contains the gamut of all the colors. Outstanding are four colors, each engraved with four translucent signs, both higher and lower. These when decomposed become twelve. They are green, red, white and sapphire, which is made up of all these colors.... This was the appearance of the likeness of the Glory of the Lord ... It is not permitted to gaze at the rainbow when it appears in the heavens, as that would be disrespectful to the Shekinah, the hues of the rainbow here below being a replica of the supernal splendor, which is not for man's gaze. The three primary colors and the one compounded of them are all one symbol and they all show themselves in the cloud. And above the firmament that was over their heads was the likeness of a throne, as the appearance of a sapphire stone."

There is no real contradiction in these passages. They show that not only were the kabbalists clairvoyant, but they were aware of the science of their times. They list both the additive and the subtractive primaries of the solar spectrum, in one of which green is a primary and in the other yellow. Black is the end result of the subtractive primaries; White is that of the additive. Sometimes Indigo is said to include all colors, or Purple. The subtractive (pigment) colors all tend toward Black when mingled together; the additive colors of light rays tend toward White when mingled together. Moreover, these kabbalists were aware of five extra colors not usually counted in the solar spectrum, of which the peach-blossom color mentioned by Goethe is one.

The Shekinah Glory consists of these colors as revealed to the spiritual vision, and the colors of the rainbow as we know them are but feeble replicas of the celestial colors.

* * *

The *vowels* are not listed in the Hebrew alphabet of 22 letters, although Aleph, the first letter, is really a vowel. They are the principle of vocalization, of speech and music as uttered by the human voice. The secret Name of God is not Jah, Jahveh, or Yahweh, or Elohim in any of its forms, or Adonai. It consists of the vowels which are placed and sung in a certain way and, when chanted by the ancient Temple choirs, were heard as a mighty thunder which shook the structure to its foundations. Only the modern pipe organ can achieve an equivalent effect to that of human voices chanting the vowels of the Great Name of God. In the Book of Revelation St. John refers to them as "the Seven Thunders" which uttered their voices. There are really more than the five vowels—a, e, i, o and u as familiarly known. In some systems they are enumerated as nine, ten or even more.

Demetrius, an Alexandrian philosopher who lived in the second century, wrote, "In Egypt the priests sing hymns to the gods by uttering the seven vowels in succession, the sound of which produces as strong a musical impression on their hearers as if flute and lyre were used." The study of the Hebrew letters shows us what those seven vowels represented: the Seven Spirits Before the Throne of God; but these Seven Spirits were named publicly only by the seven double letters.

Speech, no less than song, is impossible without vowel sounds. Just as the Hebrew letters, counted as 22, do not include the vowels, so also the early Greeks and Egyptians did not have vowels. Eventually the vowels were written down, but in the Temple Mysteries the true vowels were a secret handed from Master to disciple, and without personal instruction the meaning of the texts could not be understood except in a superficial way.

Ten basic vowel sounds are noted in modern Hebrew textbooks, for which there are fourteen vowel-points and signs. Accents also are used. Kabbalists sometimes ascribe the ten numbers to the ten vowel sounds.

The Zohar says, "What is this seed? It consists of the graven letters, the secret source of the Torah, which issued from the first point. That point showed...certain three vowel-points, *holem, shureq*, and *hireq*, which combined with one another and formed one entity, to wit, the Voice which issued through their union. When this Voice issued, there issued with it its mate, which comprises all the letters."

This mystery was not the sole possession of the Hebrews of history. It goes back to the very beginning of civilization in antediluvian Atlantis, and some form of the Mystic Word of Power is found in every known language, with the possible exception of very primitive tribes still existing today in a state of stone-age culture.

## *THE PHYSIOLOGICAL INTERPRETATION OF THE LETTERS*

Almost as obscure as the correlation with music and color is the physiological interpretation of the Hebrew letters. In this interpretation we have the kabbalistic correlation of the letters with the bodily form and organs of the Macrocosmic Man, Adam Kadmon, and with his reflection in the body of terrestrial man, Adam.

The seven double letters are so called because each one of

them possesses two sounds, one strong and the other weak, aspirated or unaspirated, representing the active and passive principles, and related to the planetary principle, which is dual. Each of the double letters represents one. of the Elohim, who are both god and goddess. The names of the seven double letters are:

*Beth*, the Mouth of Man
*Gimel*, the Hand in the act of taking
*Daleth*, the Bosom
*Kaph* or *Caph*, the Hand in the act of holding
*Phe* or *Pe*, the Tongue and back of the mouth
*Resh* or *Resth*, the Head
*Tau*, the Spine (among other interpretations)

Philosophically these stand for the seven "Opposites" as qualities: Life and its opposite, Death; Peace and its opposite, Strife; Knowledge and its opposite, Ignorance; Wealth and its opposite, Poverty; Grace and its opposite, Sin; Fruitfulness and its opposite, Sterility; Dominion and its opposite, Slavery. (Sepher Yetsirah.) They correspond to the six directions of space - East, West, North, South, Depth and Height, all sustained from the Central Point, which made the Seventh. When these seven double letters had been formed God made with them the seven planets, the seven days, and also the seven "gates" in man, which are the seven orifices of the human body, which are all really double.

The triangular bone of the lower spine, called the sacrum, had a very peculiar and important significance in all ancient kabbalism, which has not always been understood aright. This is the "bone" which was "immortal," around which the entire body was to be reconstructed in the Resurrection, and since this was taken literally and materially, many strange concepts flourished about it. Esotericists have their own interpretation, for this is the symbol of the Sacral Lotus, where the Fire-Force sleeps, and it is the force, not the sacrum-bone, which is the agent of immortality and spiritual resurrection in the deathless body of Adeptship.

The sacrum is the "os sacrum," or sacred bone, and it is mentioned many times in the Zohar. It connects with the pelvis in man. The pelvic girdle is a broad shallow basin which supports the viscera. The keystone of the girdle is the sacrum. It supports the backbone and locks the arch from behind. At birth the sacrum varies from four to seven vertebrae; these unite into one bone. Above the sacrum rises the vertebral column. The vertebral column or spine proper consists of the seven neck vertebrae called cervical, twelve thoracic vertebrae and five lumbar vertebrae, making twenty-four in all. Five round bones, about the size of peas, lie at the extreme lower end of the spine; these are the coccyx or tail bone. The human being has three more vertebrae than the animal, thirty-one instead of twenty-eight.

In Egypt the physicians had observed that there are seven neck-bones, and these were associated with the "Ladder of Osiris." Egyptologists have been considerably astonished to find that these neck-bones are also mysteriously associated with the sacrum, which is at the opposite end of the spine. The findings are not so astonishing as they seem, for the entire backbone is the Ladder of Osiris.

The twelve single letters refer to the twelve signs of the zodiac:

*He*—the Head—*Aries*
*Vau*—the Neck—*Taurus*
*Zain*—the Arms—*Gemini*
*Cheth* or *Heth*—the Breast—*Cancer*
*Teth*—the Heart—*Leo*
*Yod*—the Stomach—*Virgo*
*Lamed*—the Reins—*Libra*
*Nun*—the Generative Organs—*Scorpio*
*Samekh*—the Thighs—*Sagittarius*
*Ayin*—the Knees—*Capricorn*
*Quoph* or *Koph*—the Calves—*Aquarius*
*Tzaddi* or *Tsaddi*—the Feet—*Pisces*

Physiologically the three mother letters, Aleph, Mem and

Schin, are associated with the brain, as kabbalistically they derive from the highest Triad of Powers behind the Face of the Grand Man, Adam Kadmon, who is the Macrocosmic Adam. Unquestionably the ancient priest physicians knew that injury to the brain affected certain specific areas of the body, and so some kabbalists teach that these three mother letters govern the entire body. As the roots of Fire, Water and Air, they are the first outbreathings of the Divine Word which is made flesh in the manifested universe.

The mystic vowel sounds, which are unwritten, correlate to the tremendous powers which travel through the central canal of the spine and which resound in the seven ventricles of the brain, where they are visible to the spiritual vision as light and color. Phonetically they relate to the resonance chambers of mouth and face.

Aleph might perhaps be termed a consonant-vowel, for it is listed with the consonants yet it is a vowel, but like the other vowels its pronunciation varies and must be determined by tradition. The ancients realized that even the consonants could not be enunciated alone without some small portion of sound emanating from lungs and throat, and this is symbolized in Aleph. Ayin, or Oin, which is, like Aleph, called "silent," is ascribed to the vowel sound O as well as to Zero by some kabbalists.

## Chapter II

## THE KABBALAH: RELIGION FOR THE ASTRONOMER

### A VISION OF THE UNIVERSE

All of the concepts we have discussed thus far belong to the theosophical system known as Kabbalah in which the mysteries of the Hebrew alphabet are correlated with the several cosmic planes, or Worlds, as states of consciousness.* The Kabbalah is a vision of the universe as viewed clairvoyantly by seers and interpreted by means of the highest spiritual revelation of mystics and the intuition and reason of scientists and philosophers. The word itself means "to receive," or the oral or unwritten tradition transmitted "mouth to ear."

The Hebrew alphabet has two written forms, the Hebraic and the Aramaic. The Aramaic is called the "square letters" and the Hebrew the "triangular letters" from the way in which they were written. Aramaic and Hebrew are two dialects of the same ancient Semitic speech, to which Phoenician also belonged. Phoenician is termed Proto-Hebraic, and Hebrew is closely related to the Phoenician tongue. Hebrew is the western dialect while Aramaic is the eastern, belonging to Babylonia, Chaldea and Persia. Abraham spoke Aramaic in his native city, Ur of the Chaldees, but when he travelled west into Canaan he adopted the western dialect spoken there, the Amorite, which evolved into what we call Hebrew.

Meanwhile Persia rose to power and conquered Assyria, Babylonia, Phoenicia, Palestine and Egypt. The kings of Persia then made Aramaic the "lingua franca" for the entire section of

* The word Kabbalah is capitalized here as indicating a special theosophy, chiefly that of the Zohar.

the Persian Empire west of the Euphrates River, including Egypt. Aramaic was the speech of commerce throughout this area. In Babylon Ezra and his scribes began the work of collecting the Hebrew Scriptures and translating them into Aramaic, which in his time was becoming the common speech in Palestine; but Hebrew continued as the sacred language, treasured in the Mysteries, and was spoken as long as the nation endured. There are small differences between Hebrew and Aramaic, but these are differences of dialect since they are the same basic Semitic speech.

The fact that Aramaic was the "lingua franca" of the whole Persian Empire west of the Euphrates, spoken not only in Palestine but also in Phoenicia, Egypt, Babylonia and Persia explains why the kabbalistic names of the Archangels and other cosmic forces were so widely known in antiquity. The Book of Daniel shows this when it says that Gabriel is the "Prince" of Persia but Michael is the "Prince" of Israel. The differences in culture among these various nations speaking Aramaic more or less willingly account in part for the contradictions and discrepancies found in kabbalistic writings.

Since the ancient world knew of only seven planets, including the Sun and Moon, the 22 letters were arranged in the septenary divisions with the 22nd letter, Tau, standing alone at the end. Again we see the relationship with Phoenicia, for it was the Phoenician Cadmus who is said to have added the letter T to the alphabet, , and it was he who gave these "Cadmean" or "Kadmean" letters to the Greeks.

The Kabbalah, difficult and abtruse as its teachings seem at first to be, is readily understood against an astronomical background. The Babylonians spoke of a Tree of the Cosmos, in which the birds–planets and spirits–flew from branch to branch. Far back into Sumero-Akkadian times the basis of an astronomical religion, a religion of astronomers, was laid. The Annunaki, spirits of heaven, were not merely demons and elemental spirits but whole hierarchies of angels. The Egyptians spoke of *the Tree of the Gods in their Visible Forms* and an Ennead, or Nine Great Gods. In Babylonia the Tree was an ancient cedar or cypress or palm tree; in Egypt it was a sycamore, palm or acacia. Other nations named other trees according to size, vigor and healing properties. The silver fir is one of the most sacred. And so in the Kabbalah there is the great Cosmic Tree called the Tree of Life, as being the selfsame Tree which grew and still grows in Paradise.

## *THE TEN SEPHIROTH*

Ten cosmic Intelligences are mentioned in the Kabbalah, which are called Sephiroth. Each Intelligence taken singly is a Sephira. Biblically they are reminiscent of the Ten Commandments of Moses, but they are much more than that, for they are tremendous macrocosmic Forces, which collectively are God.

Kabbalists in the Greek Period correlated their spiritual revelations with the science of the Greeks, gathering their material from the schools of all nations; and so these Ten Sephiroth correlate with the ten spheres of Greek astronomy of which seven were those of planets, Sun and Moon; and three outer spheres which were those of the fixed stars, The Infinite and The Eternal. The Earth was "God's Footstool" or "The Hearthstone of the Universe." "The Infinite" related to Divine Mind, which ordered the revolutions of the lower spheres and was later given the name of Primum Mobile, the First Mover. Beyond this was the Empyrean, where Eternity abode incomprehensibly to mankind.

An "Invisible Sephira," Daath, is not shown on the kabbalistic diagram, but we may think of it as the Eleventh Sephira.

Kabbalists give as the home world of the Ten Sephiroth the "World of Emanations," which is the World of Spirit. They are called Emanations because the First Sephira emanates from God, the Second from the First, the Third from the Second and so out to the Tenth. But these Sephiroth are not distinct and separated from one another. The First Sephira is present throughout, for the other Sephiroth are really his unfoldings. He is named Metatron when personified in the rites, and he is "The Word" of St. John's Gospel or "The Spirit of the Cosmic Process" of Philo Judeus.

The Ten Sephiroth work through the Four Great Worlds called Atziluth, Briah, Yetsirah and Assiah, but these worlds are not divisions of the material universe. They correspond to the World of Spirit, World of Thought, World of Feeling and Desire, and finally to the physical universe in a special sense—the universe as God sees it.

All of the Ten Sephiroth appear in each one of the Four Worlds and seven planes. In *Atziluth* they appear in their own essence, as archetypal forces or Emanations, each with a God-Name. In *Briah* they appear as Archangels, each with a Name indicative of the work which he does. In *Yetsirah*, which is the World of Formation or Creation so-called, they appear as hosts of creative beings, popularly called "choirs of angels." One Sephira and One Archangel (the two are the same) are the ensouling Power of an entire choir of angels in this world. Seers compare these groups of angels to the twelve zones of the Grand Man of the Zodiac, ruled by the twelve signs. Finally, in the fourth World, *Assiah*, they manifest in the Four Elements and the innumerable hosts of living creatures which are found in the universe of space and time, every part of the physical world having its angelic counterpart or double in the World of Formations, Yetsirah. Human souls, the *Ishim*, also correlate to the divisions of the Divine Man.

The Sephiroth, as Archangels, are the same as the "Sirens" of the Greek philosophers, winged Spirits governing the ten Ptolemaic spheres, who carried the planets about in their courses and whose song constituted the music of the spheres. Later philosophers thought that the music of the spheres came from the motion of the spheres in their orbits, but the earlier mystics believed it was the Winged Spirit which sang and whose song was heard by the illumined mind.

St. John said, "God is light," and this is the basic principle of all kabbalism. Says the Kabbalah, "The Aged of the Aged, the Unknown of the Unknown, has a form and yet has no form.

He has a form whereby the universe is preserved and yet has no form because he cannot be comprehended. When he first assumed the form (of the first Sephira) he caused nine splendid lights to emanate from it, which shining through it diffused a bright light in all directions. Imagine an elevated light sending forth its rays in all directions. Now if we approach it to examine the rays, we understand no more than that they emanate from the said light. So is the Holy Aged an absolute light, but in himself concealed and incomprehensible. We can only comprehend him through those luminous emanations which, again, are partly visible and partly concealed. These constitute the sacred Name of God."

There are several substitute Names of God, consisting of three letters, four letters, seven letters, ten letters, twelve letters, thirty-two letters, forty-four letters and seventy-two letters. All of these names are substitute names and relate to the alphabetical correlation with the parts of the universe, seen and unseen. The Names are formed of the initial letters of formulas of cosmic principles or the initial letters of sentences which describe some deep Mystery of God. Some kabbalists relate ten vowel sounds to the Ten Sephiroth, as well as to the ten numbers.

## *THE TREE OF LIFE*

### *The Cosmic Christ Tree*

The Four Great Worlds are further subdivided into the seven planes familiar to all modern occultism. Within the seven planes stands the Tree of Life, the most important symbol of kabbalism; and in the Tree of Life are the "Birds" which fly to and fro on the branching pathways of the sky, which are the paths of evolution. Upon the Tree also is the Serpent, coiling among the branches–not a symbol of evil but of illumination, "the Lightning Flash."

When the student first gazes upon the kabbalistic diagram called the Tree of Life he may be puzzled to know why it is called a tree, for it consists of three upright pillars of which the central pillar is taller than the other two. The pillars are hung with circles, and these are joined by lines running this way and that. The glyph is really that of a Cosmic Christmas Tree. The circles and lines are ornaments hung upon and about the branches. A Babylonian diagram shows the sacred tree hung with ribbons and bows.

This diagram is a mnemonic device, designed by Initiates to guide the neophyte in meditation. The original diagram of the Tree must have been simply the Tree with its trunk and branches within which the great Tree Spirit dwelt, and together with it, under its protecting power, innumerable smaller spirits, and to these were added the Birds of the human species and the Serpent of Wisdom.

*The Tree as Caduceus*

The kabbalists beheld in their mysteries the likeness of the sacred Staff of Hermes, with serpents twined about it. Mercury was the messenger of the gods, and messengers from kings customarily carried a staff wound with ribbons showing their official status. However, the "ribbons" had another purpose. Secret messages were written lengthwise upon a strip of leather–perhaps snakeskin–wrapped around the staff, which were unreadable when unwound; the recipient then wound the strip upon a staff of the same dimension and read the message. The ribbons were later taken to be serpents, but this was an error, as the Greek myth indicates. Similarly, the ribbons on the Babylonian tree became the Serpent on the Tree of the Kabbalah, with its intricate paths hinting of a secret message. Again we note that the name Metatron, the highest Archangel, comes from the word Metator, "Messenger," "Outrider," or "Waymaker."

The Zohar says, ". . . the divine rod which was in Moses' hand. . . on which there was engraved the Ineffable Name radiating in various combinations of letters. These same letters were in possession of Bezalel who was called the Weaver." "Them hath He filled with wisdom of heart. . . of the craftsman and the skilled workman, and the weaver,. . ..” “So that rod had engraved on it the Ineffable Name on every side, in forty-two combinations, which were illumined in different colors.”

*The Tree as a Fountain*

Again the diagram of the Tree of Life is likened to a Fountain, which a tree resembles in its growth pattern; the roots being a shadow tree underground. The Fountain has a succession of basins, one below the other, the Water of Life and Wisdom overflowing (emanating) from the topmost and cascading from basin to basin to the lowest, which is the physical universe. The Water does not flow directly downward, however, but is led by channels in a zigzag descent, from left to right and from right to left, until it reaches the bottom. One thinks of the Persian goddess of the waters, Anahita, whose name points to Anu and Ana, the great God and Goddess of Heaven, and who survives biblically in the name Anna. The beautiful and glorious goddess Anahita plunged from mountain peaks, her rivers cascading through gorges and valleys to the sea. In Palestine the equivalent is the River Jordan with its serpentine windings.

All of the overflowings or “Emanations” are from within outward, expressing the concept of spiritual unfoldment from the highest spiritual state down to the physical world which, however, is not “lowest” but simply outermost. From this place the flowing of the waters must begin over again, returning to its source like the rivers which left their mountain summits and found their way to the ocean, whence again they rise under the powers of Fire and Air to repeat the cycle.

“The Mirror of the Wisdom of God” is one of the profoundly moving mysteries of the Kabbalah, pointing to man’s essential unity with God as Image and Likeness. Ancient peoples were as troubled by evil in the world as man is today, and so the wise men worked out this problem of the origin and nature of evil in terms of the Tree, on the allegory of Reflection and its manifold illusions. But they also recognized a True Image, which was not illusion but was Archetypal Man, an Idea in the ever-existing Divine Mind.

The student must think of the Tree of Life as growing by a lake of water in which it is reflected, while its roots, branching in the darkness underground, constitute another inverted Tree. The image cast upon the waters is inverted and also reversed in the fashion of mirror-images. Thus "right" and "left," positive and negative, masculine and feminine, bear a special relationip to each other, which is not the same as when one stands opposite another person, facing him. Two individuals facing one another have right and left reversed, so that to touch right hands they must reach diagonally across the body. Standing before a mirror image, however, one extends the right hand straight forward, and it meets the left hand of the image coming toward him, as it seems, in the glass or the water. This is the key to many secrets in kabbalistic writings, with left and right constantly confused. It is the explanation to the many misunderstandings of "clockwise" and "counterclockwise" interpretations of the kabbalistic diagrams and ciphers. One sees in it also a hint of the fact that Hebrew is written from right to left; even the horoscope is read right to left. Many ciphers are based on the various ways in which ancient people wrote thair alphabets.

In the "Mirror" we have the clue to the Hebrew doctrine of the illusion which creates seeming evil, and to the interpretation of the Tree of Life which has bewildered so many students. Another clue lies in the Invisible Sephirah, Daath, hidden in the Abyss of the Trinity and the Serpent of the lower abyss, under the roots of the Tree. Hebrew space consisted of the four cardinal directions, East, West, North and South, and to this they added "Up" and "Down" or Height and Depth. The four Great Archangels are the Throne Bearers, but Height and Depth are revealed in Daath and his reflected image in the lowest abyss.

The Invisible Sephira lies coiled in the abyss of the Trinity and is in fact its bridge or ladder. We *have* and *are* Wisdom and Understanding; we *know* that we are Wisdom and Understanding in Daath, the Invisible Sephira, whose name is *Knowledge*. Genesis shows us two Trees, that of Life and that of Knowledge.

The Kabbalah shows us one Tree, with its Reflection.

God as the Ocean of Wisdom and Becoming is described in the Kabbalah, "The Source of the sea's water and the water stream proceeding therefrom to spread itself *are two*. A great reservoir is then formed, just as if a huge hollow had been dug; this reservoir is called *sea*, and is the third. The unfathomable deep divides itself into *seven streams*, resembling seven long vessels. The source, the water stream, the sea and the seven streams, make together *ten*. And when the master breaks the vessels which he has made, the waters return to the source, and then there remains only the pieces of these vessels, dried up and without any water. It is in this way that the Cause of Causes gave rise to the Ten Sephiroth."

"The Crown (Kether) is the source from which streams forth an infinite light, hence the name En Soph, the Infinite. . . He then made a vessel as small as a point, Yod, which is filled from this Source, which is Wisdom itself. . . Upon this he made a large vessel like a sea, which is called Intelligence. . . but God need only withdraw Himself and it would dry up. . The sea is finally divided into seven streams called Greatness, Judicial Strength, Beauty, Firmness, Splendor, Foundation and Kingdom."

The student of Esoteric Masonry will find in this analogy a clue to the meaning of the work done by Hiram Abiff, the Master Workman of Solomon's Temple.

### *The Tree As the Temple of Solomon*

Again the Tree is likened to a Temple, and in Esoteric Masonry the Three Pillars, the triangles, lines and circles derive from architecture, which in kabbalism refers to the Temple of Solomon in its three historic phases: the First Temple, that of Solomon; the Second Temple, that of Zerubbabel; and the Third Temple, that of Herod, which was simply the Temple of Zerubbabel rebuilt, with Greek modifications and ornamentations. Herod restored it course by course, without interrupting the services at any time. As in Zerubbabel's Temple, priest-masons did the work in the Temple proper. The old

Temple literally melted into the new or Herodian Temple, stone by stone, which took its place. Not a stone was lost.

Solomon's Temple also included as adjuncts the palaces and courts of justice, and a military force which was the prototype of the medieval Templars who enforced the law and guarded the temporal and sacred edifices. The Temple itself was the State Church or Royal Chapel. Those who say that Masonry is the relic of the Order of Templars of the Middle Ages fail to see that the Templars were only one part of the working organism which was Solomon's Temple.

The diagram of the Tree of Life sums up all aspects of Solomon's Temple, its environs; its walls, chambers, gates, caves, vaults, storehouses, passages above and below ground, winding stairways, tower and observatory; its furniture, veils and ornamentation; its priests, servitors and sacrifices; outer and inner courts and porches.

Sometimes the Tree is likened to a pyramid, reminiscent of the tradition that Solomon's Temple was really built like the towers of Babylon in seven stages, or like that of Ur in three stages, as suggested by the several Triads of triangles on the Tree, with Kether as the point of the pyramid. Or it may have included a tower on the place where later the Tower Antonia stood as a fortress, with the Temple proper near it, as in some of the Babylonian Temple areas. In either case the Temple rooms themselves had a special meaning.

The Holy of Holies was the west room and innermost chamber, entered by the Hight Priest once each year at the Feast of the Atonement. Its furniture consisted of the Ark of the Covenant overshadowed by Cherubim above the Mercy Seat which was on the Ark; the Ark containing the Tablets of the Law, the Pot of Manna, Aaron's Rod that Budded and for many centuries the Brazen Serpent of Moses. These sacred articles were lost in the course of time, and the Holy of Holies was empty at the last.

The Holy Place was the east room of the Temple, separated from the Holy of Holies by a wall or curtain. In this room were the Seven-branched Candlestick, the Table of Shewbread with twelve loaves, the Altar of Incense and accessories and the walls ornamented with palms and pomegranates and other mystic symbols.

Before the entrance of the Temple stood the two pillars, Jachin and Boaz, and supporting the Holy of Holies but invisible to the multitude was the Third Pillar, sacred to the Mysteries of Israel and hinting of the Brazen Serpent of Moses which had been upraised on a Tau cross in the wilderness for the healing of the people.

The third pillar is Man himself, macrocosmic and microcosmic, the central pillar on the diagram of the Tree of Life. It is the Pillar of Enoch, the Initiated One, upon which at a particular time certain Wise Ones inscribed a Secret Word or Name which, written vertically in Hebrew letters, would describe the form of a man with Jod as the head and He-Vau-He as the body. This man is a divine androgyne, as shown in the arrangement Jah-Hawwa, Father-Mother God: J and E-V-E. Of this Mystery the neophyte may say, I AM THAT. Since in fact there are only three letters in the Sacred Name, *He* being repeated, the Triangle is also sacred to the Lost Word and is used in art as the symbol of the Trinity, being shown on the Tree of Life as the succession of Triads.

In the Christian Mysteries the Third Pillar relates to the Christ Sacrifice, the incarnation of the supreme Archangel, and the raising of Hiram Abiff in the person of Lazarus, who is also St. John. In the orders of architecture it is the Child, as Jachin and Boaz are Father and Mother.

The Temple structure with its two rooms stood within the Priest's Court, which held the Brazen Laver and Altar of Burnt Offerings, together with their numerous conduits of flowing water and, according to legend, a great fountain gushing forth from a subterranean spring. Beyond the Priests' Court was the Court of the Israelites, one part for men and one for women; and on all sides of the Court of the Israelites was the extreme outer Court or Court of the Gentiles. Gentiles, even converts, could not pass into the Court of the Israelites on pain of death. The famous "Porches" ran along the outside of the Court of

Gentiles. The military tower called Antonia in Roman times overlooked the whole area.

### *The Tree as a Fiery Chariot*

Again the Tree is likened to a Chariot of Fire, the chariot of Elijah wherein the prophet was caught up into heaven without passing through death. Note that the Ark of the Covenant was supported on two staves passed through rings when it was carried in the migration of the tribes from Egypt to the Holy Land, and so we may truly state that the Ark was also a Chariot. The diagram of the Tree in fact resembles a Chariot more than a Tree, and here we have the explanation of the many mystic visions of a "Chariot of Angels" wherein the soul is wafted to heaven. We are reminded also of the Cherubim which the Bible says were the chariot of Jehovah, wherein God rode when He "bowed the heavens and came down." It was their wings which overshadowed the Mercy Seat in the Holy of Holies over the Ark. There God appeared to the High Priest once each year at the Feast of Atonement as Light and as an Archangel.

Popular religions everywhere depict the human soul as always in the care of angels, protecting deities, guardian gods and goddesses. So also the Kabbalah says every human being has his guardian angel who cares for him in life and at death conducts him to his place in paradise.

The Initiate knows the Fiery Chariot in a special sense, as intimated in the story of Simeon ben Jochai, who had been condemned to death by Titus and spent twelve years in hiding in a cavern in Galilee where he wrote his great book on kabbalistic Mysteries. There he was visited by Elijah, the Hierophant of Esoteric Judaism, and there he taught his son and disciples. He passed out of the body while still discoursing on the holy doctrine, and immediately a dazzling light filled the dark cavern, whilst another light appeared at its entrance. At last the two lights disappeared and then the disciples knew that the "lamp of Israel was extinguished." When his body was being carried to the burial place, the coffin seemed to be enwrapped with vivid flame, and a flame went on before; and as the coffin was laid in the tomb a voice from heaven cried, "This is he who caused the earth to quake and the kingdoms to shake!"

Afterward his son and disciples collected his writings on the Secret Doctrine of Israel so that it might be preserved for posterity, as it had formerly been preserved by Adam who had received it from angels, who had received it from God when they formed a theosophical academy in Paradise. These angels again taught the Kabbalah to the children of Adam so that they might find the way back once more to their Source. Hence the Kabbalah is "that which is received," from the Hebrew word meaning "to receive" the secret or oral tradition.

The universe proceeds from a Trinity of Flame and "whoso wishes to have an insight into the sacred unity, let him consider a flame rising from a burning coal or a burning lamp. He will see first a twofold light, a bright white (yellow) and a black (or blue) light; the white light is above and ascends in a direct line, whilst the blue or dark light is below and seems as the chair of the former, yet both are so intimately connected with the burning matter which is under it again. The white light never changes in color; it always remains white, but various shades are observed in the lower light, whilst the lowest light, moreover, takes two directions—above it is connected with the white light and below with the burning matter. Now this is constantly consuming itself and perpetually ascends to the upper light, and thus everything merges into a single unity. . . . The creation, or universe, is simply the garment of God woven from the Deity's own substance." Therefore, "When the Concealed of all the Concealed wanted to reveal Himself He first made a point (the First Sephira), shaped it into a sacred form (the totality of Sephiroth) and covered it with a rich and splendid garment that is the world."

### *That Men May Find a Path*

We have seen that there are ten circles hung upon the Tree

of Life which are connected by "pathways." The ten circles are the ten stations of the Ten Sephiroth on the Cosmic Tree; they are connected by 22 Paths, making 32 paths in all. These are paths for meditation. The Central Pillar is called the Path of the Arrow, for it goes straight to Godhead. Upon it are hung the stations of the luminaries, the Sun and Moon, with the White Glory of Kether on the apex and the subterranean fire of Sandalphon and Malkuth at the base.

Although the Secret Doctrine was taught by the angels in Paradise in the very beginning of time, it passed through human intermediaries from age to age in the world. Adam brought it out of Eden and gave it to Seth; from Seth it passed through the patriarchal lines to Enoch, and from Enoch to Noah who preserved it through the Flood. The Angel of the Presence again revealed it to Moses on Mt. Sinai, who handed it down to the Seventy-Two Elders, or Princes, of Israel. The fact that there were 72 Elders suggests a division of each of the twelve signs of the zodiac into six parts, instead of the three decans usual with modern astrology. Later the Sons of Levi took the documents in charge, for it was Ithamar, the son of Levi, who was the first to write down the Doctrine of Moses. Levites and scribes had them in their care thenceforward. They protected the secret books through the historical period in Palestine; and during the Exile in Babylon Ezra, the Scribe of the Most High, again collected all of the sacred books together, "so that men may find a Path."

The Essenes and early Christians called themselves "Followers of the Way" or Path, and John the Baptist, like his Essene comrades, declared that he had come to make plain a Way or Path in the wilderness.

The basic number of kabbalistic Paths are the 10 Sephirothic stations on the Tree plus 22, the number of the letters of the alphabet, or 32 Paths. To this are added the 72 Paths which represent the 72 Princes of Israel who *received* the Doctrine from Moses on Mt. Sinai. The Sanhedrin or Council of the Hebrew nation consisted of 70, 71, or 72 members drawn from all the tribes.

As the number 11 points to a special Mystery we observe

again that it relates to the Invisible Sephira, which is the Mystery of Mysteries for souls in incarnation. Jod or Yod is the 10th letter; Kaph, the 11th, points to the Eleventh Sephira whose name is Daath, while 22 points to the Cross-Cube.

The Path of Daath is not described, but the mystic views it as arching over the Abyss of the Trinity and reflected in the dark waters of the nether abyss.

The 22 letters belonging to the 22 Paths which connect the ten Stations begin with Aleph, Beth and Gimel; but of these three letters only Aleph–a mother letter–penetrates through to Kether, which is the Glory Crown of the Central Pillar. In the Triad of Kether the three mother letters have their roots. The Triad or Trinity of Kether include Hokhmah (Wisdom) and Binah (Understanding). These are often said to rule the zodiac and the sphere of Saturn; but there are different arrangements. In his Divine Comedy Dante places Saturn below the Abyss of the Trinity, not above it. Hokhmah and Binah symbolize Father-Mother God. Kether, on the central pillar, represents the central equilibrating force, which harmonizes the two and makes them one. Behind Kether lies the Unmanifest, the Boundless Light of Infinity and the Cosmic Primordial Light.

Aleph, the first letter, leads the pilgrimage of flames, descending from the Inscrutable Height of Kether. It is the only vowel in the alphabet of 22 letters.

As there are Ten Sephiroth, there are three Triads or Trinities hung upon the Tree of Life, and the Sephiroth of the Central Pillar are the harmonizing Force for them all. The second Triad is that of Jupiter, Mars and the Sun–Chesed, Geburah and Tiphareth meaning Mercy or Love, Strength or Severity, and Beauty. Tiphareth is the harmonizing power of the central pillar. The third Triad is that of Mercury, Venus and the Moon, with the Moon as the power of the central pillar. Their names are Hod, Netzach and Yesod, meaning Glory, Victory and Foundation, the Moon, Yesod, being the equilibrating power of the central pillar for Mercury and Venus.

The Earth is the bottommost, and its Kingdom is Malkuth, whose Archangel is Sandalphon. Kabbalists are not in agreement about the various Names of Archangels and their rulership of the planets; but we follow in this study the listing as given by Max Heindel, although Mr. Heindel does not state the Name of the Archangel of the Earth, and we have therefore used the name Sandalphon as given by kabbalists. Sandalphon is also spelled Synandelphon. Samael is the Angel of Wrath and Satanael is the Angel of Bitterness and Despair, the two Principles of the Hell Consciousness which belong to the nether abyss and are not shown on the Tree.

The Book of Jubilees correlates the 22 letters of the Hebrew alphabet with the Six Days of Creation, as given in Genesis. According to this Book it was the Angel of the Presence (Michael) who enlightened Moses on Mt. Sinai, revealing to him how on the First Day God created the heavens and the earth and the waters and all the spirits which serve Him—the Angels of the Presence, the Angels of Sanctification, the Angels of the spirit of fire and winds and clouds—followed by other works on each of the succeeding days until at the end of six days He had completed 22 works, including the creation of mankind. On the Sabbath God rested. There are strong similarities here to the Sepher Yetzirah, Simeon's "Book of Creation" or Formations.

"Male and female created He them," is the constant refrain, and this is again shown in the kabbalistic Mysteries, with the positive and negative Powers balanced by the Power of the Central Pillar. The Kabbalah postulates two Principles in nature, masculine and feminine in essence, represented in the Two Pillars to left and right on the Tree diagram.

These are the two Powers or Principles, Father-Mother God, Jah-Hawwah, in separation; but united they are inscribed upon the Central Pillar and crowned with the Crown of Kether. Thus inscribed they represent the Son of God the Alone Begotten, the Cosmic Christ or Metatron whom Philo Judeus termed "the Spirit of the Cosmic Process" because it is He who unfolds Himself in all of the succeeding Emanations. He is "that Word" which was "in the beginning with God, and without whom was not anything made that was made."

The first three letters, Aleph, Beth and Gimel, lead the

procession of Letters, but it is only the three mother letters, Aleph, Mem and Shin—the "spirits of fire, wind and cloud" of Jubilees—which have a place in the Supernal Triad, the triune Word as it proceeds from the Mouth of God, in Breath, Heat and Sound, which the consonants form into syllables.

As each of the Sephiroth has its Archangel, so each of the twelve tribes of Israel was ruled by an Archangelic Prince, while the nation as a whole was ruled by Michael, "who is like God." The Temple at Jerusalem was the central focus for the twelve tribes, as the Sun is the focus for the powers of the zodiac. The Earth was not called a planet by the ancients but is represented by Malkuth and its Archangel Sandalphon; modern kabbalists must make a place for Uranus, Neptune and Pluto, but the three aspects of God behind the First Triad allowed for three extra principles, with Daath, "the invisible Sephiroth," ruling the Abyss of the Trinity.

Each Planetary Spirit is both god and goddess, represented by one of the double letters of the Hebrew alphabet. Each Planetary Spirit is in the likeness of Father-Mother God, Jah-Hawwah. Five planets only were known to ancient astronomers, and each planet ruled two signs of the Zodiac. The Sun ruled one sign, Leo, and the Moon ruled one, Cancer. Together the two luminaries represented the deific Principle, Light, "God is Light." The Hebrew names for the planets are:

Saturn, *Shabbatai,* rules Capricorn and Aquarius
Jupiter, *Tzedek,* rules Sagittarius and Pisces
Mars, *Modim,* rules Aries and Scorpio
Venus, *Nogah,* rules Taurus and Libra
Mercury, *Kokab ("The Star"),* rules Gemini and Virgo
Moon, *Savanah,* rules Cancer
Sun, *Shemesh,* rules Leo

The Hebrew name for the zodiac is *Mazzloth.*

## Chapter III

# THE SEVEN HOLY NAMES OF GOD
# AND THE TETRAGRAMMATON

The Seven Names of God, which are the names of seven Cosmic Principles or aspects of Godhead, are:

1. *El*
2. *Eloha*
3. *Elohim*
4. *Yahweh-Tsabbath*
5. *Elohim-Tsabbath*
6. *Shaddai*
7. *Adonai*

Two separate deific Principles are shown in this list. One is represented in the names derived from EL, meaning God, the other from the sacred Four Letters or Tetragrammaton, JHVH or YHWH. Above these seven Names are the three Names of the primordial Deity: Eheieh (I Am That), pure Being; Yahweh (standing alone), representing Yah-Hawwah, Father-Mother God; and Yahweh-Elohim, in combination, meaning Lord-God. The latter combination is also given as YaEl (Joel or Jael), translated Lord-God. The same Root Name becomes the Allah of the Arabs, for Arabic is also a language related to Hebrew.

In the English Bible the word Elohim is usually translated *God* or *the gods*, while the Tetragrammaton is translated *Lord* which is the meaning of the word Adonai, seventh in the above list. In oral readings from Scripture the Hebrews always substituted the name Adonai for the sacred Names, and the scholars who translated the Bible into English extended the practice, translating both Elohim and Jahveh or Yahweh as "Lord" in some instances. Generally, however, when we read the word God in our English Bibles, this is a translation of Elohim, while Lord is the translation of Yahweh. Scholars say that the word Jehovah was not known in ancient times, but the name Jahveh or Yahweh has been found by archeologists inscribed on potsherds and stones and in some ancient texts. The name Jehovah was created by translators who used the vowel-points of Adonai together with the Four Letters. It was unknown to Jesus and the Apostles.

The Sacred Name was spoken by the High Priest in the Temple and chanted by the choir, but it was also known to the King and to his "Architect"; but this Name is no more Yahweh than it was Jehovah. It is a "great" or "secret" Name, not a "small" or "public" name. Dr. William Albright, the noted biblical archeologist, suggests that the letters of this Name are really the initial letters of a secret liturgical sentence or group of words. The original Name was lost; but in the Christian Mysteries it was "found" once more, restored to mankind in the person of Jesus of Nazareth, who is the Living Word. The same is true of "Everyman," in whose figure the Four Letters are revealed, from *Jod* (Yod) in the head, *He* in the breast and arms, *Vau* in the torso, and *He* repeated in the pelvis and legs. Hence the esoteric mantram of Exodus, "I AM THAT I AM," the Name-Sound of God Transcendant and also Immanent, whose Voice is Seven Thunders.

The "Lost Word" consists of the primordial Thunder Sounds shaped by the Sacred Four Consonants into syllables of meaning. Their mystery is revealed in Hiram Abiff in the Old Testament and in Lazarus, St. John and the Christ in the New. Yet to our day the Word remains unspoken in the world at large, for as Philo said, "The Four Letters may be mentioned or heard only by holy men whose ears and tongues are purified by wisdom, and by no others in any place whatever." The Four Letters sound the Name of Father-Mother God: J (Jah or Yah) and H-V-H (Heva or Eve, He-Vau-He), with Man as Image and

Likeness.

The mysterious word "Amen" which appears repeatedly in Scripture and which is taken to mean "So be it," or to express thanksgiving to God at the end of a prayer or invocation, is said by kabbalists to consist of the initial letters of four Hebrew words, "Ateh gibur leolam Adonai," which mean "The Lord ever powerful." Kabbalists also interpret the sacred Four Letters as related to four words; but the name Yahwe or Yahweh, or Jah, found on inscriptions by archeologists, may also be interpreted in the same way. As we have mentioned previously, the vowels were kept as a sacred mystery in the Temple, and chanted in a certain way were thought to bring down the mighty powers of the heavens. These vowels were the magic chant, but when associated with consonants they formed a Name or Word that could be written and spoken. The sentence for which the letters of the name Jehovah, or Yahweh, stood, has been lost, but it is significant that the sacred forty-two letter name really consisted of several names which were written together. These names were Aheie Asher Aheie (I Am That I Am), Jah, Jehuiah, Al, Elohim, Jehovah, Tzabaoth, Al Chai and Adonai. (*Aheie*: see also *Eheieh* below.)

Concerning the name Elohim, Max Heindel writes in *The Rosicrucian Cosmo-Conception,* "The first part of the word is *Eloh,* which is a feminine noun, the letter *h* indicating the gender. If a single feminine Being were meant, the word *Eloh* would have been used. The feminine plural is *oth,* so if the intention had been to indicate a number of gods of the feminine gender, the correct word to use would have been *Elooth.* Instead of either of these forms, however, we find the masculine plural ending *im* added to the feminine noun *Eloh,* indicating a host of male-female, double-sexed Beings, expressions of the dual, positive-negative creative energy."

The addition of the word Tsabbath to Jahveh denotes Jahveh (or Yahweh) as "Lord" of the hosts of heaven, the angelic Hierarchies, and its addition to Elohim denotes "God" or "King" of the hosts of stars and elemental forces in Nature. The two titles refer to two aspects of the One Supreme Being and

His reflection in the stars, Sun, Moon, planets and forces inherent in matter and their spiritual counterparts.

The word Shaddai is most often used in the term El Shaddai, translated The Almighty or Almighty God, which Egyptologists say has an equivalent letter for letter in Egyptian. Adonai, as we have said, is used as a substitute word for both Jahveh and Elohim. Since the word *Adoni* means "master, lord or prince," the Hebrew sacred word Adonai is translated into English also as "Lord." Adonai was a name most especially associated with the glorious Sun and with its representative to the Hebrew nation, Michael the Archangel.

God as Trinity is expressed in the Names denoting the divine consciousness in the World of Emanations, the kabbalistic Archetypal World, which is the World of Pure Spirit or World of God, where Metatron stands alone. Their Names have been given as I AM THAT I AM (Eheieh, from which the Four Letters also derive), YAHWEH (Lord), and YAHWEH ELOHIM (Lord God). It is these who direct the Seven. Together we have then the Ten Elohim corresponding to the ten spheres of the Ptolemaic universe, which is the basis of the kabbalistic system and all other ancient astronomical theosophies. Kabbalism is thought to be of medieval origin (c. 1000 A. D.), but scholars forget that the Hebrew mystics were in touch with Greek learning not only in the early centuries of our era but before it. The medieval kabbalists were perhaps not the first of their kind to call Aristotle a Prophet of God.

In addition to these primary Names and Titles, there were other Names which were elaborated by the kabbalists of lesser sanctity, consisting of combinations of letters representing certain concepts, principles and powers; these divine Names were also "Paths."

The term *Shem-Ha-Mephorash* is properly ascribed to but one sacred name, Maimonides. Said he, "We have one divine name only, which is not derived from His attributes, viz., the Tetragrammaton, for which reason it is called Shem-Ha-Mephorash. Believe nothing else, and give no credence to the nonsense of the writers of charms and amulets . . . about the divine names which they invent without any sense, calling them appellations of the Deity and affirming that they require holiness and purity and perform miracles. All these things are fables; a sensible man will not listen to them, much less believe in them."

Some kabbalists call the sacred name of forty-two letters the Shem-Ha-Mephorash, some give that title to the seventy-two letter name. It is pointed out by scholars that the forty-two letter name consists of the names of the Ten Sephiroth run together, with the Vav conjunctive inserted before the name of the last Sephira.

However, the kabbalistic use of verses 19, 20 and 21 of Exodus XIV is of interest to every student, by which the "Ladder of Jacob," consisting of seventy-two names of angels, is found. The method seems fanciful, yet the results can scarcely be the result of coincidence. The letters of verse 19 were first taken (in the Hebrew) and written down separately, as letters, not words. Verse 20 was then taken as letters and written in reverse order directly under verse 19; after this verse 21 was taken, again in separated letters, and written under verse 20, but in direct order like verse 19. Read from above this yielded seventy-two names, each having three letters. The kabbalist next added AL and TH to these names, and the names of seventy-two angels stood revealed. These names, collectively, are God. So, also, the names of the Sephiroth collectively are God.

These three verses of Exodus undoubtedly contain some very ancient cipher or code in this arrangement of letters. We have seen that there were perhaps seventy-two divisions of the Hebrew astronomical system, instead of the thirty-six decans used today, and that there were as many "princes" or leaders of the twelve tribes, six to each tribe, who came together for the national councils. To the seventy-two Elders Moses also gave the secret Teaching, which he had received from God on Mount Sinai, and which was the source of the kabbalistic tradition for the new Hebrew nation. The names cannot be attributed to Abraham in this case, except that the prophecy of God to him was that his seed should be "as the stars of heaven," and the tribes are organized on an astronomical pattern after the time of Jacob, from whom came the Twelve Patriarchs who are founders of the Twelve Tribes.

*THE SEVEN MIGHTY ARCHANGELS WHO STAND BEFORE GOD*

In Bible theosophy certain Archangels are mentioned who are called "Princes of the People." These Archangels are race spirits who work under the God of all races, termed Jehovah-God. They are stragglers from their own life wave, who are regaining their lost status by serving the humanity of the planet Earth. They come from the Sun, and their work is described in their names. Each of these "Princes" is the focus of one of the solar and planetary rays or forces. In modern astronomy we do not call the Moon a planet, but the ancients did so; hence Gabriel, the lunar Prince, is also called an Archangel with the others, although the Moon is really the ruler of the lower, angelic, life wave.

The Planetary Spirits or Logoi are called Archangels, but they are not race spirits. They are the living Intelligence which indwells the planets of our solar system. The Earth Spirit is not named in the lists of Planetary Archangels, for the Moon is given in its place. The Earth Spirit is a great mystery, concerned with the very deepest aspect of the Christ Work for our solar system. Kabbalistically it is the sphere of Malkuth, whose Archangel is Sandalphon.

Each of the Seven Planetary Spirits, working in the three lower planes of Nature, has power over one of the seven days of the week; that is, one day each week is marked strongly by a particular archangelic Ray or power. We note that the names of the Archangels all end in "El," meaning God, while the rest of the archangelic Name describes his nature and function.

*Sunday . . . Michael,* the Sun, "Who is like God?"—a statement, not a question. Sometimes called the Splendor of God, Michael is fittingly representative of the solar orb. The race spirit Michael, who is the tutelary deity of the Hebrew nation, stands to them in the place of God, and so do the other race gods stand in the place of God to their people.

*Monday* . . . *Gabriel,* the Moon. There is both an Angel and an Archangel of the Moon. The Angel Gabriel is called the Revealer. His name means "The Man of God." It is he who announced to Mary the coming of the Christ Child. The lunar angels have charge of all generation and birth under the aegis of Jehovah-God, the God of all races. Gabriel is the giver of the man-child.

*Tuesday* . . . *Samael,* the planet Mars. His name means "Venom of God," or "Severity of God," indicating his function as angel of purgatory and bringer of death, as Gabriel is bringer of birth. Khamael is sometimes given as the name of the Mars Archangel, a name which refers to the heat or fire supposedly characteristic of that planet in human horoscopes.

*Wednesday* . . . *Raphael,* the planet Mercury, called the Friend of Man. His name means "God Healeth." The root of this name is the same as that of Orpheus. Mercury is the planet closest to the Sun, and with Apollo is the god of healing. Mercury crosses the face of the Sun about every eighth year. It was Raphael who accompanied Tobias to Nineveh, in the apocryphal Book of Tobit, and who was thought to be a man of flesh and blood, showing the Hebrew belief that an Archangel could appear on earth as a man among men.

*Thursday* . . . *Zachariel* or *Tzadkiel,* the planet Jupiter. *Zachariel* signifies "Remembrance of God." His name points to the benevolence and mercy and magnificence of God. Jupiter is preeminently the star of Princes of the Church and of Judges. Conjunctions of Jupiter and Saturn sometimes show revolutionary trends in both Church and State. *Tzadkiel* means "the Justice of God."

*Friday* . . . *Aniel* or *Haniel,* the planet Venus, Son of Heaven and Star of the Morning; the Resurrection Star, which is born in the east before dawn after dying in the west at twilight. It signifies that whereof Paul sang, "O grave, where is thy victory?" It is the Love which is stronger than death, the Grace, the Graciousness and the Mercy of God.

*Saturday* . . . *Kassiel,* the planet Saturn. The archangelic name suggests the nature of Saturn, strong, righteous and Star of the Sabbath. Sometimes Sabbathiel is applied to Jupiter, but this title belongs to whichever planet rules any Sabbath, and in Israel this was Saturday. *Tzaphkiel* is also assigned to Saturn; the name signifies Contemplation of God!

Differences in names and titles come from the many changes in calendar throughout the history of all peoples. The Essenes claimed that theirs was the true calendar, and some scholars believe that the Essenes made Wednesday their Sabbath; but if Man, Mercury or Thoth-Hermes was created on the sixth day, and this was Mercury's Day, then Thursday would have been the Sabbath Day on which God rested, while Sabbath Eve would then have been Wednesday evening. This would explain why Jupiter is termed Sabbathiel, for Jupiter rules Thursday.

Four great Archangels are very ancient. They go back to the time of Abraham in Canaan: Raphael, Michael, Gabriel and Uriel. Uriel means "God is my Light." These names relate to the Taurean Age when, as shown in Ezekiel's vision, the four fixed signs were on equinoxes and solstices. Astrology arose, however, in the Geminian Age under common signs, ruled by only two planets, Mercury and Jupiter. Reminiscent, perhaps, of this is the Hebrew calendar with its two seasons, of which spring and summer constituted one, and fall and winter the other; but astrologically there were always four seasons as marked out by the stars, and this was known to the priests and wise men.

The other names and titles show the influence of later Babylonia and Persia, from the Exilic Period, when Aramaic became the official speech in Palestine as in other areas under Persian dominance.

If the Essene calendar points back to a time when Wednesday was the Sabbath, this explains why many kabbalists still insist that Michael, the Archangel of the Hebrew nation, represents the planet Mercury, rather than the Sun or Saturn. Others say that Gabriel is the Archangel of Mercury. Again, calendar changes account for the contradictions.

The ancient Babylonians also had sabbaths, but these did not fall regularly on one day of each week but rotated so that every planet would have its Sabbath in the course of a fixed cycle. The Hebrew Sabbath, however, was set for Saturday in historic times, for Saturday was not only Saturn's day, sacred to Abraham, but completed one quarter of the Moon's cycle.

Ancient Babylonian symbols for the days of the week have been found engraved on stones as follows: Sunday, pointed star (Sun); Monday, crescent (Moon); Tuesday, spearhead (Mars); Wednesday, erect serpent beside bent horns (Mercury); Thursday, bent horns in pyramid shape (Jupiter); Friday, wedge-shaped object (Venus) and Saturday, head and neck (Saturn).

When the planets Uranus, Neptune and Pluto were discovered in modern times, astrologers sought out archangelic names for them. Ithuriel was assigned to Uranus, which means "God is my Superiority." There are many lists of angels and archangels in kabbalistic literature from which names can be taken according to the influence of the newly discovered bodies when that has been determined.

**Chapter IV**

## THE LETTERS OF FLAME

## STARS AND THE ALPHABET

he Zohar says, "In heaven above, that surrounds the universe, are signs in which the deepest mysteries are concealed. These signs are constellations and stars, which are studied and deciphered by the wise." And it continues, "He who has to start on a journey very early, should rise at daybreak, look carefully towards the east, and he will perceive certain signs resembling letters which pierce through the sky and appear above the horizon. These shining forms are those of the letters wherewith God created heaven and earth. Now, if a man knows the secret meaning of the sacred Name consisting of forty-two letters and meditates on it with becoming devotion and enthusiasm, he will perceive six Jods in the pure sky, three to the right and three to the left, as well as three Vaus, which hover about in the heavenly arch. These are the letters of the priestly benediction . . . In the bright morning he will perceive a pillar towards the west, hanging perpendicularly over the earthly paradise, and another pillar hanging over the center of paradise. This luminous pillar has the three colors of a purple web; three birds stand on it, singing . . "

The secret philosophy of the Kabbalah is more ancient than historians and scholars usually recognize; it goes back to the astronomy of the Babylonians, in which the patriarch Abraham was already versed when he left Ur of the Chaldees. The letters of the Hebrew alphabet were taken from the shape of constellations on the ecliptic and were thus letters of flame, and the letter *Yod* remains as a witness to their creation from fire. Each individual letter of the Hebrew alphabet is a flame, or combination of flames, similar to *Yod*, which is for this reason called the Workman of Deity.

Yod signifies the number 10, which is the perfect number, the number of the Sephiroth on the Tree of Life, who in their turn symbolize the forces of Spirit in operation. It has the conventional form of the free flame, the tips of which are sometimes called "jots." Every letter is really made up of Yods, or modified Yods, together with enlarged or diminished "jots" and connecting lines. In very careful writing this symbolic flame detail can be detected, and sometimes even in poor script or printing it is still evident. That the flames also point to the starry heavens is shown in the tradition that the twenty-two letters really imitate certain small asterisms of the zodiac which they picture in miniature. Thus the alphabet as a whole symbolized Light, but only a few of the letters reveal this in their present form, while the symbolic meaning still in our day lies under the veil of the Mysteries.

The Book of Ezra in the Bible shows us how the documents were collected together in Babylon, and it is believed that modern Hebrew derives mainly from what the rabbins made of Ezra's manuscripts, which were handed down from the Field of Ardath. Scholars believe that the original Hebrew in which the Bible was written was the tongue of the Jebusites of Jerusalem and possibly in that of other Ibri* tribes and in the sacred script of the Babylonian temples. With Ezra's return to Jerusalem, Aramaic became the official tongue of the scribes, as it was the language of commerce in the western Persian Empire; but Hebrew was also still used and continued to be the sacred tongue. The Bible was now read to the populace in the common

**Obri, ebree, ibri.* The term signifies those from beyond the Euphrates river. It includes all the Semites who migrated into North Arabia, Syria, Palestine, as a general appellation, with their spoken dialects of the same tongue, who worshipped Baal and Astoreth and ancestral gods, and some of whom became the "Hebrews" of history. Some Canaanite tribes were also *Ibri*, whose ancestors had been spreading westward from Mesopotamia for three thousand years.

speech, Aramaic; and this was still the common speech in the time of Christ.

A kabbalist writes, "Kabbalistic philosophy is then the Hermetic philosophy in its Babylonian form, mystically expressed in one language by means of letters belonging to an already archaic and dead one, in which some of the secrets of the past were still preserved for the private use of an initiated priesthood."

## *THE MASORETIC POINTS*

The rabbin ignored the old vowels, retaining but a tradition that some of the letters at one time had the force of vowels. In the course of time they found it needful to clarify the inconvenient old style of the Bible by dividing the strings of consonants. Five of these have two forms, one of which is termed "final." The final form is used when it occurs as the last letter of the word, and it would appear that the only definite clues possessed by the rabbin as to the dividing of the Ezraic text into words was the placement of these finals. What is called "Rabbinic Judaism" dates from the downfall of the Temple at Jerusalem 70 A.D. With Temple and national freedom and identity lost, the teachers ("rabbin") took over the task of saving their Mysteries for the future, in the vicissitudes of the Dispersion.

Aleph alone, the letter A, is named as a vowel among the twenty-two consonants, for it is the root-sound of the entire alphabet, descending from the high place of Kether. The addition of H to A was characteristic of the early change from Hebrew to Aramaic. When Sara left Chaldea with Abram to dwell in the west country, she became Sarah and Abram became Abraham.

It is said that vowel points were introduced by Rabbi Mocha of Palestine in the sixth century A.D. to help his disciples in reading the Scriptures. Knowledge of the Scriptures was the secret of the priestcraft in ancient Israel; only when it was realized that every Jew must be himself the guardian of

Scripture did it become necessary to make the Scriptures more easily read and understood.

Yet ancient Hebrew did once possess vowels, some scholars believe, as evidenced in the "conduit inscription" discovered by archeologists; and it also divided its words by points, but it used no "finals."

The vowel points are dots which are placed beside or below the consonants to indicate what vowel sound was to be used in reading the text, and this method of pointing the text was introduced by the school of the Masoretes, following the Rabbi Mocha. Their work was not completed until the middle of the tenth century, and although Rabbi Mocha is credited with having begun this method, it may actually have been started some centuries earlier. It was not until 1526 A.D. that an Old Testament printed in the Masoretic style first appeared, and so it is plain that it required many centuries of effort to convert the original documents into the form adopted by orthodox exoteric Judaism. This is a very long time in which to fix tradition, so one realizes how and by what means the Secret Doctrine of Israel was eliminated from modern Judaism.

Yet the Hebrew scholars were intensely zealous, endeavoring in all good faith to preserve Hebrew tradition in the utmost purity, and after a great deal of editing and amending and secreting of esoteric matters, the remainder was in fact preserved almost intact into our present time. It is true that many hundred small grammatical changes have been made necessary in the Masoretic text by the Dead Sea discovery, and these small changes would be immensely important to any cipher the documents may still contain, but so far as the surface meaning of the Bible is concerned, there have been remarkably few serious changes.

Running parallel with orthodox Judaism and orthodox Christianity and the traditional texts of the Bible is the Secret Doctrine of Israel, as we have to a small degree revealed it in these pages. Modern kabbalism refers continually to the book called the Zohar, written by the Jew of Granada, Moses de Leon, in the thirteenth century. This Spanish Jew was stimulated by the brilliant Arabic civilization, with its Greek and Indian overtones, for it is said that although the Arabs gave the so-called Arabic numerals to the West, the Arabs had found them in India. This new discovery must have stimulated the development of Biblical numerology, for Arabic and ancient Sanscrit also had their numerologies, and Arabic is a language which is very close to Hebrew, as we have mentioned.

Although the Zohar is proved to be a collection from all sources of Hebrew knowledge and tradition, Moses de Leon claimed that he had found in a jar in a cavern in Galilee the book of the Rabbi Simeon ben Jochai. This is the sage persecuted by Titus, whose period was from about 70 A.D. to 110 A.D., when he gathered his son and disciples together and taught them the Splendors of Wisdom, perpetuating the codes and ciphers which had been handed down by the Wise Men of Israel from the most ancient times. We have seen that these teachings included the Mystery of the Fiery Chariot as well as the inner essence of the forces of creation (Yetsirah) as symbolized in the Hebrew alphabet.

The claim of de Leon of having discovered Simeon's book in a jar in a Galilean cave no longer seems incredible, for we have seen greater finds in the Dead Sea caves and in the Egyptian cemetery at Nag Hammadi. But he added to this find, if he did truly make the find himself, the entire body of kabbalistic knowledge as it existed in his own century. This he wrote in his great eclectic work, the Zohar. Zohar means Splendor, or Light; but as we have said, its author attributed it to the Rabbi Simeon in the end of the first century A.D., and we think there is a germ of truth to his claims. He writes:

"When they assembled to compose the Sohar (or Zohar), permission was granted to the prophet Elias (Elijah), to all the members of the celestial college (Mystery School on the inner planes), to all angels, spirits and superior souls to assist them, and the ten spiritual substances (Sephiroth) were charged to disclose to them their profound mysteries, which were reserved for the days of the Messiah."

These Hebrews had rejected Jesus of Nazareth as the

Messiah, but the picture still holds for the followers of Christ Jesus. Some Hebrew mystics undoubtedly beheld the Christ in the heavens when they attained illumination, whether before or after death, and it is at any rate true that many kabbalists in the Middle Ages were self-converted to Christianity.

The Rabbi Simeon, according to this tradition, did for his era the same stupendous service that Ezra had rendered for the Hebrews during the Exile. During a time of catastrophe, when the people, their nation, their language and their religion were threatened with extinction, the Rabbi Simeon gathered the books together and imparted by word of mouth the Mysteries secreted in the very text itself. The Zohar is written in Aramaic, and it is significant that the Persian Master, Mani, also wrote in Aramaic. Moses de Leon has much to say of the mystical meanings of the vowel points.

Speaking of the verse from the Book of Daniel, "And the Intelligent shall shine," the Zohar explains, "This shining corresponds to the movement given by the accents and notes to the letters and vowel points which pay obeisance to them and march after them like troops behind their kings. The letters being the body and the vowel-points the animating spirit, together they keep step with the notes and come to a halt with them. When the chanting of the notes marches forward, the letters with their vowel-points march behind them, and when it stops they also stop. So here *the intelligent* correspond to the letters and vowel-points, *the brightness* to the notes, *the firmament* to the flow of the chant through the succession of notes, while *they that turn to righteousness* correspond to the pausal notes which stop the march of the words and bring out clearly the sense. These cause to shine letters and vowels, so that they all flow together in their own mystical manner through secret paths."

It would seem that the manipulation of the Scriptures began with the reconstruction of the Temple after the Babylonian Exile, for this was the time when Ezra brought back to Palestine from Babylon the collected Scriptures which he and his school of scribes deemed authoritative. Already at this time some of the ancient texts were eliminated and the rest pieced together to form a consecutive narrative without too many contradictions and inconsistencies, and oriented to the coming of the Messiah. The entire Old Testament was dedicated to the concept of the Davidic Kingdom with its world center at Jerusalem. The prophets of the exile and Restoration were leading spirits in this enterprise. This was the root and source of all future Christian Utopias down to and including the innermost ideal of Esoteric Masonry today.

When the written text had been established, contemporary prophecy and prophets were repudiated, and this gave rise to apocryphal and pseudonymous books and secret schools hidden away in wilderness and deserts or existing undercover in the cities. If any man claimed to be a prophet, it was decreed his own parents ought to put him to death.

At the Council of Jamnia in 90 A.D.–about twenty years after the Romans had destroyed the Temple of Jerusalem–modern Judaism was born in the body of Scriptures then deemed canonical by the assembled rabbin and sages. This was the beginning of rabbinic Judaism, while paralleling it Simeon ben Jochai transmitted Esoteric Judaism in the seclusion of his Galilean cave, and still later the Masoretes began their age-long work on the Old Testament. Today the Masoretic text is still the official Bible of orthodox Judaism as the King James is the official Bible of Protestant Christianity, but the Dead Sea discoveries have made many changes necessary in both. Masorete means traditional.

Kabbalism arose among the Jews of Europe in the centuries which say the beginning of the Crusades and the earliest epics of the Holy Grail. Maimonides (Moses ben Maimon), a celebrated Jewish philosopher of Cairo 1135-1204 A.D., tells us that the kabbalists used every device of language known to men to conceal and reveal the meaning of the Scriptures. This is what we mean when we say that the Bible is a sublime book of occultism. It is not a mere haphazard collection of primitive and obscure Hebrew texts. The entire history and culture of the Hebrew people, from the beginning, were taken by a band of mystics and Initiates and converted into symbol and allegory of the most amazing complexity. It has been said that the Bible was written by kabbalists for kabbalists of the future, the methods of reading being handed down to pious and worthy men as secrets of secrets.

Thus the Rabbi Simeon instructed the Companions "not to read so, but so." He wrote, though under a veil, the sacred mysteries of the Hebrew alphabet in the Book called Yetsirah, or Book of Creation (or Formation), and it is this book which Moses de Leon claimed to have found in the jar in the Galilean cave. Since Rabbi Simeon taught and wrote in his cavern for twelve years it might seem reasonable that a jar like those found at the Dead Sea might have been hidden there.

Certain rules attributed to Philo Judeus show that esoteric elements were already being incorporated into the Bible text in the first century A.D. and had been there at that time for an undetermined period, which esotericists trace back to Babylon.

## *THE RULES OF PHILO JUDEUS*

We give here a few of the rules laid down by Philo Judeus, who was a great philosopher of the liberal Hellenistic school of Judaism in Egypt. He lived contemporaneously with Christ and the Apostles. His work is therefore earlier than that of Simeon ben Jochai and the Sepher Yetsirah or Book of Creation, but not as old as the Book of Jubilees ("Microgenesis").

*A general rule.* Passages in Scripture which seem to say something unworthy of God, or are senseless and contradictory, are inadmissible; allegorical sentences which are used in a passage to cast doubt on the literal sense render the whole verse suspect. This would seem to mean that Philo would set some verses in the Bible aside as being of questionable value.

*Special rules.* There are hints or pointers which call attention to special esoteric mysteries in the verses of the Bible. Such hints are the doubling of a phrase, the apparent doubling of a phrase, the repeating of something already said, and a change in phraseology. An entirely different meaning may be found by combining the words in another way, and to do this it is permissible to disregard the commonly accepted way of dividing the sentence into phrase and clause. Synonyms should be carefully considered and evaluated. A play upon words points to a hidden meaning other than that which lies on the surface of the text. Sometimes a passage may be taken allegorically, and even when an allegory is not at once visible, such a meaning may be assumed from certain parts of speech and parts of words used in a challenging way. Every word must be examined in all of its meanings in order to uncover the different layers of thought. A skillful interpreter may make small changes in a word according to the rule "read not so, but so." Philo therefore did not hesitate to change breathings and accents, even in Greek words. Any peculiarity in a phrase justified the assumption that a special meaning was intended. The number of a word–that is, its numerological or letter-number–might spell out a mystery; peculiarities in forms of words, singular or plural, verb tense, gender of nouns, presence or absence of an article were not to be taken arbitrarily as errors in the text but to be examined to see if they pointed to something hidden. All kinds of ciphers were possible from the interchangeability of letters and numbers.

The importance of all this lies in the material which it gives for meditation and contemplation, for the human mind is yet in its infancy and most neophytes quickly run out of ideas when they first start to learn the art of meditation. The Kabbalah gives to the Bible student an endless array of mysteries upon which to meditate, and thus to discipline the intellect and soul, and lead them to the use of spiritual intuition and vision.

Basic to all such Bible mysteries and meanings are the 22 letters and the unwritten vowels, the letters of flame which are breathed out upon the Word of God. They are the fiery ideograms of the Word Made Flesh, not in the name and person of one man only, but in the entire living universe with its host of Star Angels.

The alphabet of flames which constitutes the starry universe is a veil which hangs before the Holy of Holies where God alone

IS. Into that hidden sanctuary the bright and burning letters conduct the human soul in meditation on the Mysteries.

# PART II

# THE HEBREW ALPHABET

# A SERIES OF COSMIC GLYPHS

## Chapter V

## THE FIRST SEPTENARY: ALEPH THROUGH ZAIN

### ALEPH

Name: *alef*—sound: silent

leph is the first letter of the Hebrew alphabet of consonants, yet it is sometimes termed a vowel, and it is called "silent," although it possesses a sound which is not easily described.

Mystically, it is said to contain within itself the essence of all the other letters, for it alone correlates with the highest of the sephirothic principles, and it represents the perfect archetypal man, the Crown of Perfection. Aleph stands for the Primordial Point or Hidden Seed, the masculine or Fire Principle of Godhead that is always present on all planes of being and in every act of creation.

From the initiatory interpretation Aleph means power generated through self-control, the first lesson to be learned by the aspirant. It is always self-control which is the law of the Lord, and blessed is he who learns to walk in the way, for it is he alone who develops the powers of the true Initiate.

Numerically, Aleph intones the ONE, which is Spirit. Its color is White, the focus and circumference of vibratory light rays, which contains within itself in latency the sevenfold color spectrum. Its keyword is *Perfection,* for it is that Mystical Point of which the Zohar says, "The Holy and Mysterious One graved in a hidden recess one point. In that He enclosed the whole of creation as one who locks up his treasures in a palace, under one key, which is therefore as valuable as all that is stored up in that palace, for it is the key which shuts and opens." (Yod, signifying 10, is the power of Aleph at the point of visibility in creation.)

As the number 1, the power of Aleph represents Unity indivisible and eternal. *One* operates ceaselessly from the Creator in the highest heaven down through all realms of being to the lowest, even to the least particle of the physical universe. The cosmic forces of Aleph extend throughout all of the sevenfold septenaries.

The true or essential being of mankind is called the Virgin Spirit, and it is this which is made in the image and likeness of God. Aleph is the signature of the Virgin Spirit, but also of its first emanation or projection which is called the Divine Spirit. The Divine Spirit is the Will Principle of the Virgin Spirit, and it is termed masculine. When the Virgin Spirit is descending into matter, this is the principle first awakened, for the being must be able to *cooperate* with the Hierophants and Hierarchies which are in charge of its cosmic career.

The path downward into materiality is called *Involution.* The Will principle initiates this involutionary trend and, again, when the nadir of involution has been reached, it is the Will principle that declares, "Now I will arise and return to my Father's house." The Will which cooperates passively with the celestial Hierarchies, obeying and carrying out their behests, is the negative pole of the Will principle, and this is all that is active in Involution. When Evolution begins, however, it is the positive aspect of the Will principle that is awake and active, as the Virgin-Spirit-as-Ego takes charge of its own cosmic career, working its way up out of materiality to join the Hierarchies of celestial Beings, a Son of God among the other Sons of God.

"In God we live and move and have our being." Each aspect or attribute of God *in*folds and *un*folds all that follows or is "below." Aleph is the first of the three mother-letters–Aleph, Mem and Schin–which correspond to the three macrocosmic "Roots" of nature, Fire, Water and Air. They correlate with the three creative sounds, tonic, dominant and sub-dominant, or the

1-3-5 notes of the octave. These three tones sound forth the chord of spirit, mind and body (or spirit, soul and body), the threefold channel in and through which man's development proceeds during each Day of God.

From this description of Aleph Biblical students can readily correlate its attributes with those of the father of Old Testament history, Abraham, who came down from Ur of Chaldea, the city of light, to live and serve in the land of Canaan. With this understanding we are better able to interpret the promise made to Abraham by the Lord:

> *That in blessing I will bless thee,*
> *and multiply thy seed as the stars of the heavens,*
> *and as the sand which is upon the sea shores;*
> *and thy seed shall possess the gate of his enemies.*

The Tarot glyph for Aleph is termed "The Magus" or "Magician," who is shown raising a staff or wand toward heaven with one hand while he points downward with the other. Various magical implements lie before him on an altar, emblematic of the spiritual powers possessed by the True Man (Virgin Spirit). With these powers he is able to descend into the lower worlds, and with these powers he rises out of them, returning to his Father in heaven. They are the powers which he had "when the morning stars sang together."

The blessed Lord Christ prayed to his Father that that Glory which he had before the world was made should be rendered visible to his faithful disciples, and it was done. In the first Tarot card we see the Christ Self, arrayed in garments of authority, with his powers laid out upon the altar of the universe. "As it was in the beginning, is now, and ever shall be, world without end, amen"–Man in the image and likeness of God.

## BETH

ב

Name: *bet* or *vet*–sound: b or v.

As Aleph was the sign of the first or Will principle of the Virgin Spirit, so Beth is the sign of the second or Love-Wisdom principle, termed the Life Spirit, or, in esoteric Christianity, the Christ Within, as Aleph is the Father Within.

Beth is the second letter of the Hebrew alphabet of consonants and the first of the double letters. The double letters have two sounds, termed "hard" and "soft." Philosophically they are linked with the "play of opposites" in the universe. Aleph represents the masculine principle of God, Beth the feminine, and these two together are the bridge connecting the heavens and the earth. The two Sephiroth signified by Aleph and Beth, therefore, have a basic significance in all of the outward manifestations of Divinity in the worlds of creation. In the highest heaven, all principles abide in exaltation. When the doors to the lower realms open, Aleph and Beth are the two wings which bear the Unmanifest into the Manifest.

Cosmically interpreted, Beth is the supreme feminine power of the cosmos in exaltation–the Love of God. In Beth abide the cosmic archetypal patterns or matrices of all forms that manifest in the universe.

Many biblical sanctuaries were located in "Beth," notably Beth-el and Beth-le-hem.

Beth means a house and is used in Hebrew both as a prefix and suffix. Beth-lehem means a house of bread. In this little town Rachel was buried, Ruth met Boaz and David longed for water from the well by the gate of Bethlehem before going to battle. All of these events conceal spiritual truths of much greater importance than their geographical or historical aspects would imply.

As Aleph is representative of the quintessential or Seed Man as concentrated in the head, or brain, so the other letters of the

Hebrew alphabet represent the various organs and parts of the divine body and the qualities behind them which collectively constitute the True Man in a state of celestial perfection.

Beth is sometimes called "the mouth of the Man." The mouth is that into which anything can be put, and out of which anything can come; that is, it takes in the substances needed to nourish the body, and it sends forth the *words of life* which are vocalized in the throat and mouth. In Beth lies the mystery of the Word Transcendent.

Numerically, Beth denotes the number 2. The duad has been called "the interval between the multitude and the monad."

Since the ancients did not use numbers but instead denoted the numbers by letters, the letters of the alphabet were ascribed to the constellations along the ecliptic. When the twelvefold division of the zodiac became common throughout those parts of the world where the Hebrews chiefly lived, they adapted their ancient system to the popular astronomy, and thus the kabbalah of the solar system, with its twelve single letters for signs, the seven double letters for planets and the three mother letters for the elements, arose. The modern Indian system still retains the use of twenty-seven asterisms along the ecliptic which are denoted by numbers, and the Zohar mentions the three divine colors which find their way through twenty-seven mystic channels on the abyss.

Astrologically, Beth stands for the cosmic emanations which focus themselves in moons, and which are therefore known to mankind as lunar forces, although they are in fact macrocosmic. The lunar forces are those which relate to formations, and therefore the moon is usually the symbol of the great mother goddesses of antiquity. Aleph on the contrary is masculine and solar, representing the Fire which is complementary to the feminine Beth.

The keyword for Beth is *Formation*. It forms the sounds into patterns before they are sent forth. Beth is the great feminine or Word Principle out of which all things are formed and without which nothing can be made, as St. John says. It is the fall and redemption of this feminine principle in humanity that is the theme of all the Bibles of every land.

According to the philosophy of numbers, Duality introduces the fatal alternative to Unity. This is the beginning of the reign of opposites wherein we discern the significance of the fallen column familiar to the Masonic craft as well as the prominent use of black, which correlates with the feminine principle, in the Temple rituals. Black is the color of Beth, for it holds all color in repose as White (Aleph) holds all colors in activity.

The Tarot figure is the High Priestess Isis crowned with the Moon. When the full power of Isis is manifest, the Moon will no longer be her diadem. It will rest, instead, beneath her feet and she, like Aleph, will be crowned with the glory of the Sun. Then man's physical body will be lifted beyond the limitations of disease and death. Man and woman will be equal in the world and mankind will know the noble fulfillment of the Song of Solomon, "The King's Daughter shall be all glorious within."

The High Priestess sits between two pillars, the one black and the other white. These are the pillars which stand before the entrance of every Mystery Temple, and they appear repeatedly in all esoteric symbolic systems. We shall refer to them many times in the following pages.

## GIMEL

ג

Name: *geemel*–sound: g.

Gimel, the third letter of the Hebrew alphabet, is another double letter like Beth. It represents a new product formed from the union of Aleph and Beth. This blending on all planes of the principles of Fire and Water produces a *new life*, which is termed Mercury by the ancient alchemists and by the modern esoteric Christians the Christ Child that must be born within.

Cosmically interpreted, Gimel is the outpouring of Aleph and Beth–or masculine and feminine conjoined–on the highest plane of manifestation. As God is in reality ONE, so also the Root Force of the universe is ONE FORCE, but in manifestation it is first dual, then triple, then manifold.

Numerically, Gimel denotes the number 3.

God's "Duality" is spoken of as his inferior and superior natures, the former constituting his manifested Self and the latter his essential Being. An ancient authority represents God speaking the following words:

"My inferior nature is the bond of union between myself and all created things. Hence it is likened to Gimel because the camel beareth rich and costly merchandise. And again, for that the camel betokeneth travel and communication becomes thus a symbol of change and of the flux and mingling of ideas borne upon the stream of memory.

"Happy is he who bestrideth the camel of my inferior nature which bringeth them who learn the secret of its mastery unto Me their lord. A task most difficult and laborious is the conquest of the power of recollection. Strength and courage and patience must they have who gain this victory, but these shall be as kings and princes in this world and even as gods in the world to come."

Physiologically, Gimel represents the throat as the channel through which certain occult life forces are continuously flowing between head and heart. More especially, perhaps, we are referred to the larynx as the point of crossing of the lemniscate currents which unite the centers of light in heart and brain. (Beth is really more than the mouth alone, but signifies also the entire cavity of mouth and throat as *holding* sound.)

In the words of the Zohar, "When the Holy One wills that his glory should be glorified, there issues from his thought a determination that it should spread forth, whereupon it spreads from the undiscoverable region of thought until it rests in *garon* (throat), a spot through which perennially flows the mystic force of the spirit of life . . . It then seeks to spread and disclose itself still further, and there issue from that spot fire, air and water all compounded together . . . . . the thought that was hitherto undisclosed and withdrawn in itself is now revealed through sound. In the further extension and disclosure of the thought, the voice strikes against the lips, and thus comes forth speech which is the culmination of the whole and in which thought is completely disclosed."

Gimel represents the third of the major Force Centers in the Image, or Archetypal Man, and it projects the threefold forces throughout the entire created universe. Hence the Law of Three generally prevails from beginning to end in the progressive world cycles.

Beth is the Word as it was with and in God. Gimel is the Hermetic Word made flesh and dwelling among the other creatures of the universe, for the head (intellect, understanding) and the heart (love, wisdom) unite at the point of equilibrium in Gimel. Gimel is the universal power which condenses in the planet Mercury.

Isaiah speaks as one in whom this equilibrium has come to pass when he says, "So shall my *word be that goeth forth* out of my mouth; it shall not return unto me void, but it shall accomplish that which I please, and it shall prosper in the thing whereunto I sent it."

The Tarot figure, which is feminine, holds aloft an eagle. Here we find a beautiful intimation of the coming of the Aquarian Age when, by subjection of the lower nature through the will power of Aleph and its transmutation into soul power by the love of Beth, the emancipated one, Gimel, citizen of the new heaven and new earth, is born. Gimel is a symbol of power and of consummation set amidst *"the fullness of strength."*

The number 3 is important in all metaphysical and kabbalistic systems. Aleph, Beth and Gimel denote the first and basic three degrees of Masonry. Gimel is the number (3) of the Master Mason, and we shall study its higher developments in 9 (3 x 3) and its esoteric, or hidden, connection with Beth, Tzaddi and Tau.

Women will be included in the exoteric Masonry of the Aquarian Age, as they are already included in the present esoteric Masonry of the Mystery Schools.

## DALETH

ד

Name: *dalet*–sound: d

The fourth letter of the Hebrew alphabet is Daleth; it signifies the number 4; and it is the third of the double letters. In Hebrew Daleth means Door.

Cosmically, Daleth is the point of transition from one world to another. The key to the door is the accumulated spiritual essence which nourishes the dormant faculties of the ego. The key having been found, the door opens upon an ever-expanding vista of spiritual glories.

"Open the door," chants the Psalmist, "that the King of Glory may come in." On this terrestrial plane Daleth is the door of Initiation through which the candidate passes when the "King of Glory" (the divinity within himself has awakened sufficiently to demand that the mystic door shall open before his spoken word.

Daleth is thus the doorway to higher accomplishments, but it is also sometimes called the Cosmic Womb–the open passageway by which man descends life after life from the higher realms to gain renewed earth experiences in the great reincarnational cycle.

Four is the feminine number and it is significant that although the division of the sexes occurred during the middle or latter half of the Third Root Race, it was not until the appearance of the Fourth Root Race that woman began to develop the inventiveness and ingenuity that will one day lead her back into a perfect relationship with her own divine or God-consciousness.

To signify the supreme importance of the work of the heart, many of the artists of the Middle Ages painted the Madonna, representing the perfected feminine principle, in an arch or doorway, an intimation of the Star of the Morning which heralds the coming of a new day. Early Christians called the

Christ "Our Lucifer," that is, Our Day Star, Son of the Morning.

Daleth is represented Biblically by the vision of Jacob's ladder upon which the angels of God descend and ascend as the consciousness of the Initiate (Jacob) expands to comprehend the meaning of the various degrees or stages extending from earth to heaven.

Signifying the number 4, Daleth is representative of the sacred Quaternary, known Biblically in the Four Letters of the Name of God, or Tetragrammaton, Yod - He - Vau - He (JHVH). These four letters are the mystic formula which opened to Moses the wonders and powers of the seen and the unseen. It conceals within itself the magical essence of the word AMEN, used by ancient Egyptians and Hebrews and also by the early Christians as an invocation of cosmic Truth. Its Tarot picture is the youth seated upon a cube (in the Egyptian series)

Man, a creature of impulses and passions, must pass through door after door, in life after life, until he attains unto a likeness of the Divine, which is his ultimate goal.

Note that each one of the Hebrew letters represents some attribute which man is learning to unfold within himself. Daleth, or Four, represents the "Perfect Square," and implies both balance and harmony, a lifting into a higher plane of consciousness wherein one finds strength and freedom to fashion a more perfect life here and now, and to attain wisdom and power in the spiritual realms. Its keywords are *Realization, Freedom* and *Aspiration.*

## HE OR HEH

Name: *He* as in "head"–sound: h.

The meaning of the fifth letter, HE, is Life. The importance of this letter is shown in the fact that it occurs twice in the sacred Tetragrammaton JHVH. According to certain kabbalists, the letters are taken alternately as masculine and feminine, beginning with Jod as masculine, while H - V - H hints of the Divine Feminine in God-head, in this position representing Polarity on the high creative level.

The letter He means a window. Solomon sings in his Song of Songs: My beloved looks forth at the windows. Daleth is the Door by which the soul descends into incarnation or ascends in Initiation. *He* is the window looking out to the heavens. *He* is the *breath of life.*

The number 5 is often represented geometrically by the five-pointed star called the Pentangle or Pentagram, sacred in all spiritual and magical mysteries. It signifies the human being in his present status, midway between the animal and the god. One of the most important meanings of the number five is its position as half of all that is contained in the Unity of ten. The work of five, He, is so to train the human will that it becomes one with the Divine Will.

Five is therefore the number of the Seal of Solomon, the holy five-pointed Star of the Disciple, the Fiery Star which raises the Initiate into higher realms of consciousness. The Seal of Solomon is also called the Endless Knot, because the five-pointed star can be drawn continuously with one line, and it symbolizes the spirit of man tied into the physical body which, with its head and four limbs, may be inscribed within a star, or a star inscribed within the bodily form. When the fire forces of the spirit have grown strong enough, the Star rises aloft.

In these studies we are following, be it noted, the system in which twelve only of the Hebrew letters correlate with the signs of the zodiac, these are the twelve singles. The seven double letters correlate with the seven ancient planets, while the three mother letters stand alone above all, symbolic of the elements. More anciently, the twenty-two letters symbolized asterisms along the ecliptic. *He* is the first of the twelve single letters. (Aleph is one of the transcendental mother letters.) He therefore represents Aries.

In the Tarot the letter He is represented by a masculine figure, and the numerological character of the number 5 is that of mobility, movement, change, variety, progression and the ability to achieve high attainment. Although the pentagram (five-pointed star) is its perfect symbol, it is also symbolized by a square with a central point, which is 4 plus 1, the perfect square with 1 added.

In the formation of the letter He we can trace the eventual blending of the two powers which were separated at the time mankind was divided into sexes. This blending is the Mystic Marriage. It was beautifully illustrated in ancient Egyptian Temple ceremonial when the aspirant was brought into the presence of the great god Osiris, there to receive his blessing as he listened to the triumphant chants of the Temple choirs. For here he perceived that he had indeed achieved that high estate in which neither feminine nor masculine was predominant over the other, but both functioned in harmonious equality.

This was exemplified in the hymn which was chanted during the ceremony of Initiation:

O Fatherhood! O Motherhood!
Thou blessed Two in One!
Absorb me evermore in Thee
And find my soul's completeness!

And so also modern mystics chant of the *Father-Mother-God omnipotent.*

The exquisite Temple dances performed by virgin maidens during these initiatory ceremonies represented the mystical rapture engendered in the aspirant during the Mystic Marriage Rite of the soul clad in its starry "golden wedding garment."

## VAU or VAV

ו

Name: *vav*—sound: v or w.

Vau, the sixth letter, conveys the meaning of Light and

Love, as God Powers which are present in every created being. It is the third letter of the Tetragrammaton JHVH. It is also second of the single letters. Vau denotes the number 6.

The Bible states that God is Light and also that God is Love. St. John tells us that when the God Power of the Love-Light is sufficiently developed or unfolded within us, we shall love our fellow-men as God has loved us, and it is then that we shall know all the wonders and glories of the new heaven and the new earth.

Since–in the system which we are using–the twelve singles relate to the signs of the zodiac, we find that Vau, the second of these single letters, relates to Taurus, the sign ruling the neck. The center of creation is located in the throat when generation has been transmuted into regeneration, and then the perfected man knows and can can speak the Creative Fiat.

Vau signifying the number 6, its symbol is sixfold, being the double triangle or interlaced triangles, which is the seal of wisdom, revealing that through the inner light the power comes to investigate "the beyond." Man can now live in both the creative and the formative worlds and consciously relate the workings of the two.

The kabbalist notes here that the hexagram or interlaced triangles, is the symbol of David as the pentagram, or five-pointed star, is the symbol of Solomon. Solomon's Star shows control over the elements and forces of nature, David's Star is the Star of the Messiah of prophecy. Here again is the union of 5 and 6, yielding the Master Number 11.

The number 6 is formed from two sets of 3, which represents a tremendous power whether used for good or ill. If used on the lower plane, it can lead to *De*-generation, but if used on the higher plane it leads to *Re*generation. These two paths are indicated on the sixth Tarot card, "The Lovers." The inner Christ Light is beautifully simbolized as a blazing sun from the center of which radiates the Love Principle in the form of Cupid, the god of love. We think of Cupid as presiding solely over human affections. Not so the ancients. In their mysticism Cupid aimed his arrow at man's pineal gland rather than at his heart, symbolizing cosmic or universal love attained through Initiation.

Thus in the Egyptian Tarot system the "Genius" is shown holding an arrow which points unmistakably toward the pineal gland. The neophyte stands between two maidens who represent worldliness and spirituality respectively. The esotericist knows that when the pineal gland force center is aroused into activity, the whole body becomes full of light, and the life is dedicated to loving, selfless service for the upliftment and blessing of all. This is the high ideal given in the sixth Tarot card and in Vau, the sixth letter of the Hebrew alphabet.

*To every man there openeth*
*A way, and ways, and a way.*
*And the high soul climbs the high way,*
*And the low soul gropes the low;*
*And in between, on the misty flats.*
*The rest drift to and fro.*
*But to every man there openeth*
*A high way and a low,*
*And every man decideth*
*Which way his soul shall go*
*–John Oxenham*

The power of the Christed One, Vau, is placed between He, the Breath of Life, and Zain, the Victor. Thus its meaning is clearly shown. Until the Christ Consciousness is developed, the youth does not recognize the difference between love and sense gratification, but when the Christ is truly awake, the lower love loses its power.

## ZAIN

ז

Name: *zayeen*–sound: z

Zain is the seventh letter of the Hebrew alphabet; it is used to denote the number 7, and it is the last letter of the first septenary. It is third of the single letters. Zain represents the seven steps or degrees leading to Illumination. Its keyword is *Victory*. It stands for the right directive influence of the spiritual Will expressing through the Christed or spiritualized consciousness.

Cosmically, it represents power which, focused by Will, permeates and interpenetrates all worlds.

Physiologically and astrologically, this third of the single letters represents the arms and Gemini—two projections of power, a positive and a negative—under Gemini, whose dual nature they reflect.

The number seven of Zain is a point of transition between the higher and lower realms. After passing through the six degrees of the creative and formative worlds, man is ready for another degree, which is represented by the number seven. Next to Unity, it is the number most frequently used to denote perfection. Zain, following and completing the "six days" or steps, heralds rest, attainment, at-one-ment, completion.

Sometimes seven is called the Number of Perfection. It is formed of the "perfect square" of four, to which has been added the trinity of three, or the Will-Wisdom-Activity principles of God-in-Man. The Bible tells us that when God viewed His fresh new creation he pronounced it good and then rested on the seventh day. The Kabbalah says that God had made several earlier creations which He did not pronounce good and which He had to destroy, a clear reference to the processes of evolution which unfortunately the orthodoxies did not retain.

The seventh Tarot is called "The Conqueror." This means not a conqueror of worlds or men but a conqueror of self, a supreme spiritual achievement. The seventh Tarot Arcanum contains the symbols of the Red Lion and the White Eagle. Alchemically, the blood of the Lion and the gluten of the Eagle are important symbols of transmutation. In the great mystic brotherhoods which have existed since man became man there are exalted Beings who never know the limitations of time or distance, for they can communicate instantaneously by means of thought transference. The same power will one day belong to all mankind, but this cannot be so long as men harbor thoughts of evil, fear, hatred and suspicion toward one another.

Zain is sometimes represented by a scepter and sometimes by a sword–the latter being the symbol of Truth, also of Victory. Hence Zain typifies the attainment of high spiritual Truth and the Victory which is complete self-conquest.

This self-conquest leads up to the illumination which is attained at the end of the first septenary of initiatory degrees. It is said that the incarnational cycle proceeds in groups of seven, that is, that certain lines of causation or karma work themselves out in series of seven lifetimes, during which a likeness can be traced from one embodiment to another. At the end of the seventh incarnation of any one series there is a complete change, and the next cycle of seven unfolds an entirely different type of causation. It is also said that our incarnational cycles take us through the twelve signs of the zodiac, these twelve signs being ruled by the seven planets. Again, the world periods of the cosmic evolutionary scheme are given as seven in number, and the Hebrew alphabet divides into three sections of seven letters each, with Tau as the consummation.

## Chapter VI

## THE SECOND SEPTENARY: CHETH THROUGH NUN

### CHETH

Name: *Chet*–sound: CH as in German "doch"; H or KH
(at the end of a word pronounced "ach.")

heth or Hetch, the eighth letter of the Hebrew Alphabet, is the beginning letter of the second septenary. Numerically, it is used to denote the number 8. It is the fourth single letter in order of alphabetical procession. The first seven letters express universality and are cosmic in their import. The second series of seven represent man's endeavor to attain and express that universality. Aleph, the first letter of the alphabet and leader of the procession of letters, has unlimited power on all planes. Cheth or Heth centers in the formative realms and its forces have not yet attained their full complement of power.

As fourth of the single letters, Cheth associates with the sign Cancer, which is the fourth sign of the zodiac. Numerically it is in sympathy with Daleth (4 and 8), its eightfold character signifying the dual feminine, relating man to the Eternal through intuitive perception. Intuition is that soul wisdom which discriminates unerringly between the true and the false, the real and the unreal, and *Intuition* is the special keyword of Cheth.

Physiologically, Cheth relates to the breasts as symbols of the fountain of life flowing from the bi-une Spirit Power. It stands symbolic of the great cosmic Hierarchy of Beings who work through the sign Cancer in the zodiac. Cancer is the great

Mother sign of the zodiac, the Madonna of the Skies. (Virgo is the Virgin). The keywords of Cancer are *Service, Love,* and *Sacrifice.*

Heth means "a field," and cosmically it represents the union of two worlds. It is the *field* of unlimited possibilities in human nature which is worked by the true or Spiritual Man by way of the mind to bring about what is esoterically termed the union of the lower and the higher Self. In reality there is never more than One Self, the Virgin Spirit which is True Man, but this True Man throws a shadow-image of himself into each of the cosmic planes, and on each plane he has a different name and a different vesture or garment. Each plane is a field of experience for the Spirit as he *in*volves into matter and *e*volves out of it, and this is the signification of Heth. The cultivation of the Field of Heth requires great labor. It was only from the Sons of Heth that Abraham could purchase the center of spiritual understanding, Machpelah.

Heth (eight) has been called "a field of cosmic possibilities," referring to the varied life experiences of the ego's vast incarnational cycles. The keynote of love and sacrifice which characterizes Cancer and Heth apply also to the feminine Daleth (four). The Book of Genesis says that man's body was formed of the dust of the earth, and it is implied that all pain and suffering result from the limitations of this "dust."

The picture of the Hebrew letter Cheth or Chet resembles the ancient erections of stone found in many places. Jacob slept with a stone for a pillow, and dreamed a dream of the Ladder of Heaven upon which angels ascended and descended. That this Ladder referred to the human being in general is shown in the words of Christ Jesus, "Verily I say unto thee . . . thou shalt see the angels of heaven ascending and descending *upon the Son of Man.*"

The picture of Cheth shows two pillars crossed with a third, resembling a doorway with posts and lintel. Two other similar letters are He and Tau, but only Cheth has the perfect balance of the two pillars upon which the crossbeam rests.

Bible students are familiar with the columns Jachin and Boaz which stood before the door of Solomon's Temple, and they know also of the two columns of wind and fire which flanked the entrance of the Temple of the King of Tyre. It is not so well known that in Egypt these same two columns confronted the devotee or the Initiate and that he walked between them to enter the sanctuary. Within the Temple he was again required to pass between two columns before he could enter the Holy Place. These inner columns differed from the outer, being united by a crossbeam under which the neophyte must walk, indicating that he had brought to equilibrium the two natures within himself, and only those who had accomplished this work were worthy to enter.

The eighth Tarot card is known as Justice and shows a female figure holding a balance in her hands, in which she weighs each thought, word and deed of every human being who lives upon the earth. If one lives a life of selfish worldly pleasure or devotes his time to the satisfaction of personal ambitions alone, his life's harvest will prove sparse and unfruitful. On the other hand, if one devotes himself to unselfish loving work in the vineyard of Christ, his field of life will produce a harvest that is rich, bountiful and filled with soul satisfaction.

In exact proportion as we send forth, so in good measure will it be returned to us again. This is the message which the Hebrew letter Cheth has for mankind.

## TETH

ט

Name: *tet*–sound: t.

Teth is the ninth letter of the Hebrew alphabet, significator of the number 9, and fifth of the singles. It has the sublimated power of 3, representing the 3 x 3 of the Master Initiate who has ascended the nine steps of the Lesser Mysteries to the fullness of knowledge, and suggests the Ennead (ninefold

Hierarchy) of the Egyptian gods and the Osiris "who sits at the top of the staircase." In Greece we find Nine Muses, and esoteric Christianity adopted the ninefold arrangement of the celestial Hierarchies. In Greco-Egyptian lore we learn of Thoth-Hermes, or Hermes Trismegistus the Thrice-Great (3 x 3), who spoke the words of life by which the creation came into being and who taught these words to the other gods.

In the kabbalah the ninefold constitution of the universe is reflected in the Sephiroth, with the extra Tenth, and in the ten major vowel sounds (thirteen vowels are named). In the kabbalistic diagram of man's constitution there is a similar triple arrangement of Triads, representing the threefold spirit, the threefold soul, and the threefold body (personality), with the Mind (Hermes) as the crux or crucial point.

The keyword is, I AM THOU AND THOU ART I AM--an Hermetic axiom.

In the Hebrew alphabet the twenty-two consonants united with the ten major vowels give a total of thirty-two letters; and sometimes this is counted as thirty-three, with Shin being written in two forms. This makes Tau the 33rd letter, if the vowels are scattered through the consonants according to an esoteric pattern. In Scottish Rite Masonry there are 33 degrees, the 33rd degree being "honorary," and outside the actual ladder of degrees. It may be conferred even upon an Entered Apprentice. In the York Rite there are no degrees, but there are ten steps, again reminiscent of the staircase of the Mysteries.

Through 3 x 3 the aspirant is lifted up, renewed and transformed upon three planes of consciousness, the physical, the psychical and the spiritual. Gimel, the letter third in the alphabet and signifying the number 3, is the Master Mason. Teth, ninth in the alphabet and signifying the number 9, is 3 x 3. The series culminates, the 3 x 3 is fulfilled, in Tau, taken as the (honorary) 33rd letter. Again, in the Egyptian Mysteries we see an arrangement of 30 steps or stages to which the base and summit add two, all associated with the Tet or "backbone of Osiris." The Tet of Osiris is sometimes said to be the sacrum of Osiris to which the pillar is added, but usually the figure is placed at the top of the pillar. This is the pillar of the tree (the acacia) in which the body of Osiris was found by Isis. Sometimes a head is placed above the Tet, sometimes the face is shown in and through the Tet, but the symbolism is the same. We shall speak of this further in the discussion of the Tau.

Masonically, the Master's Word inscribed with two triangles relates to the same Mystery of Threes, for that Word is the Name of God, the four-letter Tetragrammaton JHVH, which is really only three letters with the H repeated.

Teth or Nine has been called the "serpent number," reminiscent of the serpent which Moses raised up upon his staff in the wilderness. Nine, and the Serpent, relate to Initiation, which is the supreme lesson awaiting humanity. The serpent of the mysteries is not fully unfolded until man passes through the Nine Lesser Mysteries. The Bible has been termed the serpent book of the ages and contains many references to symbolic meanings of the serpent.

The most ancient form of Teth was the cross, referring to the serpentine fire force which wreathes itself about and through the staff of Hermes. Through the misuse of this fire force, mankind took upon itself "coats of skin," which must be acquired at birth and repeatedly cast off in death until at last the disciple is the Initiate over whom death has no power. He then embodies within himself all the powers of Teth. Mankind is still bound to the cross of the body, awaiting the day of liberation. Christ Jesus, the divine Exemplar, was nailed to the cross and resurrected that all men might learn to follow in His steps.

It may be noted that although both Teth and Tau are pronounced T, there is no picture of a cross of any sort in the modern Hebrew alphabet, but esotericists treat of this sign in the Mystery tradition and archeologists have found a crossmark in ancient Hebrew inscriptions.

According to Greek legend it was the Phoenician Cadmus, or Kadmus, who introduced into the Greek world the alphabet, or Cadmean letters, and especially the sign T or Tau. We find both T and X in the Greek alphabet. (See Webster's Collegiate

Dictionary: *Alphabet.*) However, neither T nor X is the last letter of the Greek alphabet; the last Greek letter is Omega, while T is the nineteenth letter and X the twenty-second. The Greek alphabet differs from the Hebrew in that the vowels are inserted, and it consists of twenty-four letters. In Masonic legend we read that it was Methusael, a descendant of Cain, who "invented the sacred characters, the Books of Tau and the symbolic T by which the workers descended from the genii of fire recognized each other."

* * *

Teth being the fifth of the single letters, it represents Leo, the fifth zodiacal sign. Biblically, Leo signifies the royal house of Judah, especially David and Solomon. The king is called "the lion of the House of Judah." The Queen is Cancer, a sign which is sometimes called "the mouth of the Lion." Sheba is the Wisdom Queen and, Max Heindel points out, represents humanity collectively.

As Leo is the fifth sign, it governs the fifth house of the horoscope which is the giver of children. Here the esotericist observes that every human soul is the child of the Great King of the Universe, Father-Mother God, a Royal Prince or Princess in the Hierarchy of Heaven. He recognizes that the union of Leo with Teth indicates the Mystic Marriage of the soul with God, the transmutation of the lower into the higher self. The heart is ruled by Leo. Out of the *heart* are the *issues of life.*

Associated with Solomon as the Grand Architect who had charge of the building of Solomon's Temple is the Master Workman, Hiram Abiff. As Solomon, the Lion of Judah, is represented in Leo, Hiram is represented in Aries. His hammer resembles the symbol of the sign Aries. In the ancient Hebrew calendar there were but two seasons named for the entire year; Spring and Summer were one season, and Fall and Winter the other. Hiram and Solomon were both rulers of the first, the Spring-Summer season. The Masonic legend intimates that Hiram secretly married the Queen of Sheba, so that in addition to being born a Prince of the Son of Fire, he also married the Wisdom Queen.

Certain little-known Masonic legends tell of a quarrel between the Master Builder and the King through rivalry for the Queen of Sheba. It is said that Hiram cast a great brazen sea—not only was it the vessel to contain a sea, but it was also the sea of molten metal itself—and through treachery this masterpiece was ruined. Hiram heard a voice calling to him to leap into the molten sea, which he obeyed, and descended through nine arch-like strata of the earth to its center. There he met his ancestor Tubal-Cain (or Cain in some accounts).

We are told that Tubal-Cain had lived contemporaneously with Noah, and when both he and Noah knew that a deluge was at hand, Noah built an Ark to save the Sons of Seth, while Tubal-Cain caused his people to dig great caves in the mountains where they might take refuge from the waters. However, all of his race perished except for himself and one son; yet from this son the race of the Sons of Fire replenished itself down to the time of King Solomon when Hiram Abiff, the Master Workman and flower of the race of Cain, united his labors with Solomon's for a great and magnificent undertaking which should turn the earth into Paradise.

The friendship of the two Kings was shattered by rivalry over the Queen of Sheba, and Hiram leaped into the brazen sea, but the fire could not harm him, for it was his own element.

Tubal Cain prophesied to Hiram that a son should be born to him and that although he might never behold this son, presumably born of the Queen of Sheba, yet his descendants would, in the fullness of the ages, inherit the earth, a beautiful race of divine men. Take note that the Sons of Cain and the Sons of Seth are one and the same race—humanity. The Sons of Fire are Sons of the Spirit, not sons of flesh. They represent a new and higher cycle in human evolution.

Hiram Abiff receives from Tubal Cain certain significant objects—a new hammer and a new word. These he takes with him and returns to the surface of the earth, where he brings his great labor to a successful conclusion, but is afterward murdered by the three ruffians, in the legend which is known to all Masons. According to esoteric Christian teaching, Hiram was reborn as Lazarus and raised from the tomb to immortality by the Christ. It is also taught that Lazarus took the name of John as his Initiate-name and was writing of his own Initiation when he wrote of the raising of Lazarus. Hence, Masons not only revere the "Head of John the Baptist"–who is the "head," source, of the new initiatory school preparing for Christ's coming–but also the Gospel of John. (The "Head" may also be compared to the Tet of Osiris.)

In this story, as in the Hermetic texts, the ancient formula occurs, "WHO THEN AM I, AND WHO ART THOU?" Hiram asks this question of Tubal Cain in the center of the earth, and the reply is given, "I am the father of thy fathers, I am the son of Lamech, I am Tubal-Cain."

We note that the name Hiram, if spelled with consonants only, is H - R - M, which is the root of the name Hermes, the vowels being inserted differently in the Greek. In the Hermetic Mysteries, Hermes or Mercury is called the First Man, referring to the time when mankind received the germ of mind and the Lords from Mercury came to earth to establish the Lesser Mysteries, nine in number. Max Heindel says, THE MIND IS THE PATH. In Greece in its great period Hermes was revered as the Ideal toward which mankind should strive. Esoterically, again, we understand that the "First Man" is Spiritual Man, the Thinker, the Image and the Likeness of God.

The ninth Tarot card pictures the high soul wisdom of the 3 x 3 Initiate as a man leaning upon a staff or rod and bearing in his hand a lighted lantern. The *Staff* is the Staff of Hermes, the *Lantern* is the Light of the Mysteries. Both are found within the soul sanctuary of every human being. Biblically we see them in the Brazen Serpent of Moses and the Blossoming Rod of Aaron, which were hid in the Temple at Jerusalem for many centuries. Their initiatory meanings will be further discussed under the letter of fulfillment, the last letter of the Hebrew alphabet, Tau.

Masonic esotericists will observe that the 18th degree of the Scottish Rite Masonry involves this same 3 x 3 Mystery of Teth, or Nine. It is the degree of the Rose Cross. When Teth is understood esoterically, one lifts himself to the high consciousness wherein he discovers deeply hidden initiatory truths, and there is none to hinder or forbid. As the aspirant meditates upon the wonderful and far-reaching meanings to be found in Teth and the number nine, he realizes more and more clearly the reason for the esoteric axiom that "Nine is the number of Initiation."

We shall understand Bible Mysteries better if we bear always in mind that the Hebrews have two archetypal ancestors. The one is Abraham, but the other is Melchizedek, who had neither father nor mother but was like to the immortal gods. He was a King in Canaan, ruling at Salem, the early name for Jerusalem, and was by some Hebrew mystics called Michael the Archangel, and again some said that Michael taught the Hebrew language to Abraham. The *King* could not be a *High Priest,* but Jesus, the descendant of David and Solomon, is termed not only "Messiah" but "High Priest *after the Order of Melchizedek.*"

It is Melchizedek who is the symbol of the hidden side of the Hebrew religion, as we may understand when we recall that the Sons of Cain were called "bene Elohim," sons of the gods.

In the course of centuries the inhabitants of Canaan—including the Grecian Philistines—who were conquered by the Hebrews, assimilated their conquerors, and the resulting race became the Hebrews of history. It is for this reason that we say that Melchizedek is also an ancestor of the Hebrews, though in a special sense. The Hebrews looked upon the Greeks as Sons of Cain, but they recognized their kinship, and this kinship has been substantiated by recent archeological discoveries.

## YOD

י

Name: *yod*—sound: y as in "yes."

Yod (I, J, Y) is the tenth letter of the Hebrew consonants,

and sixth in the series of single letters. Astrologically and physiologically Yod is connected with the virgin of the skies, Virgo, and thus also with the six-pointed star representative of the House of David. Virgo is the sign which rules the digestive organs of the body, the stomach and intestines, but Yod, spiritually interpreted, refers to the ego's assimilation of spiritual essences.

Having passed through the Nine Lesser Mysteries, the masculine principle has evolved through Aleph, Gimel, He and Zain to manifest a high spiritual power in Teth, the Initiate. The feminine principle has ascended through Beth, Daleth and Vau to Cheth, the new body builded through the transmuted powers of regeneration. Now all are summed up in Yod. Yod occurs within every letter of the entire series of twenty-two. These letters symbolize the way of evolution for the masses and the path of Initiation for the few.

Yod represents the ego on the physical plane, the I-Am when reborn into the power of a joint heir with Christ. Yod-He-Vau-He was the Sacred Name of God to the Hebrews; Yod is the number of Adeptship.

The keyword of Yod is *Omniscience. Aleph,* the white fire of Godhood, lowers in vibration in order to manifest. Yod is this same fire after it has come into manifestation as spiritualized Will.

The glyph in the Tarot representing Yod is the Wheel of Fate or destiny presided over by the Sphinx. Upon the wheel are four letters which mean "wheel", ROTA, but as the wheel revolves, these letters seem to form the word Taro. Also inscribed on the wheel are the four sacred letters of the Tetragrammaton, Yod He Vau He, signifying that God and no other is the ruler of destiny, both for man and the universe. Yod is the initial letter of the Tetragrammaton.

The sphinx represents cosmic consciousness, which harmonizes with the universality of Yod. We have seen that Aleph, signifying 1, is the Primordial Point, silent but all powerful behind manifestation and acting as a hidden force throughout. Jod, signifying 10, is the selfsame power manifesting openly in the universe in letters of flame upon the heavens and in the powers of the human spirit and life forces of all kingdoms. The *Zero* is the mystery behind and within the *One* of Aleph, which is shown openly in 10, or Yod.

Numerically, Yod indicates 10 or the masculine and feminine powers conjoined. A kabbalist writes, "The decad means fully accomplished. It is the grand summit of numbers which, when reached, cannot be passed." Yod is the great masculine significator. It is the first letter of the four-letter name of God, and when written vertically upon the archetypal Man, it resides in the head, while the letters He-Vau-He describe the body. St. Paul was referring to this mystery when he said that the man is the head of the woman.

Jesus, the Master of the New Testament, and Joshua, the Master of the Old Testament–Jesus is the Hellenized form of the name Joshua–are examples of the androgynous powers of Yod or 10, the masculine merged with or containing the feminine.

In every world religion the Divine Equality (polarity) is shown as the basis of Initiation, and for every World Teacher there is a World Madonna–from Isis of the Egyptians to the blessed Mary of the Christians, and among the sages of the Hebrew Mysteries, the Shekinah, whom all Initiates, like Moses, "marry." The Shekinah survives as a symbolic reminder of Anath, the ancient goddess of Canaan, who was the wife of Jahveh, a goddess panoplied for war like the Greek Athena and reminding her children that wisdom and love are mightier than the sword.

The Shekinah represents the same divine attribute as the "female Holy Ghost" of the early Christians. She is the Bride of whom John writes in the Book of Revelation. Hebrew mystics said that all those human spirits whom God created were conceived by the Shekinah. She is the Mother Goddess of esoteric Judaism, and like the Angel Ecclesia of the Christians, she is "Mother Church" carrying all souls in her bosom to the throne of the Father.

The Union with Shekinah is the first of the supernal

Initiations which open the Paths from the world (Malkuth) to the higher planes. Malkuth is called "The Kingdom," and Shekinah flies to and fro in that Kingdom caring for her loved ones.

Ten is often termed the Universal Number, or the All-Number. Its significance is allegorically shown in the Parable of the Ten Virgins, five of whom were wise and five foolish.

There were ten Virgins who carried their lamps as they went forth to meet the bridegroom, but when he tarried, they fell asleep. Then at the hour of midnight came the cry, "Behold, the bridegroom cometh!" The virgins awakened and five discovered that they had no oil in their lamps, so they sought to borrow from their sisters. But the five wise virgins said, "Not so, lest there be not enough for us and you, but go ye rather to them that sell and buy for yourselves." While the foolish virgins went to purchase oil the bridegroom arrived, and the five wise virgins went in with him to the marriage feast, and the door was shut. Then the five foolish virgins came seeking admittance, but the Bridegroom replied, "Verily I say unto you, I know you not."

The foolish virgins are those who squander their sacred life force (oil) in worldly and sensual pleasures and so have no light within themselves to greet the Bridegroom when He comes; in other words, they have not made themselves worthy of the Christ Life of Initiation.

Many keys to Bible interpretation are hidden in the sacred meaning of numbers. Ten (10) is the number of man and woman working together as they travel the Path of Discipleship. Five (5) is the number of the five bodily senses, and also of the activity by means of which the inner lamps of the "golden wedding garment" are kept alight. An ancient utterance long antedating biblical literature is the admonition, "Learn to count aright that thou mayest have oil for thy lamp." So long as man is subject to the lure of the physical senses he can never discover the true meaning and purpose of life. When he has overcome that lure he becomes the five-pointed star and understands the real import of the Master's words, "I am the Light of the World."

The oil forfeited by the five foolish virgins was the divine creative essence within themselves. When that force passes up the spinal cord and reaches the head, it illumines the two spiritual organs located therein, the pituitary body and pineal gland, which then shine forth with rare radiance. This accomplished, the disciple bears within himself his own lighted lamp and is ever ready to welcome the Bridegroom. He who is thus illumined never fails to attract the attention of a Teacher. "When the pupil is ready, the Master appears."

## KAPH OR CAPH

כ

Name: *kaf*–sound K, or CH as in the German "doch," like Cheth; the third picture is the letter as it appears at the end of a word, called a "final."

The letters from Aleph to Jod represented the numbers 1 to 10, but with Kaph the significance changes, the number does not coincide with the placement of the letter in the alphabet. Although Kaph is the *eleventh* in the procession of letters, it was written as the sign of the number 20. We therefore have for this letter, and for those that follow, a *numeral* interpretation and also a *numerological* interpretation in addition to the mystic meaning of the letter as such.

Kaph is one of the double letters, having two sounds, and like all of the doubles it represents the play of opposites in nature. As 20 it is the second manifestation of the decad, revealing the cosmic powers of Beth, 2, on another level. The double of ten, it shows the mastery of the lower selfhood by the ego. The dual nature of Beth, signified in the number 2 and its second place in the procession of letters, reflects the mystery of the Double Feminine symbolized in the New Testament as Mary of Bethlehem and Mary of Magdala. The Feminine is the Cosmic Love Principle of God, and Love is never other than good and holy in its pure essence, but when it is attached to wrong objects, disorder enters into nature, and with it sorrow and suffering. It is the mind which directs the cosmic forces in manifestation, and therefore when the mind is linked with the spirit, the High Feminine manifests; when it is linked with the senses, Love falls into darkness and degradation.

In the mysticism of the Kabbalah the same mystery is shown in the dual nature of the Shekinah, the feminine or Wisdom Attribute of Godhead, who enters into human souls, like the Holy Ghost of Christian mysticism, and may be said to be the selfsame Principle.

The first ten letters, like the Ten Commandments show the path for the masses, in which morality is the keynote, Cosmic Law reflects in the Ten. With the eleventh letter the tests and trials begin which eventually enable one to become a "Follower of the Way," the straight and narrow way of Initiation. Remember that the early Christians were called Followers of the Way, and for this reason. Every disciple, ancient or modern, must walk this same Way and accept the trials imposed upon him. This Path is described in the initiatory interpretation of all of the twenty-two Hebrew letters. As we proceed in our study we realize increasingly their importance to an adequate understanding of the truths concealed in Biblical names. With Kaph a crucial point has been reached.

Kaph symbolizes the Initiate. We have noted previously that the number 9 represents Initiation; 11, which is a higher number, represents the Initiate himself.

Physiologically, Kaph represents the hands in the act of holding. The hand is a channel for the inflow and outflow of spiritual power; the attitude of holding suggest the keyword, *Strength.* We are again reminded of the names of the pillars, Jachin and Boaz, which are established in the strength of the spirit. The Tarot picture is that of a virgin holding closed with her hands the mouth of a lion.

The two parallel upright lines which are the modern signature of the number eleven (11) remind us that these two columns have guarded the entrance of every initiatory Temple the world has ever known. We may mention in passing that the Arabic numerals originated, it is thought, in India but were transmitted through the Arabs and incorporated in the Arabic numerology, whence they passed into the Hebrew and finally into the Anglicized Kaballah. Many intricate codes have been constructed from the combination of several sets of letter-numbers. As we have pointed out, the Hebrews did not have numbers but used the letters of the alphabet for numbers, as the Greeks and Romans did also.

## LAMED

ל

Name: *lamed*–sound: l.

*Sacrifice* is the keyword of Lamed, the twelfth letter of the Hebrew alphabet and seventh of the single letters. Numerically, its value is 30, which is the round number of earth years in Saturn's orbital revolution; and the picture which represents Lamed resembles the astrologer's symbol for Saturn. As seventh of the singles, Lamed associates with the sign Libra, sign of the scales, of Law and Equilibrium, in which the planet Saturn is exalted.

Physiologically, Lamed is associated with the kidneys, the bodily organs for purification, astrologically ruled by Libra, the sign of balance. The Gnostics said that Libra was the birth sign of the "New Adam."

Lamed, embodying the vibrations of 12, marks a state of cosmic consciousness, for it implies the complete conquest of the personality when subjugated by the forces of Spirit. This work requires a preparation that is long and arduous, taking many earth lives for its consummation. Those who have made any progress upon the Path know how difficult it is to subdue the personal inclinations. *Self* truly becomes the Dweller on the Threshold for the average individual.

Goethe, who was an occultist as well as writer and scholar, has stated that some attributes may be developed by solitude and seclusion, but that character can be built only through contact with our fellow beings in the everyday busy world. Many think, when they take up spiritual studies, that it is needful to spend much time in seclusion devoted to mystical dreaming. This, however, is only a small part of the Great Work, for it is only as we learn to give of ourselves in loving self-forgetting service for the upliftment of others that we begin to make real spiritual progress.

Max Heindel had traveled far upon the illumined Path when he wrote, "An Elder Brother will only grasp my extended hand when I extend my other to the younger ones coming behind me in order to lead them to the Temple door. This will open to them if they seek prayerfully, if they knock persistently, and if they work manfully."

We have noted that beginning with Kaph, each of the letters represents some experience encountered upon the initiatory path. The very first lesson set before the aspirant whose inner powers are unfolding is the necessity of Sacrifice.

Out of these sacrificial experiences, if they are accepted in the right spirit and assimilated, come elevation of consciousness and spiritual perception. Cosmically, therefore, Lamed stands for such elevation and expansion as eventuate in man's fulfilling his destiny and being crowned with eternal light.

Numerically, Lamed's power of 30 again associates with the Triune Powers of Spirit; it is the triple power of 10. As twelfth in the procession of letters, however, it is again three, (1+2=3), showing that man must be purified by continued communication with the higher dimensional worlds. Truly, humanity hangs upon the cross of matter and suffers the wounds inflicted by the goad of karma until, by its own efforts, through sacrifice, love and service, it releases itself. The Tarot glyph for Lamed is the Hanged Man, which refers to the ego in the present earth period, who is crucified between his higher and lower natures.

## MEM

Name: *mem* or *mim*–sound: m; second picture represents the final form, used when the letter appears at the end of a word.

Mem is the second of the three mother letters and thirteenth in the procession of letters. It signifies the Mother as the great Sea of Life out of which all life has come. Aleph, the first mother letter is Fire, and Schin, the third, is Air. When Aleph is called "ether" this does not mean "air" but "fire," the Fire of God. Mem is the primordial Ocean of Life out of which the material universe solidifies. Its numerical value is 40, the fourth level or expression of the decad, and its keywords are *Infinity* and *Transmutation.*

As thirteenth letter, Mem shows the Trinity projected from Unity. These two divine numbers 1 and 3 again produce the 4, which represents time, space and materiality, the wheel of becoming, the Divine Quaternary of the Pythagoreans.

Mem is the "manna" of the Hebrew alphabet. Paracelsus writes, "If I have manna in my constitution I can attract manna to myself from heaven. Saturn is not only in the sky, but also deep in the ocean and the earth. What is Venus but the artimesia that grows in your garden? And what is iron but the planet Mars? That is to say, Venus and the artimesia are both of the same essence, while Mars and iron are manifestations of the same cause."

Mem as a mother letter reminds us that the prenatal epoch, in which the prospective mother holds within herself the promise of new life, may be the most important period of her entire incarnation; for through the law that like attracts like she may, if her own mind is exalted, bring into the world a Master Soul noble in character and in mind and beautiful in body.

## NUN

Name: *noon*–sound: n, the second picture represents nun as a final.

Nun (N), the fourteenth letter of the alphabet, means a fish, one of the symbols of the Initiate. Nun represents "the Son of Man," and its keyword is *Individualization.* Joshua, the Jesus of the Old Testament, was the "Son of Nun," an Initiate Priest. Nun has been called "the Developed Man." It is eighth of the single letters.

Cosmically, Nun stands for augmentation and extension, attributes of the evolved individual. Its numerical value is 50, which becomes the fifth power of the decanate, and relates to the number 5, the forces of the ego (true spiritual Selfhood) working through the mind toward the spiritualization of the personality. Spiritualization of the mind itself is the ultimate work of all occult initiations and the ultimate goal of evolution. It is when the mysteries of the mind are understood that the Initiate becomes the Adept or God-Man.

Signifying the number 50, Nun has been the cryptogram for many abtruse philosophical concepts, symbolized in the "fifty gates of understanding." It was extremely important to the Essenes and the Messianic Mysteries which they held sacred and secret.

The name Joshua in the Old Testament is the name given in the New Testament as Jesus, the meaning of the name being, "God is My Savior." The letter Nun was the code letter-number for the Messiah who was expected at exactly this time when Jesus of Nazareth was born and grew to manhood.

The fish was the symbol by which Christians knew one another. The fish was the sign of Jonah, who had been seemingly swallowed by death yet was cast out alive to bring his mission to a conclusion. Jonah means "dove," showing that he was an Initiate Priest of the Moon Goddess, and the number 50 relates to the round number of weeks in the lunar year (literally 52). Throughout antiquity the number 50 is found to be sacred to the lunar calendar, having a special importance in the worship of the Moon, who is not only the ruler of the night sky but also of the waters of the oceans.

As the eighth of the single letters, Nun correlates zodiacally with Scorpio, and physiologically with the sacred centers of generation and regeneration. Generation becomes regeneration when the life essences have been transmuted into the divine waters of everlasting life. The Master said, "If one drinks of these waters he shall never thirst again." It is then that the body of the Initiate is truly the holy temple of the indwelling Godhead.

The fourteenth Tarot Arcanum shows an angel maiden with outstretched wings, representing high idealism and aspiration. In her hands she holds two vases filled with precious fluid which she pours from one to the other. In the Waite Tarot series we see that beside the angelic figure there is a nebulous pathway which ascends to the very summit of a distant mountain peak where it seems to disappear into the golden glory of a vast sun.

When the aspirant reaches the summit to which the Path leads, he can proclaim to the world from *first-hand* knowledge, "I know that my Redeemer liveth"; for it is in that high and holy place that he learns the true secret of immortality or Eternal Life.

The precious substance contained within the two vases is the emanation or essence of the high spiritual life. Great Initiates always emanate from themselves a rare perfume, perceptible to all who come within their aura. The approach of the Blessed Virgin Mary is always announced by a fragrance as of the rarest lilies.

The poet Tennyson, in one of his idealistic fantasies, wrote:

*From the meadows your walks have left so sweet*
*That whenever the night wind sighs,*
*It leaves the jewelled print of your feet*
*In violets blue as your eyes.*

We may not all be spiritual enough to cause flowers to bloom in our footprints, but we may so live, so love and so serve all whom we find in need, in both inner and outer worlds, as to bring a blessing with our presence and leave a benediction as we depart. This is a beautiful ideal held forth for our emulation by the Hebrew letter Nun.

## Chapter VII

## THE THIRD SEPTENARY: SAMEKH THROUGH SCHIN

### SAMEKH

ס

Name: *samekh*—sound s.

Samekh is the fifteenth letter of the Hebrew alphabet and its symbol resembles a serpent holding its tail in its mouth. It signifies the number 60. "In the letter Samekh," says the kabbalist, "is found the spirit of evil. Samekh is the first letter of the third-final series. In this series the power of the flesh-body and the human will are predominant." It is the ninth of the single letters.

The symbolism of the serpent with tail in mouth is one of the earliest developed. Christ Jesus said, "Be ye therefore wise as serpents, and harmless as doves;" a true Initiate admonition.

Again the kabbalist says, "Samekh is the great cosmic bow, the string of which hisses in the hands of the profane." The serpentine force in man exalts him to the highest estate where he knows himself to be a god or, on the contrary, degrades him to a state of animalism.

Astrologically, Samekh belongs to Sagittarius, sign of aspiration, idealism and attainment on physical, mental and spiritual planes. The pendulum swings in its full arc, from the heights to the lowest point and up again to the heights.

Physiologically, Samekh correlates with the lower spinal column and sacral plexus, whence the currents of the serpentine spirit fire ascend.

Numerologically fifteen, which is its place in the procession of letters, the 1+5=6, correlating again to the numeral value of 60. It is the sixth expression of the decad. All of the sephirothic powers express on each and every plane of being, and so the powers of 60 represent a sixth expression of the whole gamut of cosmic and egoic forces.

"Things which are seen are temporal," said one who knew, in regard to the transitional state. The Tarot picture shows the contrast between Aleph and Samekh, for Aleph is the White Fire of God expressing on the plane of eternity; Samekh is the Fire which burns in the sense world, with its constantly shifting and changing values, a plane of continuous transition. There are two Masters, one representing the forces of Light and the other the forces of Darkness. The first points the way to immortality by lifting the staff (the life current) toward the head (purity and regeneration). The second points the way to sense indulgence which leads to degeneration and death.

Man is free to choose his own path. *"Le demon est Deus inversus."*

It is perhaps significant that some kabbalists relate the sign X to this letter, which is occasionally written Xmach; and again Masonic legend suggests deep underlying mysteries.

A Masonic historian suggests that the path of blood traced out by the wounded Hiram Abiff, staggering from door to door of the Temple, actually describes an X-cross. We note further that X is the cross of St. Andrew, upon which he was crucified, and that he is the patron saint of Constantinople, having founded the first Christian church there. St. Andrew is the patron saint of Scotland also, where the Scottish Rite Masonry originated.

It is said that the banner of Constantine which bore the "flaming (red) cross" and the words, "In this sign conquer," may in reality have had the Greek Chi and Rho in an emblem; for the Greek Chi is an X, and together with Rho, R, forms the beginning of the name Christos.

# AYIN

Name: *ayeen*–sound: silent.

Ayin is the sixteenth letter of the Hebrew alphabet and tenth in order of the singles. 1+6=7. It is also the symbol for the number 70, the seventh plane of expression of the decad. Through the powers of 7 Ayin becomes a divine symbol.

Cosmically, it is the beginning of expanded consciousness. This letter aptly describes how man–though surrounded by upheavals and changes and caught in the swirl of suffering and disaster–is gradually but surely becoming conscious of a divine power that will aid him. The Bard of Avon had this awareness when he penned the lines:

*There's a divinity that shapes our ends,*
*Rough-hew them how we will.*

Seven signifies the conjunction of the square (materiality) and the trine (spirit). As we all know, materiality has been in the ascendency. In Ayin there is an urge or a beginning toward spiritual elevation. The candidate on the Path is still in darkness, but he is groping toward the light. And we have the supreme Initiator's promise, "Ask, and it shall be given you; seek, and ye shall find; knock, and it shall be opened unto you."

The Tarot glyph is a tower struck by lightning. Adam and Eve–generic terms for mankind, for male and female–are seen in desolation and isolation, for the tower (protective aura) that formerly shielded them no longer does so. They are falling into materiality (coats of skin) and only by their own individual efforts and labors can they be restored to their spiritual estate. Christ Jesus cannot of Himself save men but He can and does help man to save himself. We cannot buy salvation any more than we can buy nourishment for our bodies through someone else eating food for us.

Ayin, therefore, signifies the futility of material living.

Astrologically, Ayin is under Capricorn with its frequent and sudden explosive reactions. Such explosions, however, herald the coming of a new and nobler era.

Physiologically, Ayin represents the liver as center of the desire body, under Mars exalted in Capricorn. This center is the arena of conflict between the high and the low; and it is also the center of transmutation.

Ayin is indicative of the fall into matter, yet it is represented by a divine number. That the spiritual and the mundane are waging a war for mastery is evidenced by the conflict currently engulfing the world. The final "dread and terrible days" are at hand, but the victory is almost in sight.

The keywords are *sudden change.*

Change levels all, as does death. Human pride and false interests will be displaced in the new age currents which are already flowing. By cooperative endeavor and creative idealism shall be made manifest the Good that is for all.

## PHE

פ

Name: *Pe* as in "pet," and *Fe*–sound: p and f; the third picture is Phe as a final.

Phe or Pe is the seventeenth in the procession of Hebrew letters; and it is also one of the double letters, having two sounds; and it is in addition one of the "finals," or letters which are written in a special way when they occur at the end of a word. There are five consonants which have these "final" significators; they are: Kaph, Mem, Nun, Phe and Tsaddi. These "finals" are not to be confused with the "doubles," which are: Beth, Gimel, Daleth, Kaph, Phe, Resh and Tau. Numerically, Phe is the significator of the number 80, which is the eighth sublimation of the decad. As there are Ten Sephiroth, so there are, in reality, ten cosmic planes upon which all of the

Sephiroth manifest. The grand divisions, however, are the four given in another place: Atziluth, the World of Emanations; Briah, the World of Creation; Yetsirah, the World of Formations; and Assiah, the World of Action.

Again as numerological seventeen, Phe's place in the procession of letters, yields 8, (1 plus 7). We have shown that 8 represents the double feminine, the Feminine in Exaltation and the Feminine in Generation.

Physiologically, Phe is the pituitary gland, which when awakened points toward thought transference, intuitive knowing and other extended faculties making for a race that is "super" human. We are as yet "a little lower than the angels," but Phe intimates that which we shall be in that day when "we shall be like Him for we shall see Him as He is." Its keyword is *Immortality,* and its Tarot symbol is an eight-pointed Star. The seventeenth Tarot card is named "The Star," a title not conferred on any other Arcanum.

Phe, "the Star," is "the true Light that lighteth every man that cometh into the world." This is the star of the blessing which is being poured upon a transformed world and which is being assimilated by a new and transfigured humanity.

We noted in the fourteenth Tarot Arcanum a beautiful angel maiden who was conserving the sacred Elixir or Life, or the Holy Spirit essence within herself.

In the seventeenth Tarot Arcanum we find this same angelic maiden–but here she represents a higher phase of spiritual development, for having conserved this great force within herself until it has become a truly transcendent power, she is now pouring it forth in blessing upon the world. She holds the same two vases we observed in Arcanum fourteen, but this time she is pouring forth the precious contents, one upon the sea, and the other upon the land.

Here we find the union of the two Feminines–the lower is uplifted and united with the higher. This produces a tremendous force which is cleansing, purifying, uplifting and transforming.

## TZADDI

צ

Name: *tsadee*–sound: ts; the second picture shows its form as a final.

Tzaddi is the eighteenth letter of the Hebrew alphabet in order of procession. It is a single letter. Interpreted esoterically one may observe in Tzaddi the upheaval wherein earth and its humanity are engulfed at the present time. Tzaddi is a pruning hook or scythe, and it "journeys toward a final solution." Numerically it signifies 90.

Cosmically it denotes that the spiritual forces are persisting in their efforts to arouse latent spirituality in man.

The number 18 is 1 plus 8, or 9, which is also the mystic 3 x 3, indicating that inner work is being accomplished on man's three lower vehicles–mind, desire nature and body. That the work is being accomplished under the auspices of 9 proves its ultimate and complete success, for this number foreshadows *accomplishment.*

Tzaddi has an esoteric connection with both Teth, the ninth letter, whose name suggests the "Tet" of Osiris, and the Tau, which has the sound of T but also of S. It also connects with Schin, which has the sounds both of Sh and S.

A lone scorpion is in the center of the Tarot glyph. This symbol indicates that the beginning of the New Age will not be all good. Forces of darkness will become more aggressive as the Good shows itself increasingly dynamic. The scorpion (sex) will be one of the great evils. After a period of libertinism, new codes of conduct will be established which are based on a higher understanding of the creative fires and their true power when uplifted and used on mentally creative planes.

Tzaddi prepares us for the highest power of Nine (9). We noted in the study of the ninth Arcanum that 9 is the number of Initiation and also of humanity. In the study of the ninth Tarot Arcanum we noted the development of Wisdom, which is the foundation of all true Initiation. In the eighteenth Tarot Arcanum we note the number 9 in its relationship to the ninth cosmic plane, for it signifies the ninth phase or plane of the decad.

The Hebrew letter Tzaddi is astrologically correlated with the Hierarchy of Aquarius whose keywords are *Brotherhood* and *Unity*. It is the eleventh of the single letters.

The eighteenth Tarot Arcanum is divided into two parts. In one part the landscape is covered with darkness, in the other it is revealed in light. Not only the landscape but also the great sun is shown half in darkness and half in light. In one of its meanings the dark side represents the Piscean Age which is now waning, and the light side the Aquarian Age which is just beginning to dawn. The Piscean Age has been a time of pain, sorrow and despair when the world has been filled with wars and rumors of wars—every nation armed to the teeth, looking with fear, suspicion and oftentimes hatred on its neighbors. The spiritual signature of the Piscean Age has been the Crucified Christ.

The Bible contains many dramatic pen pictures descriptive of the incoming New Age, among them, "There shall be no more sorrow, pain or tears, for the former things have passed away."

In the glory of the New Day all mankind will be united into one vast brotherhood whose keynote will be "The greatest good for the greatest number." The idealistic concept of life in the New Age will be centered in the beautiful teaching of the Lord Christ, "Do unto others as you would have them do unto you."

When the Aquarian Age has fully dawned mankind will have learned to overcome death which has been the greatest enemy of the Piscean Age. The spiritual signature of the New Aquaria will be the Risen Christ.

Tennyson sang truly in these words:

*The old order passes, making way for new.*

## KOPH or QUOPH

Name: *kof*—sound: k

Koph or Quoph is the nineteenth letter of the Hebrew alphabet. It signifies a spiritual force directed into constructive endeavors. The twelfth of the singles, it correlates with the zodiacal sign Pisces. Numerically it signifies the number 100, and 10 x 10.

The positive and negative forces of the cosmos in their interplay surround and interpenetrate man's physical body, his mortal mind and his spirit in order to augment and accelerate their vibratory rhythms. Apollonius of Tyana, Pythagorean philosopher, said, "Until the ego becomes conscious of the two distinct currents acting within it and can thoroughly distinguish between them, it is not yet ready for initiation into the higher degrees of living."

Quoph is connected physiologically with the physical body in its entirety. The lords of Pisces aid man to immortalize his new body of light. Its keyword is *Transfiguration*.

The Tarot glyph shows a youth and a maiden within a walled area, symbolizing the limitations of the physical world. The sun's rays pour down upon them, and this brings to mind the Master's injunction, "Suffer little children to come unto Me." As a child is born from higher realms into the physical state, so is man's true self born from its sleep in materiality into the spiritual state.

The two children stand hand in hand (masculine and feminine in perfect balance) within a circle of flowers (spiritual awakening), while above them hangs the symbol of universal regeneration. The glory of John's vision is made plain in Quoph. It is the beginning of the new heaven and earth where there is no more pain, disease, poverty or death, and earth has been transformed into an eternal summerland. The prodigal son has returned to his Father's house and is received with rejoicing. The door swings wide upon a nobler life, whereof Christ said, "Ye must be born again." Here man enjoys perpetual youth in a state of supreme love and happiness.

Some writers have ascribed the nineteenth Arcanum to the rulership of Pisces, others to that of Gemini, and still others to Leo. This diversity of opinion is probably due to the degree of illumination with which one is dealing. The keynote of Pisces is *Transfiguration.* The keynote of Gemini is *Equilibrium,* while Leo is concerned with the accomplishment of the *Great White Work.* In Waite's Tarot series the nineteenth Arcanum depicts an infant seated upon a white horse, which represents the innocence and purity which must always accompany the harmonious blending of the masculine and feminine forces within man. The child seated on the white horse typifies the complete transmutation of the lower into the higher, the material into spiritual.

The inner message and meaning of the Hebrew letter Quoph, and also the nineteenth Tarot card, are centered in the harmonious blending of the masculine and feminine forces within the body, a blending known in all Mystery Schools as the Mystic Marriage Rite.

Nowhere in mystical literature has this Rite been more exquisitely described than in the story of King Solomon and the beautiful Queen of Sheba. Solomon was the wisest man of the Old Testament Dispensation. He was also the highest Initiate of his time. The word Solomon means The Wisdom of the Sun. The word Sheba means Seven, which has reference to the seven mystical degrees of the Temple teachings. These are:

1. The Quest
2. The Awakening of Love
3. The Attainment of Knowledge (Many are called but few are chosen, for few there are who pass beyond the Third degree.)
4. Detachment (Here the Path begins to narrow.)

5. Unification or Blending (The Mystic Marriage Rite)
6. Annihilation (To become lost in God and to say with Christ, "Of myself I am nothing–God is all in all."
7. Divine Consummation

Solomon spent three years preparing for the coming of the Queen of Sheba. This refers to the three degrees preparatory to entering the Path of Initiation.

As Solomon awaited the Queen's coming he built two great walls which extended from the border of Israel to the gates of Jerusalem (the City of Peace). One of those walls was built of gold (the masculine power), the other of silver (the feminine power), and between the two he fashioned a great lake in which were mirrored all the beauties and wonders of the world. Attired in regal garments Solomon stood upon this lake to greet the beautiful Queen. The lake symbolizes the Akashic Records wherein are mirrored all important events which have occured upon this earth plane. It is here that in certain degrees the Initiate is permitted to read the record of his long past incarnational cycles.

The Queen arrived, robed in golden gossamer, adorned with the beautiful sevenfold colors of the rainbow. Both Solomon and Sheba are clothed in their wedding raiment, which must be fashioned by the Initiate before the Mystic Marriage Rite can be observed.

Sheba brought to Solomon priceless gifts in rare jewels of pearls and moonstones–feminine jewels which represent the beauty and holiness of the high feminine which Sheba symbolizes.

Solomon's gifts to Sheba were eight green rose trees from the mystic land of Damascus (green being the color of eternal life) and rare jars of healing waters from the magic Pool of Siloam. The body of the Initiate is often referred to as a "flower body." One possessing this body also has the ability to heal, as the Christ demonstrated many years later when he taught His disciples how to free others from blindness and obsession in the mystic waters of the Pool of Siloam.

The beautiful Marriage Song written to commemorate this high mystic rite is known as the Song of Solomon. This is not a sensuous love song, as so long believed, but is an Halleluia ("Praise God") of rejoicing, and strikes the highest spiritual keynote of the entire Old Testament.

The coming of Solomon represents the the beginning of the Quest, and the arrival of the Queen the entrance into the second degree, or passage through the veil of Love.

The blending of the two poles of spirit constitutes the Mystic Marriage, such as the Marriage at Cana described by St. John, and this is the real significance of Solomon's beautiful Marriage Song. Veiled for those not ready for the quest under the likeness of a vividly beautiful love song, the Song of Solomon is to the illumined a revelation from the very Holy of Holies, wherein he stands face to face with the Light Eternal, now no longer seen "as through a glass darkly," but with transcendent clearness.

In some of the verses King Solomon sings to his beloved, while in others the loved one sings to him. In this antiphonic arrangement is indicated the interaction of the two poles of spirit which express as Will (Epigenesis) and Imagination (the image-building faculty) whose interaction brings new creations into being.

Solomon in his matchless song refers in many ways and through many symbols to this blending of the two poles of spirit, this great Balance achieved interiorly, which is also the theme of the Zohar.

At the time of the separation of the sexes, the masculine aura partook of the golden glory of the Sun and the feminine of the silvery beauty of the Moon. King Solomon unites them again in the body of the Initiate, which he calls the raiment of his beloved, when he sings:

> We will make thee borders of gold, with studs of silver.
> A bundle of myrrh is my well-beloved unto me.
> (Song: 11, 13, 14.)
>
> I am the rose of Sharon, and the lily of the valleys. As the lily among thorns, so is my love among daughters. (Song: 2:1,2.)

The Hebrew word for Nazareth means a flower, and this flower is usually referred to as the lily. Thus Jesus of Nazareth literally means "Jesus, the Flower," or "the Lily," that is, Jesus, the pure one. The body of the new race will be a flower body, beautiful and fragrant. Man's place in evolution is between the flower kingdom and the gods. Both the rose and the lily refer to the awakening of certain centers of spiritual power within the body of man. The rose symbolizes the positive force and the lily the negative.

"My beloved is mine and I am his; he feedeth among the lilies." (Song: 2:16.) In this lovely verse King Solomon sounds the keynote of purity, the high note achieved through chastity, conservation and transmutation. Only through regeneration can the greater and the lesser selves be reunited in the Mystic Marriage, at which time the whole being exults in the ecstatic chant, "My beloved is mine, and I am his; he feedeth among the lilies."

"If the life is attuned to God every action is set to music." Both music and color form the setting of Solomon's soul chant. It breathes the fragrance of rose gardens and the deep loveliness of midnight skies studded with the light of blue-white stars.

"My beloved is mine and I am his, and he feedeth among the lilies," constitutes the chorus or sacred mantrum of the Song and sounds the keynote of the Fifth Degree, Unification. This, translated literally, means that when one learns to seek God as the first and supreme Reality he learns that God is seeking him with that same eager intensity, and the blending or merging of human consciousness with God-consciousness is productive of this same ecstatic note of the soul's awakening, "My beloved is mine and I am His."

At this point there is another change in the numerical alphabet. The letter Jod was the tenth, and it was used to signify the number 10. The eleventh letter, however, Kaph, signified not 11 but 20, and each letter thereafter signified the tenth number, until with Koph we find that the number signified is 100. The remaining three letters, Resh, Schin and Tav, represent the numerals 200, 300, and 400. Their significance in mystical numerology still revolves around the number of their place in the procession of letters, however. Nineteen, 1 plus 9, gave 10, which harmonizes with the tenth cosmic phase of the decad shown in the numeral 100.

Note that although both Kaph and Koph or Quoph have the sound "k," their numerical value differs; and the letter Koph is best thought of as Q, rather than K. Kabbalists often spell the word kabbalah with a Q–Quabbalah.

## RESCH

ר

Name: *resh*—sound: r

Resch, R, is the twentieth letter in the procession of letters, while numerically it signifies 200. The four letters which complete the Hebrew alphabet gather up into themselves the quintessential powers and significances of those that have gone before. According to the Zohar there are eighteen cosmic worlds, indicated by the first eighteen letter. Now we enter upon four planes which pass beyond the outer planes of matter and its limited consciousness, entering into the wide pastures of the Infinite and the Eternal.

Physiologically Resch has special reference to the pineal gland, which is the "seat" of the human spirit in occult philosophy. It stands for the ego, the thinker, and his power of creative thought or epigenesis. Epigenesis is the name for the fire of creative genius which is really latent in all beings.

Numerically Resch is 200, which reduces to 2, the number of the first manifestation of the feminine or formative principle, Beth. Its keyword is *Redemption*—for Resch signifies the end of the struggle for self-mastery, the culmination of the Great Work.

The Tarot glyph is an angel with wings of fire. He carries a trumpet decorated with a banner marked with a cross. This represents completion of the mystery of spirit as it is concerned with man's eventual and final unfoldment. Below the angel is an open grave from which issue forth a man, a woman and a child (symbolic of the human race). This is one of the most exquisite portrayals of the processes of Illumination and Resurrection ever given to man.

As the angel sounds the keynote of the Sun, the three figures rise from their graves (mortality). The stone of limitation (the five senses) is rolled away, freeing the spiritual consciousness for the glory of resurrection morn, as angelic hosts sing throughout the heavens, "He is risen from the dead."

Note the similarity of this glyph to the initiatory vision of St. John in Revelation, when he saw the angel clothed in the Sun descending from heaven.

## SCHIN

Name: *sheen* or *seen*—sound: sh and s

Schin is the twenty-first in the procession of letters, but numerically it signifies 300. It is a double letter, having two sounds, S and SH, and it is the last of the three mother letters—Aleph, Mem, Schin. As Aleph was Fire and Mem Water, Schin is Air. The three mother letters have been termed "the Trinity of Light." Aleph represents the head center of Light; Mem the heart center of Light; and Schin the body center of Light, the light which is vibratory power. Schin, the final letter of the third septenary, unites within itself the threefold powers of all of the three mother letters.

Schin, like the Cosmic Air which it typifies, is the power of expansion. Again it is called "the continuation of the arrow to its goal." Without this intrinsic impulse *to expand, to continue,* the human soul would have remained forever bound to the wheel of destiny, the karmic cycle of repeated births and deaths throughout all ages. Thus Schin represents the Christ Principle

Within which is *emancipation, the liberty of the Sons of God.* Note that Samekh, the fifteenth letter, is a serpent-symbol; but Schin is representative of the Macrocosmic Breath, the Breath of Life, which is a "serpent" of Air, not Fire.

By the time of the Greco-Roman Period in which Jesus appeared as the Christ, mankind had become so enmeshed in karmic reactions that no human teacher could extricate him, nor could he free himself. Therefore divine intervention was necessary, and the Christ came, saying, "I am the Way, the Truth and the Life." In these words we may discover the foundation of the Christian Mysteries. When man sets his feet upon the upward path, his ability to progress and to attain is endless and without limit.

Numerically Schin, being 300, and twenty-first in the alphabet, 2 plus 1 or 3, reduces in both instances to 3. The Trinity is always emblematic of fulfillment or completion. Here there is no more a fallen Eve but only the Mary who is lifted up.

The Tarot glyph is a female figure in the center of an ellipse. Her legs are crossed–as are those of the hanged man for the letter Lamed–to form a cross. In the four corners of the card are the four Recording Angels of human destiny: the lion (Leo), the bull (Taurus), the eagle (Scorpio) and the man (Aquarius). These four mighty Beings release the cosmic currents of Fire, Earth, Water and Air respectively, elements of all earthly manifestation.

Man is under the protection and guidance of these vast cosmic Beings until he shall awaken and develop the Godhood within himself. This development is known in all Mystery School parlance as "the exaltation of the Divine Feminine." In this celestial state the heart becomes the body's center of creation, and love is the primal impulse of the individual life.

Beneath the central figure is that of a young girl playing a three-stringed harp, symbolic of complete harmony between spirit, mind and body. The three-toned chord sounded through Aleph, Mem and Schin is perfected in eternal harmony.

The song of Schin may be translated in the biblical words

that mark the end of man's evolutionary course upon the planet earth, "Him that overcometh will I make a pillar in the temple of my God, and he shall go no more out." Earth's lessons are completed. The human cycles are finished. The egoic sheath is now the shining raiment of the Virgin Spirit. Schin denotes the final steps of Initiation.

Ancient Egyptians regarded Schin as a symbol of the universal soul. Its physiological relationship to the lower extremities refers not so much to the flesh-and-blood body as to the ethereal form:

*A body so clear and transparent of hue*
*One might see the moon shine through*

This body is represented in the Tarot glyph by the form of the maiden surrounded by the four sacred signs.

*Perfection,* ideal of attainment for the human race, is the keyword of Schin.

## Chapter VIII

## THE TWENTY-SECOND LETTER: TAV OR TAU

Name: *tav* or *tau*—sound: t, th, sometimes s

### *GOD GEOMETRIZES*

Tav or Tau is the twenty-second and final letter of the Hebrew alphabet of consonants, and last of the seven double letters. The three septenaries were completed with Schin. Tav or Tau concludes the entire alphabet. It signifies the number 400. As twenty-second in the procession of letters, Tau incorporates the powers of two 2's, symbolizing the lower and the higher Feminine, which are shown biblically in Mary Magdalen and the Virgin Mary, always together at the foot of the cross.

In our discussion of Teth, the ninth letter, we said that there was no X or T in the symbolism of the exoteric Hebrew alphabet and that the T was introduced into the Greek alphabet by Kadmus the Phoenician who gave to the Greeks their "Kadmean letters." A faint remembrance of ancient cultural and racial ties with the Greeks still lingered in the centuries just before the advent of the Christ, as we learn from the first Book of Maccabees, wherein we are told how Onias the High Priest wrote to the Lacedemonians, reminding them of this ancient kinship, and received this reply from Areus, King of the Lacedemonians, "It is found in writing that the Lacedemonians and Jews are brethren, and that they are of the stock of Abraham; now therefore, since this is come to our knowledge, ye shall do well to write unto us of your prosperity. We do write back to you again that your cattle and goods are ours and ours are yours. We do command therefore our ambassadors to make report unto you on this wise."

Both T and X are found in the Greek alphabet, and the apocryphal Hebrew legends also have something to say about them, and from this source the symbolism enters modern Freemasonry. An X-mark does occur in old Hebrew alphabets.

Apocryphal Masonic legends ascribe the Books of Tau and the symbolic T to Methusael, the descendant of Cain, as we learned in our study of the letter Teth, which is also T in sound; and we reviewed the story of Hiram Abiff, the Master Architect of Solomon's Temple, who plunged through the raging molten sea to the center of the earth where he met his ancestor Tubal-Cain and received from him a disk and a hammer, with which he returned to the surface of the earth and completed his masterpiece. Afterward he was attacked by three ruffians, but succeeded in throwing into a well the golden plate upon which was inscribed the Master's Word, which was thus lost. Rosicrucian legends state that Hiram Abiff was reborn as Lazarus, taking the name of John in Initiation, and becoming the author of the Fourth Gospel. Only in John's Gospel do we have the story of the raising of Lazarus, and only there does Mary Magdalen receive the supreme honor of being first to see the Risen Christ.

Four, and therefore 400 (the number of Tau), which is 4 raised to a supernal plane, relates to the number of the planet Earth. When Hiram arose from earth's center *he bore within himself* the mystic symbols; the disk and the hammer which became the ROSE AND THE CROSS.

The wonderful Books of Tau recorded the history of the Sons of Fire and detailed all of their wondrous wisdom and their secrets of the arts, crafts and sciences including also those deep mysteries pertaining to Earth's center, into which Hiram had been initiated by Tubal-Cain.

A hint has come down to modern man as to the esoteric significance of the Tau in Lucian's satire, "Trial in the Court of Vowels," in which he writes, "Men weep and bewail their lot and curse Kadmus with many curses for introducing Tau into the family of letters; they say it was his body that tyrants took for a model, his shape that they imitated, when they set up the erections on which men are crucified. *Staurus* (cross) the vile engine is called, and it derives its vile name from him." The legendary Kadmus is variously ascribed to a period close to that of Moses, approximately twelve or thirteen hundred years B.C. Scholars and historians are not unanimously agreed on the dates for Moses and the Patriarchs of the Bible; some ascribe the Mosaic period to the century following the Pharaoh Akhnaton, and many Hebrew historians believe that Moses was indeed a disciple of the monotheistic Pharaoh of Egypt who led the Hebrews and a few surviving Egyptian Aton-worshippers out into the wilderness and on to the borders of the Holy Land. Nor is this an unreasonable deduction, since verses closely similar to some of Akhnaton's hymns are still to be found in the Old Testament, although all trace of the Pharaoh was destroyed in Egypt, and even in the Zohar the tradition lingers that the name Adonai is found in the orb of the Sun.

From the Book of Exodus we learn that the Hebrews were builders, working on the pyramids in Egypt. The famous motion picture, "The Ten Commandments," portrays these scenes vividly, showing Moses as the architect in charge of the building operations. Important to these builders in Egypt was the Tau-cross, used for measuring the rise of the waters in the Nile. Together with the Pythagorean triangle, it constituted the most important of the builder's tools; it is well known that the so-called Pythagorean triangle was used by both Babylonians and Egyptians before the time of Pythagoras. Pythagoras was deeply indebted to the sages of Babylonia and Egypt, and reverence for Egypt continued throughout Greek history.

A triangle is the symbol of the pyramids, which are composite triangular structures. Some pyramids are built on a triangular base, but the Great Pyramid of Gizeh, and similar pyramids in Egypt, has a square base with triangular sides sloping to the apex where, however, the capstone is missing. Similarly, some Bible historians believe that Solomon's Temple was in reality a stepped pyramid, like that of Bel at Babylon, or perhaps like the three-staged pyramid of the Moon God of Ur in Chaldea whence Abraham came. The esotericist notes with interest the following parallels: that in the foundation of the pyramid of Bel, there was *an empty sepulcher* supposed to be that of the god Bel, who should one day return to be the savior of mankind; that in the Great Pyramid are two chambers, both containing empty sepulchers; that in the Holy of Holies of the Hebrew Temple was the Ark of the Covenant, and that legend says that the Holy of Holies and the Ark were both reminiscent of the King's Chamber and Sepulcher in the Great Pyramid. The Ark of the Covenant suggests an esoteric "measure of a (divine) Man." MAN HIMSELF IS THE ARK OF THE COVENANT.

A further consideration of "The Measure of a Man" is that in the Egyptian Osiris Mysteries the death of Osiris was enacted in which the evil Set made a coffin to fit Osiris and enticed him to lie in it; the coffin was then locked and thrown into the Nile River. It floated down to Byblos in the Egyptian Delta; this Byblos is often confused with the Byblos in Syria, where also the Osiris Mysteries were celebrated.

Isis found the coffin lodged in an acacia or tamarisk tree, which had grown up around it. The tree was cut down and made into a pillar. Isis took the pillar with her and hid the body, but Set found it and cut it into fourteen pieces. Again Isis searched for the fourteen parts of the body of Osiris and found all but one, which had been eaten by a fish.

Mystery legends vary according to the lesson which they teach in dramatic form; but one of the Osiris stories says that Isis again buried the fourteen parts where she found them, and so throughout the land of Egypt there were Temples sacred to one part or another of the body of the god. The shrine at Busiris, in the Delta of Lower Egypt, held the sacred relic of his backbone and sacrum, while in the shrine at Abydos, in the mountainous high south of Upper Egypt, the sacred head was the relic of the Mysteries. At one time in Egyptian history the Osirian Festival as a whole must have included a pilgrimage up and down the entire length of the Nile River from one shrine to another. The second and culminating form of this legend shows Isis as successfully putting the parts of Osiris' body together and raising him to immortality as god of the underworld and symbol of the Resurrection of all mankind.

Ancient astrologers also saw "the Measure of a Man" in the zodiacal stars, from Aries to Pisces, where the Divine Child of the Sky Goddess Nut was visible, and some divined by means of a "coffin" inscribed among the stars.

Solomon built his Temple on Mount Moriah at Jerusalem, which was the old stronghold of Melchizedek. This is one of the sacred mountains of the world. It was on Mount Moriah that Abraham became the adopted son and heir of Melchizedek in the Supper which is the prototype of the Last Supper of Our Lord with his disciples.

David procured the site for his proposed Temple, which Solomon built with the aid of King Hiram of Tyre and the Master Builder, Hiram Abiff who, the Bible tells us, was the son of a workman of Tyre and a widow of the tribe of Dan-Naphtali. (The two tribes in the north were virtually one and their names interchangeable.) We may add that Hiram Abiff was, however, no common workman but a prince in his own right. The tribe of Dan was a builder's tribe, and there was a Temple in the district of Dan and also in Ephraim (Samaria) for many centuries as well as other sacred shrines throughout the entire land.

Moriah is a mystery mountain. It is honeycombed with passages, many of them artificial, created when the site was enlarged to make possible the buildings necessary to the governing of the land by Solomon, and by later Kings who also enlarged the top of the hill. The westernmost chamber of the Temple was the Holy of Holies, which contained the Ark of the Covenant.

It was on Mount Moriah that Abraham offered up Isaac but substituted a ram in his place, in the ancient Chaldean manner; and so it was here in the forecourt of the Temple that the Brazen Altar was set up, on which were sacrificed many thousands of animals each year.

When Jesus of Nazareth was crucified, however, it was not in the Temple area but on Mount Golgotha, which adjoined the estate of Joseph of Arimathea. Yet in the Temple the "Shadow of the Cross" was visible to those who had eyes to see. From the Brazen Altar the upright of the cross ran straight and true to the Ark in the Holy of Holies; and across it lay the Holy Place with articles suggesting the crossbeam in the manner of their arrangement.

The relationship of geometry to the human body was a natural correlary of the architectural knowledge of the Egyptian priests who were able to observe in the bodies dissected by them or their assistants the architectural principles which caused them to think of the human body as a Temple in which the spirit dwelt as a god.

In the early centuries of our era, the Christian Fathers at Alexandria still knew of the nature of the brain, and of small organs lying within it, and of the fact that certain parts of the brain influenced specific localities of the body. They spoke of a fiery essence generated in the brain which passed through the spine, and while we may think of this physiologically as the spinal fluid, it is evident that they also knew of the electricity or life-force which flows through the nerves and the magnetism which holds the body together. Part of this was the result of experimentation, but much of it came from the visions of clairvoyance. Thus the seer visually beheld the "fire" and the "forces" which flowed in blood, bone, muscles and nerves, and this knowledge is hinted of even in the writings of the Church Fathers.

The T which was the builder's square and which consisted of two right angles was the basis of the Tet, which is the backbone of Osiris, also known as the Ladder of Osiris. The backbone of Osiris is pictured as nine (or 33, 3 x 3) steps which suggest a series of T's placed one upon another. It is the symbol of the Acacia tree, and a head or face is sometimes seen upon it.

Upon the ladder of the spine the life forces both descend and ascend, flowing through the central canal of the spinal cord as a stream of light. Eventually these forces pass through the twenty-eight plus three vertebrae at the top of the spine, which are ruled by the three fiery signs, Aries, Leo and Sagittarius; and as these are vivified a new cycle of unfoldment begins. These are the 31 vertebrae of the human spine, which attune man to the solar cycle, whereas the spine of the animal with 28 vertebrae is attuned to the cycle of the Moon. The Osiris pillars often show 30 steps or stages plus a base or a capital which may also be double or triple.

At last the forces enter the head, flowing toward the point at the root of the nose where the seed atom of the mind is located, and where the Divine Spirit (Will Principle) of the spirit has its citadel. Just below, and nearby, is the pituitary body, above the roof of the mouth. Impinging upon the root center in the frontal sinus, the forces set into vibration "the Crown of Thorns," which means that the cranial nerves are being sensitized and are becoming responsive to the vibrations from the spiritual worlds.

It was the activity of this ascending fire-force as it reached the center in the frontal sinus that was viewed by Egyptian seers and portrayed as the Uraeus serpent upon the crown of the Pharaoh, signifying that he was an Initiate in the Mysteries.

These are the Mysteries of Thoth-Hermes, or the letter T, the sign by which the Master Workman called forth to labor upon the Temple of Solomon and the sign by which Moses called their Egyptian brethren forth in an earlier time to labor upon the pyramids of Egypt. The fact that T may also have the sound S, the hiss of the serpent, suggests an esoteric relationship between Samekh, Schin, Moses' staff and the Tau cross, and Aaron's Rod that budded, as well as with the letter Teth and the number nine.

When Moses led the Israelites out of Egypt and when they were wandering in the desert, many were grievously stung by scorpions. Moses raised up a serpent on his staff, commanding them to look upon it and be saved. This is the Hebrew Caduceus, emblem of the God of Healing, who in the ranks of the ancient Hebrew gods corresponds with Mercury of the Greeks. All students of biblical history know that the Hebrew "angels" are in fact no other than the "gods" and "goddesses" of the pagans, as many ancient pictures and statues clearly show. Mercury and Iris were chief of the "angeloi" or "messengers" of

God; both are winged, and Iris is surrounded with a rainbow halo.

By the Serpent raised up on the Staff *within himself* Moses performed his miracles, healed the multitude in the desert, provided manna and water, and led them to the borders of the promised land. By the same power *within himself* the Lord Christ multiplied the loaves and fishes, healed the sick, raised Lazarus from the tomb and performed for himself the miracle of the Resurrection.

But the work of Tau is not complete until it is joined to the circle. This is the Work of the Mysteries of Isis. When a circle was added above the T-cross it became the Ankh cross, or Cross of Life, sacred to the divine Mother Isis. Isis it was who resurrected Osiris from the dead, collecting the parts of his body together and speaking over them the "words of life" which she had obtained from the Sun God. Her sign surmounts the Tet.

The circle drawn over or upon the cross has also a special connotation in the serpent of the rainbow. The commonly accepted picture of the rainbow is that of an arc of colors in the heavens opposite to the Sun, but if one ascends to a high place in the mountains the rainbow is seen as a circle. Mountain-dwelling peoples would have known this. The rainbow is the Circle Glory of the Divine Feminine, symbol of the Shekinah Glory in kabbalism, the Covenant of the Rainbow.

And so it is that in Temple symbolism the two pillars are crowned with globes and with pomegranates, which are the sign of the Sun and Moon and also of the Divine Mother and her life-giving powers.

Following upon this, the relationship of the T, the T-square, and the equal-armed cross is obvious. The equal-armed red cross is often termed "the solar cross," but the symbol for the Earth always was, and still is, the circle divided into fourths by two intersecting diameters. In many of these ancient mysteries we must know that the priesthood understood that the Earth was round and knew that it journeyed around the Sun in its orbit; the priests knew, too, that Venus was one star, not two. And so the secret of Freemasonry and of Moses is that the tomb of

Osiris is the Earth itself, from which he rises unto his throne of the Sun in the heavens.

In esoteric Christianity it is the Christ Ray which penetrates to the core of the planet Earth, and when the 3 x 3 Initiate has gone through the Nine Lesser Mysteries founded by Hermes Trismegistus, he is joined to the Liberator and is released from the Wheel of Death and Rebirth, for at the center of the wheel there is rest. The central Earth Mysteries are symbolized geometrically in The Point, the Square and the Circle, all drawn in one figure.

Masonic symbolism shows a widow weeping over a broken column. This has been interpreted as signifying Isis weeping over the broken column, which contains the body of Osiris, and also as the Queen of Sheba weeping for Hiram Abiff. Esoterically it is the Divine Feminine who weeps over the chaos caused by the misuse of her powers by mankind.

Tau is the emblem of humanity–the widow, the Queen of Sheba, weeping over the slain Hiram; Mary weeping for the Christ; Isis weeping for the slain Osiris; the Voice of the Shekinah crying in the streets, "Unto you, O man, do I call."

The Tau shows us the human spirit bound to the cross of matter. The entire cycle of evolution (the way of the masses) and of Initiation (the way of the few) are bound up in this mystery of the Divine Feminine. In the "fall" of this principle in man lies the origin of the cross, which is a universal symbol, not the exclusive property of any one people or nation. All Mystery Temples have two columns before the portal, emblematic of the masculine and feminine in equilibrium. These will be the symbol of the religion of Initiation of the Aquarian Age. It is significant that among the early Christians *Resurrection* and *Exaltation* were synonymous terms.

So long as the "fallen" Feminine, or Love Principle attached to wrong objects, gives rise to the cross as a universal symbol, so long will Mars, the lord of war and separation, reign supreme over the lives of men; and so long will earth continue to be known as the "Sorrowful Star."

It now becomes clear why the two female figures are always

pictured together at the foot of the Cross in the Rite of the Crucifixion. The path trod by Christ Jesus was not laid out for himself alone. Each and every disciple must tread the same path, to the same goal. Tau, as the twenty-second letter, is 2 plus 2 or 4, and again the 400 which is the same principle raised to a cosmic level and potency.

Four is the number of letters in the Tetragrammaton: Yod-HeVau-He (which becomes the I.N.R.I. of the New Testament). These are the letters engraved upon the Rod of Aaron which is preserved in the Holy of Holies, within the Ark of the Covenant, which is Man himself in the image and likeness of God. There also to our own day is the mystical Staff of Moses, called the Brazen Serpent by means of which he performed miracles. "All things are possible in My Name," the Power of Four.

The Tarot glyph for Tau is symbolic of the human race being left without protection of the Divine Feminine until it has passed through all manner of trials and tests. This is shown in the broken obelisk, covered with hieroglyphics. We see a lightly clothed man, laden down with a burden which hangs front and back, blindfolded and is oblivious of the crocodile which lurks behind the fallen obelisk waiting to devour his prey. The man leans on a thin frail staff which fails to warn him of the gaping jaws into which he will surely fall. The Sun is partially eclipsed by a shadow, symbolizing *fear*, but also *hope*, since the Sun will shine again in due course. Truly,

*Things are in the saddle*
*And ride mankind*

## *THE POINT OF PERFECTION*

In every human being there lies concealed the Point of Perfection which is the Fire of Aleph. Upon this Point without dimension are inscribed all of the geometric figures which form the archetypes of the cosmos.

Within every human soul the Dual Powers of Aleph and Beth make manifest the hidden mystery of the Point of Perfection.

Within the Head of the human body is the Triangle of Light, and the three mother letters, Aleph, Mem and Schin are the Triple Glory which form the halo around the head.

From the Triple Glory have come the other nineteen letters, descending to the outermost and returning once more to be lifted up on the Tau. The Point, the Square, and the Circle have shone in the heavens for a cycle of time and return to their source.

Man, consisting of a series of triple formations, has fulfilled his labors, and has become once more one of the Sons of God, the Bene Elohim. The disk and the hammer (Tau) have become the Rose and the Cross.

The mystic septenaries ended with Schin, picture of the glorified man of the future. Tau belongs to the present, which must pass away when mortality is swallowed up in immortality, and the cross, formed by the feminine pillar fallen across the masculine, disappears from the esoteric symbolism where the two upright pillars stand firmly in nobility and strength before the entrance to the Temple. Matter has been transmuted into Spirit, and Time swallowed up in Eternity.

To those who are still wandering in the wilderness of sense gratification and materialism, Tau remains the cross of sorrow and suffering, and its keyword is *Destruction*; but when the serpent is raised up on the staff of Moses, and they lift their eyes to gaze thereon, they are healed, for this staff with its serpent, or Serpent Staff, is the FIERY GOD POWER WITHIN. Its keyword is CONSUMMATION, as revealed in the words spoken by Christ Jesus on the cross, taken from the 22nd Psalm, "It is finished."

The course has been run from Aleph to Tau.

It is completed.

## THE SUPERIOR NUMBERS

We have shown in another place that after the number 400 has been reached with the letter-number Tau, the count returns once more to Kaph, which is the first of five letters having a "final" form. That is, this letter and four others are written in a special way when they fall at the end of a word.

K, Kaph, the eleventh letter, which in its ordinary form denotes the number 20, is used in its final form to denote 500.

M, Mem, the thirteenth letter, which in its ordinary form denotes 40, is used in its final form to denote 600.

N, Nun, the fourteenth letter, which in its ordinary form denotes 50, is used in its final form to denote 700.

P, Phe, the seventeenth letter, which in its ordinary form denotes 50, is used in its final form to denote 800.

TZ, Tzaddi, the eighteenth letter, which in its ordinary form denotes 90, is used in its final form to denote 900.

For 1000, a word translated "many" is used in the Old Testament, which also signifies tribe or family. The Egyptian symbol for 1000—one of the very first hieroglyphs to be deciphered by Egyptologists—is the lotus. A botanist has said that upon the stamen of the blue Egyptian lotus one may see the symbol of two interlaced triangles—the family emblem of David, and sign of the Messiah. This is not the five-pointed Star which is the Seal of Solomon and the "Endless Knot"—it can be drawn without lifting the pen from the paper—and symbolizes the Silver Cord and the forces of the ego in embodiment. Nor is it the eight-pointed star of Phe, which associates with the Star Sirius.

It was commonly held in antiquity that the average cycle of reincarnations was one thousand years; hence the Messiah was to come one thousand years after David. The exact time would be shown by signs in the heavens and signs upon earth. Again we note that the lily has a special significance for Israel as a nation.

Tzaddi we see as the eighteenth letter-number, signifying 90 and 900. As there are eighteen kabbalistic worlds, so there are eighteen "Lesser Mysteries"—the 3 x 3, or Ennead, repeated-after which the Initiate enters the School of the Greater Mysteries as they were created by the Christ. There are seven Schools which teach the Nine Lesser Mysteries (sometimes called Seven); there are five Schools which teach the Four

Greater Mysteries. These Four Greater Mysteries correlate with the four terminal letters, Koph or Quoph, 100; Resch, 200; Schin. 300; and Tau, 400.

In Freemasonry the number 18 denotes the Degree of the Rose Cross, which is one of the seven Schools devoted to the Nine Lesser Mysteries.

From the time of the introduction of the Arabic numerals into Europe there is a revolution in the mystical numerology of the kabbalists; and since the new knowledge was applied to the ancient texts, a certain confusion may be observed.

However, the basic principles of Kabbalah do not change. The Hebrew theosophy is based throughout on the Ptolemaic astronomy of the second century A.D., which looked upon all mathematics and all cosmic phenomena as manifestations of the Will of God. Each number had a sacred power and a sacred meaning, in the Pythagorean tradition. Mathematical processes were revelations of divine Wisdom. Further unfolding of mathematical mysteries was simply the continuing revelation of God's infinite and therefore illimitable Wisdom.

On the basis of numbers, when Zero was added to the scheme, the higher numbers were read as pertaining to divine powers on ever–ascending planes of consciousness, and this was shown by the addition of zeros. The Zero separated the real Decads, but *One* was still basic, symbolizing the Unity of Infinity and Eternity. The number *Ten* 10, was the same Unity acting in the worlds of manifestation, through Ten Aspects or powers. The 100 was the tenth power or level of expression of the 10, a further unfolding in terms of the Age. The number 100 denotes an Age. This may have been determined on the reckoning of the precession of the equinoxes, which was well known to ancient astronomers, but their figures were not the same as those used today. One ancient figure yields the rate of precession as 1 degree in 100 years. The Indian texts show 1 degree for 600 years. The modern figure is 1 degree for 72 years (or nearly so), and some Egyptologists declare that the ancient Egyptians actually used a number very close to this.

Because 1000 was the reincarnation number, it was

associated with the coming of World Saviors. Hence the coming of the Messiah was looked for in Palestine, and other ancient nations were also looking for their Savior at the same time. Virgil wrote of a Savior before the time of Christ, and his prophecy was taken to refer to the Caeser Augustus. Egyptologists tell us of an ancient Egyptian prophecy of the coming of a Shepherd-King for whom the people waited throughout their history as a nation.

Egypt and the Greco-Roman world, and also Persia and India, held that the creation of the universe had taken place in the myriads of years before their time; but the Hebrew-Christian scholars in later centuries in Europe, calculating from the genealogies of the Old Testament, placed the creation of the world by God as 3761 B. .C. (Hebrew) and 4004 B.C. (Christian). Other dates are found in the apocryphal books. These dates would seem to refer to the rise of a new astronomy in the area extending through Persia, Assyria and Babylonia, Palestine and Egypt, as shown in the Old Testament.

The modern kabbalist is under no compulsion to accept these traditional figures and their interpretation. The kabbalistic principle, however, still holds true, for it is the recognition of the fact that God's Intelligence is present throughout the universe, and that in the unfolding of new mysteries of mathematics and astronomy, man is receiving a new revelation of God's Will for himself and for the universe.

Today the mystic must harmonize the spiritual revelations familiar to him with the further unfolding of science and mathematics, for he continues to hold with his ancient predecessors that all knowledge, all mathematics, all number, is in very fact the revelation of the continued unfolding of God's Will in time and space. It is for us to learn to read the divine script aright.

## Chapter IX

# PARABLE OF THE LETTERS

eachers of all ages have used little lesson-stories to impress the memory and awaken the understanding of their pupils. In the New Testament such stories are represented in the parables which the blessed Lord Christ gave to his followers. These stories are sometimes homely and whimsical, but they always clarify a particular teaching and make it striking and memorable. A mere admonition may be forgotten, but when it is illustrated with a vivid story it is impressed deeply upon the emotions as well as the mind. And so it is that in the Hebrew writings, as in all mystical literature everywhere, parables abound, sometimes quaint, sometimes beautiful and inspiring, but always pointing up a profound lesson.

From the Zohar of Moses de Leon we have taken the parable of the letters of the Hebrew alphabet. Not only is this parable a helpful lesson on the Hebrew letters as such, together with related words, but it contains many hidden gems of mystical wisdom and understanding. The letters are personified as feminine angels enthroned before God before the dawn of creation, for the letters had to be in existence when He spoke the creative fiat. The letter-angels address God as Lord of the World, meaning not the physical world which was not then created but the spiritual universe with its ranks of angels, archangels and other divine beings. The letters present themselves before God in reverse order, beginning with Tau, because the lower worlds are a reflection of the higher ones, as in the Hermetic axiom, "As it is above, so it is below," and they will be reversed when they appear in the mirror or crystal of time and space.

All ancient mystic teachers used the symbolism of the mirror to explain or elucidate the mysteries of the created universe in relation to its archetype in the heaven worlds. And so it is that we find the letter-angels appearing before the Divine Face as in a mirror which is yet empty of images, with Tau, the last letter advancing first, "The first shall be last, and the last first."

Historically we note that Hebrew is written from right to left, hence the letter-angels who appear before God in reverse order, from T to A, suggest an opposite arrangement, such as we find in the Greek alphabet, which uses the same letters but writes them from left to right, which is the case in English also. We are reminded of Lucian's satire on the trial of the letters in the court of the vowels, quoted in another place, which was evidently inspired by just such mystical playing with letters as we find in this parable.

The parable of the letters was related by Rab Hamnuna, the Venerable, in commentary on the verse in the book of Genesis, "In the beginning, God created."

* * *

When the Holy One, blessed be He, was about to make the world, all the letters of the alphabet were still embryonic, and for two thousand years the Holy One had contemplated them and toyed with them. When He came to create the world, all the letters presented themselves before Him in reversed order. The letter *Tau* advanced in front and pleaded, May it please Thee, O Lord of the World, to place me first in the creation of the world, seeing that I am the concluding letter of EMeTH (Truth) which is engraved upon thy seal; and seeing that Thou art called by this very name of EMeTH, it is most appropriate for the King to begin with the final letter of EMeTH and to create with me the world.

The Holy One, blessed be He, said to her, Thou art worthy and deserving, but it is not proper that I begin with thee the creation of the world, since thou art destined to serve as a mark on the foreheads of the faithful one (Ezekiel ix:4) who have kept the law from Aleph to Tau, and through absence of this mark the rest will be killed; and further, thou formest the conclusion of MaWeTH (death). Hence thou art not to initiate the creation of the world.

The *shin* then came to the fore and pleaded, O Lord of the World, may it please Thee to begin with me the world, seeing that I am the initial letter of Thy name Sha DDaI (Almighty), and it is most fitting to create the world through that Holy Name. Said He in reply, Thou art worthy, thou art good, thou art true, but I may not begin through thee the creation of the world, since thou formest part of the group of letters expressing forgery, SheKeR (falsehood), which is not able to exist unless the Koph and Resh draw thee into their company. Hence it is that a lie, to obtain credence, must always commence with something true. For the *Shin* is a letter of truth, that letter by which the Patriarchs communed with God; but Koph and Resh are letters belonging to the evil side, which in order to stand firm attach to themselves the Shin, thus forming a conspiracy (QeSheR). Having heard all this, the Shin departed.

Enters the *Zade* and says, O Lord of the World, may it please Thee to create with me the world, inasmuch as I am the sign of the righteous (Zadikim) and of Thyself who art called righteous, as it is written, "For the Lord is righteous, he loveth righteousness" (Ps.xi:7), and hence it is meet to create the world with me. The Lord made answer, O Zade, thou are Zade, and thou signifiest righteousness, but thou must be concealed, thou mayest not come out in the open so much lest thou givest the world cause for offence. For thou consistest of the letter Nun surmounted by the letter Yod (representing together the male and female principles). And this is the mystery of the creation of the first man, who was created with two faces (male and female combined). In the same way the Nun and the Yod in the Zade are turned back to back and not face to face, whether the Zade is upright or turned downwards. The Holy One, blessed be He, said to her further, I will in time divide thee in two, so as to appear face to face, but thou wilt go up in another place. She then departed.

The letter *Pe* presented herself and pleaded thus, May it

please Thee, O Lord of the World, to create through me the world, seeing that I signify redemption and deliverance (Purkana, Peduth), which Thou are to vouchsafe to the world. It is, hence, meet that through me the world be created. The Lord answered: Thou art worthy, but thou represented transgression (Pesha), and moreover thou art shapen like the serpent who had his head curled up within his body, symbolic of the guilty man who bends his head and extends his hand.

The letter *'Ayin* was likewise refused as standing for iniquity ('Awon), despite her plea that she represent humility ('Anavah). Then the SAMEKH appeared and said, O Lord of the World, may it please Thee to create through me the world, inasmuch as I represent upholding (Semikah) of the fallen, as it is written, "The Lord upholdeth all that fall" (Ps. CXLV, 14). The Lord answered her, This is just the reason why thou shouldst remain in thy place, for shouldst thou leave it, what will be the fate of the fallen seeing that they are upheld by thee? She immediately departed.

The *Nun* entered and pleaded her merits as being the initial letter in "Fearful (Nora) in praises" (Ex. xv, 11), as well as in "Comely (Nawa) is praise for the righteous" (Ps. xxxiii, 1). The Lord said, O Nun, return to thy place, for it is for thy sake (as represented in the falling, Nofelim) that the Samekh returned to her place. Remain therefore, under her support. The Nun immediately returned to her place.

The *Mem* came up and said, O lord of the World, may it please Thee to create by me the world, inasmuch as I commence the word Melkh (King), which is Thy title. The Lord replied, It is so assuredly, but I cannot employ thee in the creation of the world for the reason that the world requires a King. Return, therefore, to thy place, thou along with the Lamed and the Kaph, since the world cannot exist without a MeLeKh (King).

At that moment, the *Kaph* descended from its throne of glory, two hundred thousand worlds began to shake, the throne trembled, and all the worlds quaked and were about to fall in ruins. Said to her the Holy One, blessed be His Name, Kaph, Kaph, what doest thou here? I will not create the world with thee. Go back to thy place, since thou standest for extermination (Kelayah). Return then to thy place and remain there. Immediately she departed to her own place.

The letter *Yod* then presented herself and said, May it please thee, O Lord, to vouchsafe me the first place in the creation of the world, since I stand first in the Sacred Name. The Lord said to her, It is sufficient for thee that thou art engraved and marked in Myself and that thou art the channel of my will; thou must not be removed from My Name.

The *Teth* came up and said, O Lord of the Universe, may it please Thee to place me at the head in the creation of the world, since through me thou are called Good (Tob) and upright. The Lord said to her, I will not create the world through thee, as the goodness which thou representest is hidden and concealed within thyself, as it is written—O how abundant is thy goodness which thou hast laid up for them that fear thee (Psalms 31:20). Since then it is treasured within thyself, it has no part in the world which I am going to create, but only in the world to come. And further, it is because thy goodness is hidden within thee that the gates of the Temple sank into the ground, as is written—Sunk (Tabe'u) in the ground are her gates. (Lam. 11:9). And furthermore the letter Heth is at thy side, and when joined you make sin (Chet). (It is for that reason that these two letters are not found in the names of any of the tribes). She departed immediately.

Then the *Zayin* presented herself and put forth her claim, saying, O Lord of the World, may it please Thee to put me at the head of creation, since I represent the observance of the Sabbath, as it is written—Remember (Zakhor) the day of the Sabbath to keep it holy (Ex. xx:8). The Lord replied, I will not create the world through thee, since thou representest war, being in shape like a sharp-pointed sword or lance. The Zayin immediately departed from His presence.

The *Vau* entered and put forth her claim, saying, O Lord of the World, may it please Thee to use me first in the creation of the world, inasmuch as I am one of the letters of thy Name. Said the Lord to her, Thou, Vau, as well as He, suffice it to thee that thou art of the letters of my Name, part of the Mystery of My Name, engraven and impressed in My Name. I will therefore not give thee first place in the creation of the world.

Then appeared the letter *Daleth* as well as the letter *Gimel* and they put forth similar claims. The Lord gave them a similar reply, saying, It should suffice thee to remain side by side together, since "the poor will not cease from the land" (Deut. xv:11), who will thus need benevolence. For the Daleth signifies poverty (Dalluth) and the Gimel beneficence (Gemul). Therefore separate not from each other, and let it suffice thee one maintains the other.

The *Beth* then entered and said, O Lord of the World, may it please Thee to put me first in the creation of the world, since I represent the benedictions (Berakhoth) offered to thee on high and below. The Holy One, blessed be He, said to her, Assuredly, *with thee I will create the world,* and thou shalt form the beginning in the creation of the world.

The letter *Aleph* remained in her place without presenting herself. Said the Holy One, blessed be His Name, Aleph, wherefore comest thou not before me like the rest of the letters? She answered, Because I saw all the other letters leaving thy presence without any success. What, then, could I achieve there? And further, since thou hast already bestowed upon the letter Beth this great gift, it is not meet for the Supreme King to take away the gift which He has made to His servant and give it to another. The Lord said to her, Aleph, although I will begin the creation of the world with Beth, thou shalt remain the first of the letters. My unity shall not be expressed except through thee, on thee shall be based all calculations and operations of the world, and Unity shall not be expressed save by the letter Aleph.

Then the Holy One, blessed be His Name, made higher-world letters of a large pattern and lower-world letters of a small pattern. It is therefore that we have here two words beginning with Beth (Bereshith bara) and then two words beginning with Aleph (Elohim Teth). They represent the higher-world letters and the lower-world letters, which two operate, above and below, together and as one.

# PART III

# A COMPARATIVE STUDY
# OF
# THE
# BIBLE AND THE TAROT

## Chapter X

## TAROT ORIGINS

o one today knows the real origin of the Tarot picture cards. They have been traced as far as the thirteenth century in Europe, but students of the Tarot symbolism believe that in the nature of the symbolism as such, there is evidence that it has come down to us from the Temples of ancient Egypt and Babylonia.

The first outstanding scholar of the Tarot in modern times was the Count de Gebelin, the French archeologist, who in the years c. 1773 to 1782 set forth the theory that the Tarot cards originated in Egypt. On the basis of this understanding a set of cards was later drawn up with Egyptian pictures in imitation of the vignettes which are inscribed at the head of each chapter of the Book of the Dead. These pictures, however, follow the patterns of the "Bohemian" Tarot, which had been circulating in Europe, especially in Southern France, and were used for fortune-telling by bands of wandering gypsies. A.E. Waite takes credit to himself as having been the first to introduce the Tarot to the English-speaking public in 1887 in a digest of the writings of Eliphas Levi.

Egypt's magic had come down to the Middle Ages of Europe in a legendary form from the ancient Greeks and Romans, who had looked with superstitious awe upon the might and the glory and the wisdom of the Egyptians. Medieval Jews of Spain and Egypt (notably Maimonides–Moses ben Maimon–of Cairo and Moses de Leon of Granada) were in touch with a still living tradition of Egyptian wisdom in the Gnostic documents hidden away in crypts and temples in ancient lands. It was in the last half of the eighteenth century, when the American colonies were breaking away from the British Empire, that the Coptic document *Pistis Sophia* appeared in England. A letter written in

1773 states that a Dr. Askew found this document in a book shop, and references to it are found in print as early as 1770. Dr. Askew's heirs sold the *Pistis Sophia* to the British Museum in 1785.

Meanwhile, the Scotsman, James Bruce, was inspired by higher powers to travel to Abyssinia (Ethiopia) to learn if any copies of the Book of Enoch still survived in the first century, as shown in the Book of Acts of the New Testament. From 1768 to 1773 Bruce sought for the Book of Enoch and succeeded at last in finding three copies which he brought back to England. One copy he gave to the Library of Paris, one to the Bodleian Library of Oxford and one he placed in the family archives.

The book *Pistis Sophia* was written in Coptic, which is the last form of the Egyptian language used in Egypt, written down in Greek characters. The Book of Enoch which James Bruce found was inscribed in Geez, the ancient language of Ethiopia. Scholars and historians believe that no one in Europe could read these documents at the time they appeared there; yet there were many strange unfoldments of history during the nineteenth century which intimate that a Gnostic revival was taking place, arising from some unknown source. During this century Rosicrucianism and Freemasonry took a fresh hold upon European and American thought. The Pyramid of Gizeh was adopted as a symbol by the new American nation. As higher degrees were added to the basic degrees of the Blue Lodge in Freemasonry, evidences of kabbalistic thought were more and more conspicuous, and Egyptian influence more and more in evidence.

Now we are in a position to understand the eminent scholarship of the Count de Gebelin and his interest in things Egyptian. An intelligent youth, he grew to manhood in an era in which these and other mysterious documents were being discovered and somehow, somewhere, by persons unknown, translated into the languages of Europe.

It was in this same era that the Egyptian hieroglyphs were first deciphered. The honor for this is generally bestowed upon the young Champollion (1790-1832); but earlier than Champollion, an Englishman had already succeeded in deciphering some of the hieroglyphs, an Englishman by the name of Thomas Young (1773-1829). His brother was the poet Edward Young.

In the Egyptian rites of Freemasonry created by Cagliostro (who lived from 1743 to 1795), scholars have discovered evidence which indicates that Cagliostro may indeed have known the meaning of certain Egyptian hieroglyphs.

When we consider that this was also the era of the great Count St. Germain, "the Wonder Man of Europe," we have a hint of the truth; for it is said of this man that he spoke every living language of occident and orient, and was equally learned in the dead languages. It was believed that he had travelled throughout the world to many far off and mysterious places.

According to Max Heindel, there are in existence on earth five schools which teach the Four Great Initiations and seven schools which teach the Nine Lesser Initiations. He intimates that one at least of the five schools of the Greater Mysteries is located in Palestine, for the Christ founded all of these Greater Mysteries; one of the schools of the Lesser Mysteries he states is located in southern Germany–the Order of the Rose Cross, of which he was the representative, and another he mention as existing in Egypt. In early lectures he also intimates that a Temple of the Lesser Mysteries is situated in the Himalayas.

It is noteworthy that not only the Hebrews but also the Egyptians and ancient Indians had a "kabbalah" that is a mystical interpretation of the letters of the alphabet, which were looked upon as sacred revelations from God. The Word itself, the Living Sound, came from God, and every letter, every word, of the sacred language might be read both as a letter and as a divine ideogram which revealed the deepest and most abtruse mysteries of Spirit.

The Tarot is of intense interest to the occult student because it contains an outline of Initiation; and as some form of Initiation has formed the heart of every world religion, the truths contained in the Tarot symbolism are universal and belong to no one race, creed or culture, but constitute a textbook for every serious aspirant on the Path of Light.

The Tarot system consists of twenty-two Arcana, or Arcanes as they are also termed. This word means something hidden, secret, mysterious. These Arcana outline the Path from its beginning to its end in the supreme attainment. Having twenty-two Major Arcanes, its likeness to the Hebrew Alphabet is at once apparent and suggests a connection with esoteric Christianity as arising from the ancient Hebrew Mysteries. For each of the Major Arcanes there is a letter of the Hebrew alphabet, a number from 1 to 22 in direct sequence, and in another order from Hebrew numeration, and also an astronomical signature. Writers are not in agreement on these various symbols as attached to the Tarot cards; A.E.Waite intimates that he himself has the true key, which he does not choose to reveal, but he adds that the symbolism is so rich in meaning that any study of the Tarot is rewarding.

The Bible is one of the profound cipher books of the world. From Genesis to Revelation it outlines the Path of Initiation. Like the Tarot, the Bible has its exoteric interpretation, available to the many; it has also its esoteric interpretation, which is to the exoteric as the soul is to the body, as the great Christian scholar and mystic, Origen of Alexandria, observed.

Perhaps the greatest value of the Tarot teaching is its appeal to the intellectualist in religion. The devotee is generally termed "the Mystic" while the scientist or philosopher is termed "the Occultist." Yet the philosopher and the mystic may be one and the same individual, for as the philosopher he may rationalize all of the occult mysteries, while as a mystic he experiences them and comes to know God "face to face" or to "taste" God, as the mystic states.

The philosopher who endeavors to understand the Bible Mysteries takes the Bible narratives and discourses into his consciousness by a process of reasoning in which every character and situation, every text and commentary, relate to formulae of Initiation. Thus his understanding forms a bridge over which he enters into the experience of the inner truths of the Scriptures.

Here he meets the mystic on his own ground.

Again we may say that the philosopher *reasons about* Wisdom; the mystic *experience* ("tastes") Wisdom. The Hebrew mystic-philosophers who created the Kabbalah endeavored to combine both Paths, signified in the two Sephiroth Chockmah and Binah, Wisdom and Understanding. So also the Tarot ciphers are aids to meditation and knowledge for the occultist and revelation for the mystic.

In the present studies we are not interested in the fortunetelling aspect of the Tarot, but we are concerned entirely with the inner or spiritual significance, which pertains to the Path of Initiation as represented in the twenty-two Major Arcana or Arcanes.

We are using the cards known as "the Egyptian Tarot," with Egyptian pictures of designs. They reflect the overwhelming fascination of all things Egyptian upon the minds of eighteenth and nineteenth century Europeans; but they are merely imitative of the Egyptian vignettes from the Book of the Dead, drawn by some unknown artist. In some instances we refer to A.E. Waite's Tarot, the pictures for which were drawn under his personal direction; these are medieval European in setting and style.

Some modern mythologists who have studied the Tarot observe that these cards may be linked with the Druid Mysteries. We have noted earlier that the Druid alphabet, like the Hebrew, consisted of twenty-two letters. This, however, is a problem which involves the Anglo-Israel theory, which holds that the Druid religion was really a form of the ancient Hebrew religion, and that Jesus visited Glastonbury in England in his youth, and that Joseph of Arimathea was the first Bishop of Christendom and founded the first Christian Church in Britain. This problem cannot be discussed in these pages but some of the deepest mysteries of Christianity are conerned therewith.

Here we deal solely with the Major Tarot Arcana, and we endeavor to show how each one of these Arcana, or Arcanes, may be correlated with a story and a teaching in the Bible.

## Chapter XI

## THE FIRST SEPTENARY OF ARCANA

### ARCANE I

*The Magus*

The First Arcanum is that of the High Priest or Magus, the divine Magician. He is robed in white, symbol of his attainment through purity. His head is encircled with a golden crown, typifying the awakening of the spiritual organs located therein. His waist is engirdled with a golden serpent typifying eternal Wisdom. One hand holding a scepter points upward to heaven, meaning that his high attainment has united the forces of both heaven and earth. He is a majestic figure and typifies the perfected masculine principle. He embodies the God-Power of Aleph and the number 1, which is God-in-manifestation.

Biblically he is representative of Adam in Paradise before Eve (the rib) had been taken out of his side. He is masculine as he looks upon the world spreading out before him, for the feminine is hidden within. As a result of the division into sexes, mankind descends from the Mount of Paradise and enters the lower realms of matter, space and time where the Opposites hold sway, and Paradise is but a remembered dream of bliss. The Magus has found the secret Path leading back to that Mount of Glory.

The word table in Hebrew refers to something which is spread out, or in which something is enfolded. Esoterically, it refers to an aura of protection. Upon the table before which the Master stands are arranged four articles which are symbolical of his Path of high attainment. The first is a Wand or Scepter, which represents the God-power awakened within him. The second is a Cup, which symbolizes transmutation (the personality transformed into spirit). The third article is a Sword, symbol of victory, the victory of renunciation, of learning to walk the way of pain and sorrow in perfect peace. The fourth article is a golden coin which typifies truth, as enunciated by the Lord Christ to His Disciples in the words, "Seek ye *first* the kingdom of heaven and all else shall be added unto you."

## ARCANE II

*The High Priestess*

The Second Arcanum is that of the High Priestess and is termed the Gate of the Sanctuary. The Priestess is seated on a throne between two columns, one white, the other black. These typify the contesting forces of the "opposites" so-called White against Black, with which every aspirant becomes familiar when he enters the Path of Attainment. The "opposites" include Day and Night, Good and Evil, New and Old and all those "opposites" in the natural order which are a mingling of happiness and despair, comfort and discomfort, sickness and health, hot and cold, poverty and wealth, etc.

The head of the Priestess is crowned with the crescent, indicative of fecundity and fertility. Her face is hidden by a veil. Her breast is adorned with the great solar cross representative of universal creativity. She is therefore the symbol of the Great Secret or Hidden Feminine. She is in truth Mother Nature in her most secret and sacred aspects, prolific in her production of life, rich in the abundance of gifts to her children. Her mysteries are also most sacred and most secret, and she is identified with the Hidden Wisdom, for upon her lap she holds a scroll or Book which is partially concealed by her mantle, and this tells us that the aspirant must make himself worthy to partake of the knowledge and power conferred by the Book of the Wisdom of Nature. This is the Principle of which the Bible speaks when it says, "Wisdom is justified of her children" (the Initiates). Of her the Egyptians said, "I am Isis. No mortal man hath ever me unveiled."

The opening chapters of the Book of Genesis describe mankind made in the image and likeness of God. The First and Second Arcana are a pictured representation of this perfected man and woman, the Archetypal Man. We meet the two Perfected Ones again in the New Testament in the persons of Jospeh and his wife Mary, the parents of Jesus.

On the high plane of divinity or God-Consciousness, the High Priestess denotes the Glory of Shekinah, the manifested Presence of God as she begins to reveal Herself to her children, the Initiates. This is the "upper" Shekinah of the Kabbalah; the Shekinah of the Mysteries. In the next Tarot card we are shown the "lower" Shekinah, not as a "fallen feminine," but as God's manifestation in the realms of Nature. The disciple is taught to relate these two aspects of the Divine Feminine as being the manifestation of God on the inner and the outer planes of Nature.

## ARCANE III

*The Isis-Urania*

The Third Arcanum is termed the Isis-Urania. Here we see again the beautiful figure of the High Priestess. This time, however, her feet are resting upon the moon. Her body is radiant with the golden nimbus of the sun, and her head is crowned with the glory of twelve stars. She is seated upon a cubic stone which is covered with eyes, and upon which is also inscribed the picture of a cat, the animal that sees both in light and in the dark—the whole a composite symbol of clairvoyance. The Urania holds a scepter which points heavenward. Upon the other hand rests an eagle which represents the power of the New Age. This card is also termed the Venus-Uranis, or Celestial Aphrodite, as shown by the emblem of the planet in the upper left corner.

Kabbalists look upon the Iris-Urania as symbolic of the Feminine in Exaltation. Her twofold Mystery, shown in the Arcanes II and III, are signified biblically in the two H's of the Tetragrammaton: J-H-V-H. The letter He is also associated with E, the Hebrew alphabet having no vowels, but is generally termed H. The Tetragrammaton is the Greek name for the Sacred Four Letters which in the Hebrew stand for the Ineffable Name of God: Jod-He-Vau-He. The sacred Name was never pronounced except by the High Priest in the inmost sanctuary of the Temple, and certain substitutes for the Word were chanted under cover of the holy choir, for even these substitues might not be used lightly. The word Adonai was such a substitute. It was only at special times that the Name was pronounced by the High Priest, and it was accompanied by the loud blast of the trumpet so that the magic intonation might never be heard by the unworthy.

*Yod* represents the perfected masculine principle of the First Arcane. *He* typifies the eternal feminine of the Second Arcane. *Vav* or Vau represents the vessel of transmutation, in which the *He*, of generation is lifted to become the second or renewed *He*, the redeemed feminine of regeneration.

In the mystical interpretation of the New Testament the alchemical mystery of the Word is shown in the life work of Mary of Bethlehem, the blessed mother of the holy Master Jesus. She descended to earth for the sole purpose of becoming the mother of the Savior. She was born into the most exalted ranks of the Essene Order; and when the times were propitious, she left the innermost cloister of the Order to become a Householder so that she might prepare for Christ's incarnation. Thus in her role of Householder she represents the first *He* or Feminine in Generation. After her mission was accomplished, she was lifted by the rite of the Assumption to become the second *He* or Feminine in Regeneration, wherein she passed into the celestial realms. to become "Queen of Heaven," companioned at all times by the celestial hosts. Thus she remains for all time the perfect type-pattern of the Exalted Feminine (e-V-E), whom St. John describes in the Book of Revelation, "a woman clothed with the sun and with the moon under her feet (having overcome all earthly propensities) and upon her head a crown of stars"–showing that she had achieved to the power of the liberated ones and would henceforth collaborate with the great Hierarchies who surround our solar system and who transmit to it the powers emanating from the twelve zodiacal constellations.

## ARCANE IV

*The Cubic Stone*

In this picture we see portrayed a man (the aspirant), seated on a cubic stone, with one leg crossed over the other. In his right hand he holds the scepter of the Magus—the staff with a ring—which is pointing toward heaven, while the left hand gestures toward the earth, showing that materiality must be conquered before he can soar heavenward. Upon his breast is a dove, meaning that purity is a supreme power of attainment. The cubic stone represents the long and arduous work of preparation. The Masonic fraternity has a very beautiful teaching in connection with this. The candidate is admonished that his supreme work is to change the rough ashlar into the perfect cubic stone.

There are many references throughout both the Old and New Testaments to the building of the perfect stone (which has reference to the "soul body" in the Western Wisdom Teaching).

In the life of the great Hebrew leader Joshua (who is the "Jesus" of the Old Testament) there is an interesting story relating to the *work with stones.* This is one of the Twelve Labors through which he is prepared for his eminent leadership.

*Joshua 4:9-20*

> And Joshua set up twelve stones in the midst of Jordan, in the place where the feet of the priests which bare the ark of the covenant stood: and they are there unto this day. And these twelve stones which they took out of Jordan, did Joshua pitch in Gilgal.

When the Initiate leaves the unillumined wilderness behind and enters into the land of light he sets up twelve stones in Gilgal. The twelve stones are the twelve spiritual centers in the body which are "set up" into activity when a certain stage of development has been attained. Seen clairvoyantly, these centers appear as whirling vortices of energy, hence their symbolical placement in Gilga, a name which means a "circle" or "whirlwind." They are the *lotus blossoms* in the language of oriental occultism and the *roses* that bloom upon the cross of the body in Western esotericism.

The stones, it is stated, are there "unto this day." In other words, the centers of light and power which Joshua had aroused to active expression are present today in the body of every human being, though latent in the great majority. The process of their unfoldment is one of the principal subjects dealt with by the Bible writers.

St. Peter, by reason of his spiritual accomplishments, was numbered among the first three of the Immortal Twelve. To him the Master said, when he changed his name from Simon to Peter, "You are now Peter, and upon this Rock *(of Initiation)* My Church is founded."

## ARCANE V

*The Master of the Arcanes*

Here the Priest of Isis is sitting between two columns decorated with palm branches indicative of triumph. Every aspirant must at some time be worthy to stand between the two columns of the Sanctuary, for they typify equilibrium between the masculine and feminine principles in both man and nature. In one hand the Priest holds a staff with three bars which indicates mastery of the physical, the mental and the spiritual. At his feet kneel two figures, one white, the other black, representing the mastery of the good and evil forces within himself and in the world around him. This entire Arcanum is symbolic of triumphant mastery. The most important work of every aspirant is to learn self-control. He can never hope to control the forces of nature about him until he has learned to control the forces of nature within himself. This is one of the prolonged and arduous labors which make the Path so difficult.

One of the wisest teachers of the Old Testament dispensation had learned this lesson well for himself, and he taught it to his disciples when he said, "Greater is he that controlleth himself than he that taketh a city."

## ARCANE VI

*The Two Ways*

In this Arcanum we see a youth standing between two beautiful maidens. One is crowned with leaves of gold—for she is Athena, the Goddess of Wisdom. The other is crowned with the leaves of the vine—she is Aphrodite, the Goddess of Love. These two maidens represent two diverging Paths, and every aspirant must make his choice as to which path he will take—the path of Spirit or the path of sense. The supreme Master said, "Many are called but few are chosen." This is the Place of Dedication. Above them a figure hovers, pointing an arrow toward one, indicative of the heavy karmic debt awaiting him who chooses the negative path. All of the important characters in the Bible have passed this way. In the Book of Genesis Abram and Lot, when they came to this testing place, parted company. Abram chose the way that led to Caanan, the Land of Promise, while Lot chose to pitch his tents in the plain adjacent to Sodom, a city given over to such wickedness that it was at last destroyed utterly. Lot and his family were saved only through Abram's intercession, for Abram had reached that high state of mastership wherein he was instructed, guided and companioned by the angelic hosts.

## ARCANE VII

*The Chariot of Osiris*

Here we see a warrior seated upon a cubic chariot; in one hand he holds a sword indicating victory, in the other hand is a staff surmounted by a square (control of matter), a circle (union with the eternal Truth), and a triangle (harmonious workings with the Divine).

The chariot is drawn by two sphinxes, one white, the other black—symbol of the positive and negative forces of nature over which he has gained mastery. There is a starry canopy above his head, supported by four columns. These four columns typify the four elements on which all forces of nature depend: Fire, Air, Water, Earth.

Every Wisdom Book, whether ancient, medieval or modern, contains varied descriptions of Initiation correlated with these four elements. The Water Initiation means control of the emotions; the Fire Initiation the purifying of the desires; the Air Initiation the spiritualizing of the mind; and the Earth Initiation, the mastery of the physical body. Throughout the Old and New Testaments many fascinating experiences are described which relate to these four Initiations. We turn now to the great hero of the Book of Exodus—Moses—in whose life these four Initiations are clearly defined.

There are four paths leading to Illumination, correlative to the four elements and to the four sheaths that make up the fourfold vehicle through which the human spirit evolves. In each body the spirit generates a certain type of energy; from each element it derives a distinctive power; with each Initiation added soul faculties become operative. Moses, in whose life the path of

Initiation is outlined with exceptional clarity, took all of these four steps of Illumination, each of which we will discuss in the sequence in which Moses took them.

We have shown that after Moses had overcome his lower nature he went into the Midian desert but soon found himself not on parched ground but beside a well (esoteric truth). Seven maidens (soul qualities) were drawing water (attracting spiritual sustenance). Moses (the awakened aspirant) helped them (gave conscious cooperation).

Ater this "baptism with the waters of life by the Seven Virgins of Light," to use a phrase taken from an ancient initiatory chant, the victor over the emotional life was qualified to take up the work of a yet higher degree of Illumination.

The Initiation by Water took place beside a well. The next higher Initiation, by Fire, occurred on Horeb, the "mountain of God." Even so every aspirant climbs the ladder of being and enters increasingly into first-hand knowledge of the inner secrets of nature. The veils of matter are lifted, and objective nature is seen to be but a symbol of the world of reality. The very word "Mysteries" is related to the Greek word "mystor" meaning veil.

The bush that Moses looked upon burned but was not consumed. It was not enveloped in flames but in light. It is only the flame that consumes. The spirit of fire nurtures and builds. Flame bears much the same relationship to fire that the physical body does to the indwelling spirit.

A complete mastery of the lower nature is a prerequisite to Initiation by Fire. Passion must be raised to compassion, and the love that once burned for the gratification of self must have been transmuted into a consuming love for all mankind. As the sea belongs to the water element and the desert to fire, so does the mountain choose for its home the air. Moses, having taken the Initiation by Water at the Red Sea and Initiation by Fire in the Wilderness, is now qualified to take a third degree, the Initiation by Air on Mount Siani.

With the Initiation of Earth, the mystery of matter is mastered. The atomic vibration of the body can be altered at will, and the life of the physical instrument prolonged indefinitely. This is the last and most difficult of the four Great Initiations and is attainable only after renunciation of the little self, as Moses showed when he said that he would rather his name be blotted out of the Book of Life than that his recalcitrant people should be destroyed for their misdeeds.

The Earth Initiation gives admission into the deeper strata of the Earth and the ability to manipulate certain forces of the physical planet. It bestows upon its possessor, literally, the "keys to heaven and hell."

## Chapter XII

## THE SECOND SEPTENARY OF ARCANA

### *ARCANE VIII*

#### *The Balance and the Sword*

The Eight Arcanum shows a maiden holding an uplifted sword, symbol of Truth. In the other hand she holds a pair of scales.

One of the most dramatic episodes recounted in the Egyptian Book of the Dead is that of the weighing of the heart when the soul comes to Judgment soon after death. The weighing of the heart determines his place, whether it is to be in the upper or lower abodes, with gods or demons.

This symbolic weighing of the heart bears an interesting significance for the occultist, who understands that the seed atom of the physical body is located in the apex of the etheric heart and contains an indelible record of every thought, word and deed of that individual during his earth life. It is from this record in the heart that the values of each earth life are assessed at the time of death.

The aspirant has made much progress along the Path when he can bravely face his trials and errors and acknowledge that he alone is responsible for them all.

All Wisdom Books—and this includes both the Bible and the Tarot—lay much emphasis upon the fact that there is a great and immutable Law of Destiny under which man on this planet lives, moves and has his being. The eight Arcanum bears testimony to this in its every detail. The maiden wears a crown of iron about her brow, symbolizing the immutability of karmic Law; her eyes are bandaged, to signify that justice is meted out in perfect impartiality.

The biblical story correlative to this theme is that of Belshazzar, King of Chaldea (O.T. Vol. III. P. 485).

Belshazzar was proud, haughty and insolent. He showed his contempt for the Hebrew captives by commanding that the gold and silver vessels, which had been used in the Temple at Jerusalem and were held sacred, should be brought to his banquet hall, there to be used in scenes of wildest revelry. The splendor of the royal banquet with its throngs of guests, its flowers, the flowing of heavily perfumed wines and the wild abandonment of merrymaking, has long been a favorite theme for artist and poets. It was while the orgy was at its height that the mysterious hand appeared upon the wall and wrote in a mystic script, "MENE, MENE, TEKEL, UPHARSIN," "Thou art weighed in the balance and art found wanting. Thy kingdom is divided and given to the Medes and the Persians."

And even as these letters were inscribed on the wall in letters of fire, the soldiers of Cyrus were surrounding the city and forcing an entrance through the canals, whose floodgates had been opened from within to allow the waters to recede, affording a passageway for the Persian troops. The supposedly impregnable city fell, taken by surprise, and Belshazzar, a prisoner to Cyrus, was later killed when he attempted to lead his people in an uprising.

At this time the purity and beauty that had belonged to early Babylonian religion were largely lost, and the sacred rites had degenerated into gross superstition. As often happens in periods of decadence, the people and their leaders were no longer able to contact the spiritual Hierarchies who had previously guided them, and failing this they came under the influence of earthbound discarnate entities and succumbed to idolatry and sorcery with their attendant cruelties. All early races possessed a type of involuntary clairvoyance: hence it was an easy matter for them to read etheric records wherein is inscribed the outline of the most important events to occur in any individual life. Belshazzar had been given his opportunity for leadership and had failed ignominiously. The record of that failure was written in the ethers, and it was this record which was revealed in his last fateful celebration.

Archeology adds its mute testimony to this romantic story. An ancient temple of the goddess of harvests has been found in Babylonia and upon the walls are letters which were ancient even in the time of Belshazzar, and these letters might well have been interpreted to have a meaning as related in the Bible. Belshazzar was interested in the antiquities of his nation, as were other kings before and after him. Such kings often rebuilt abandoned temples or temples lying in ruin under the cities when these were accidentally discovered by masons and workmen. Inscriptions on the walls of these temples might be read and interpreted by sages and seers together, combining their powers of scholarship and seership.

## ARCANE IX

*The Veiled Lamp*

This Arcanum shows us the picture of an elderly philosopher carrying in his hand a lighted lantern, which he has partially concealed by his mantle. The light symbolized Wisdom, and the fact that it is partly concealed by the philosopher's mantle indicates that Wisdom is never to be lightly worn. The aspirant must prove his worthiness, and for some length of time, before the light of Wisdom can be revealed to him.

In the words of the Psalmist, "Thou wilt light my candle; the Lord my God will enlighten my darkness." The candle flame is not a mere figure of speech. It is visible to the spiritual sight, and many illumined artists show it burning above the heads of the angels, nature spirits, and also of human beings. We see it again in many of the cards of this Egyptian series.

Solomon, famed for his great learning, exhorted his sons to seek Wisdom above all things, saying, "Happy is the man that findeth wisdom and that getteth understanding, for the merchandise of it is better than silver, and the gain thereof than fine gold. She is more precious than rubies, and all the things thou canst desire are not to be compared to her" (Prov. 3: 13-15).

In the New Testament the Ninth Arcane is associated with the "Widow's Son of Nain," or Nine, the great Initiate of the Christ era, known as Lazarus, who later instituted the work of the Rose Cross in medieval Europe and founded the scientific School of the Mysteries which pertains to this era.

The glyph shows with what reverence Truth is received by

the illumined mind and how carefully it is preserved. In the teachings of the Rose Cross the Initiate who has passed the Ninth Initiation is ready to take the First Great Initiation in which there is revealed "the Mystery of the Mind" and the "Religion of the Father." This is the mysterious flame hidden beneath the cloak of the Nine Lesser Mysteries.

In another reading the "Old Man of the Mysteries" represents the Wanderer through the world, the Virgin Spirit on its pilgrimage through matter with its manifold illusions, as shown by the pilgrim's staff upon which he leans while walking, and by the manner in which he holds his cloak to protect the flame of his lamp. He is sometimes called the Hermit, and as such he portrays the biblical characters of Elijah and John the Baptist. Elijah is the Great Light, the Hierophant, of esoteric Judaism. The kabbalists teach that he is the reincarnation of Moses. According to the Christian kabbalist, Elijah was reborn as John the Baptist, as shown in the words of the Christ, "This is Elias." In John the Baptist the Light of the ancient Mysteries of the Holy Land passes over into the New Mysteries of the Dispensation of the Kingdom of Christ.

## ARCANE X

*The Sphinx*

We weave with colors all our own
The tissue of the life to be;
And in the field of destiny
We reap as we have sown.

—**Whittier**

The tenth Arcanum again sets before us the action of cosmic Law. We see here the revolving Wheel of Life. It is to this Wheel that all are bound as it revolves between heaven and earth, carrying the spirit upward into high realms after death, and then downward again into lower realms incident to physical rebirth. Each earth life is a day in God's great School, and each pupil must return day after day, life after life, until every lesson this earth has to teach has been learned.

We have shown two cards here—that of the Egyptian series popularly called the "St. Germain," although there is no proof that Count St. Germain was responsible for these cards, and that of the A. E. Waite series. Mr. Waite interprets the four strange figures shown on the Egyptian wheel as representing the four Beasts of Ezekiel's Vision, which we see again in the XIXth Tarot.

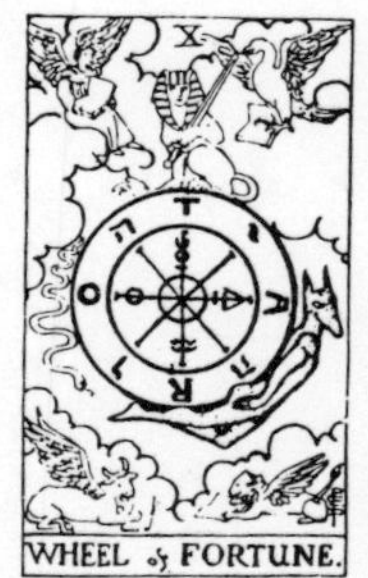


Poised atop the revolving wheel is the figure of the Sphinx, which remains calm, unmoved by the rapid revolutions of the Wheel. She is the Divine Watcher, the very essence of Life who yet remains aloof, over and above the movements of life in the particular, the mystery of the Virgin Spirit consciousness which is made in the image and likeness of God; evolving from lower to higher *forms* on the great wheel, while in its own pure essence it remains perfect and unmoved.

There are two strange figures attached to the wheel, one of which seems to be carried upward, the other downward. These represent the forces of good and evil—the god Knephta and the evil Typhon—and the figure representing evil seems in imminent danger of being thrown off the wheel entirely, in accordance with the fact that good always triumphs in the cycle of ages, while evil is predestined to annihilation since it is not a thing in itself but only a misconception of Reality. If it seems that these two forces, good and evil, still strive to conquer the spirit of mankind, further observation shows that Good alone has power and is constantly ascending, while evil is constantly descending and being thrown off from the wheel. It has no persistence, no real and enduring life.

The Wisdom books of all the world contain the definite message that good will ultimately triumph over evil. The Tenth Arcanum of the Tarot repeats this message when it shows the good ascending toward the Sphinx while the evil descends toward the abyss.

At the base of the axis which supports the Wheel are two cobras which represent the positive and the negative forces manifesting throughout nature. Each of these forces strives unceasingly to gain the ascendancy over the other. It is this conflict of opposites which produces most of the inharmony in the life of mankind, an inharmony destined to continue until man has learned to balance the two forces within himself. Only when harmony has been established within will harmony be reflected on the outward world of time and space.

The four dominant phases of human life are symbolized in the Sphinx—birth and childhood, maturity and parenthood, rulership and power, and finally death. The Bull and the Eagle have special rule over the karmic debts of the planet earth in its present material state; Aquarius and Leo belong more especially to the future when man has become the winged citizen of the skies, both in a physical or scientific sense, journeying to far-away universes, and in a spiritual sense, becoming an angelic being winged with Wisdom and Love.

We stand now on the threshold of the Aquarian Age, the Age of the Winged Man of Heaven. The Aquarian Age is only about two or three thousand years in duration, as measured by time, but it is the seed of an entire new order, and its germination belongs to the wondrous adventurings of Spirit in the Macrocosm.

The signs of Lion and Man in the skies typify the incoming Aquarian Age with its keynote of Love and Brotherhood, giving a preview, as it were, of the high destiny awaiting the human race when the current Piscean Age of darkness and sorrow has passed away.

A further, deeply esoteric, meaning is also discernible in this Tarot as relating to the occult forces which rise through the spine to the brain, where they awaken the power of the spiritual centers of the brain itself and also of the glands in the head which are important in the alchemy of soul-growth.

## ARCANE XI

*The Maiden and the Lion*

Here we see a young maiden who, without any apparent effort, is opening and closing the mouth of a lion.

It has often been said that man's first Bible was the starry script of the skies, where all the mysteries of life and death are revealed to him who knows the language of Archangels.

In the Eleventh Arcanum the lion represents the constellation Leo, the keynote of which is Love. As previously stated, the maiden is the constellation Virgo, the keynote of which is Wisdom. The ancients believed that Virgo had a special relationship to the human race, followed by Gemini and Aquarius. These three constellations are all represented by human figures, Gemini the Twins, Virgo the Maiden, Aquarius the Man. When the Maiden has control over the Lion, the human spirit has achieved a union of Wisdom and Love and possesses all power over heaven and earth.

As the sun reaches the highest point in its northernmost ascension, the Christ likewise ascends into the spiritual realm described biblically as the throne of the Father, the abode of the God of this solar system. God is Love and God is Light. Love and Light are keynotes of the Hierarchy of Leo, the Lords of Flame (Love). Under the supervision of the Lords of Flame, and united with the powers of the Father, the first aspect of the trinity, the Lord Christ works with the supreme power of Love, the stabilizing force of the earth. Here He becomes the channel for that Love power whereby He rotates the earth on its axis and revolves it in its orbit around the sun. This love power is reflected by the Hierarchy of Leo to its opposite sign, Aquarius; hence, it will be the power animating the new Aquarian Age.

In September the blessed Christ Ray turns from the glory of the highest heavens and begins the descent toward physical realms. Throughout this month of the tender, yearning beauty of nature is like that of no other season, for the Christ is brooding over the earth with the same gentle sorrow He felt as He wept over Jerusalem long ago. His tears were shed because He knew the long ages of pain and suffering through which humanity must pass, in having chosen darkness rather than light. His great heart grieved over the dark clouds that would encompass Jerusalem, the heart city of the planet to which He had dedicated Himself in service and upon which He was pouring out His great love.

September is a special month of preparation for a disciple. One of the keywords of Virgo is *sacrifice*. An earnest disciple, preparing himself by means of sacrifice and self-renunciation to take part in the coming winter feasts, mediatates often upon the spiritual keynote of Virgo, "If any man would be first, the same shall be last of all, and the servant of all." (Mark 9:35.)

## ARCANE XII

*The Sacrifice*

This Arcanum depicts a human figure suspended head downward between two columns, hanging by one foot, the free leg crossed upon it to form an inverted triangle. From his hands, which are bound together beneath his head, golden coins are dropping upon the ground.

In the sixth Arcanum we saw the aspirant beginning his work upon the Path. There it was essential that he develop discrimination and will-power—discrimination to know right from wrong, the better from the good, and the best from the better—and the concentrated will to act upon his discernment. Now in the twelfth Arcanum the disciple has progressed so far that *Selflessness* is demanded of him. He may not achieve his ideal immediately, but he must be one-pointed in his dedication. The supreme Master said, "Greater love hath no man than this, that he lay down his life for his friend."

Upon the initiatory Path, however, it does not mean necessarily that one must *die* to prove his selflessness. One may be crucified in the renunciation of a great personal love for the sake of a spiritual ideal; a promising career may be abandoned because of a disabled parent, or to assume the responsibility of a child. In many ways a disciple can be tested to prove his selflessness, but if he is earnest and sincere and his renunciations are for the betterment and upliftment of others, his spiritual recompense is sure.

The golden coins dripping from the hands of the hanged or sacrificed man signify the high idealism which motivates his action, and causes him to become an example set up for the emulation of others. The great Indian Saint Gandhi was such a one. St. Peter met death hanging head downward upon a cross.

Humility is an essential part of selflessness. This was sublimely illustrated in the life of St. Peter. Despite his marvellous spiritual attainments, the legends state, when he came to his martyrdom he asked to be crucified head downward, because he felt unworthy to be placed on the cross in the manner his Master had been.

The glorious golden Christ, the supreme Master of the world, evinced this same spirit of humility, saying, "Of myself I can do nothing; the Father in me, He doeth the works." Christ Jesus admonished his disciples repeatedly, "Let him that would be greatest among you be the servant of all." The Coin of Spirit is pure gold of renunciation, which opens for the soul the Gates of the inner worlds.

## ARCANE XIII

*The Reaping Skeleton*

Here we see a skeleton, scythe in hand, with which he is mowing down the figures of human beings, who have fallen into a trench or grave, from which heads, hands, feet and limbs obtrude.

We have said that both the Bible and the Tarot teach the One Law—the Tarot in symbolism, the Bible in direct statement and also in allegory. "Whatsoever a man soweth, that shall he also reap." If a man sows the wind, he will necessarily reap the whirlwind.

The figure of the skeleton in this Arcanum represents the fleetingness of all earthly things; but behind the skeleton, across the horizon, arches the great rainbow, symbol of hope and of the promise that man's spirit is eternal.

## ARCANE XIV

*The Two Urns*

The fourteenth Arcanum shows us a handsome youth, illuminated by the great yellow sun which shines above him. In his hands he holds two urns, one gold the other silver; and from the gold urn he pours a rare electric and magnetic fluid into the silver urn. He pours this elixir most carefully, so that not a drop of the precious liquid is lost. Great wings spring from his shoulders and smaller ones from his feet.

Wings belong to the air, which gives evidence that this youth belongs to the Air Age of Aquarius. When St. Paul taught his disciples, "Ye are the temples of the living God," he foresaw a time when this truth would be outwardly evident, visible to the eye in the perfect body of the New Age Pioneer.

The two urns with their precious fluid are physiologically symbolic of the voluntary and sympathetic nervous systems, the golden urn representing the masculine or cerebro-spinal system and the silver representing the feminine or sympathetic system. At the present time most of the work which the human spirit performs consciously in the body is under the control of the cerebro-spinal system. Man has little control over the activities governed by the sympathetic or automatic nervous system which regulates the life processes. But are the life processes of the human body in fact automatic? The occult scientist says that these processes are also governed by intelligences invisible and unknown to the material scientist; and the work of the sympathetic nervous system, which is called feminine, is hidden, secret and mysterious. The feminine always signifies Life, and Life is as yet concealed by a veil. But in the New Age—as contemporary events already hint–humanity will awaken within itself the Divine Feminine of Wisdom and will be able to control and direct, consciously and voluntarily, all of the life processes of the body, thus achieving the foretaste of immortality.

One of the most beautiful mystic prophets of the Old Testament dispensation was Zechariah. In his Book he details something of the wonders of the body of the New Age pioneer.

> *Zechariah* 4: 3, 11, 14
>
> And two olive trees by it, one upon the right side of bowl, the other upon the left side thereof.
>
> Then answered I, and said unto him, what are these two olive trees upon the right side of the candlestick, and upon the left side thereof?
>
> Then said he, these are the two anointed ones, that stand by the Lord of the whole earth.

From an historical viewpoint the two olive trees "that stand by the Lord" refer to the High Priest Joshua and the King Zerubbabel. But there is also an initiatory interpretation pertaining to the alchemy of the two nerve systems which play so important a role in human regeneration. For this work man must do for himself. The Hierarchies cannot do it for him. They have been teaching him to build the living temple. Now he must show that he has learned his lesson and begin to build for himself.

The sympathetic nervous system is the stronghold of the vital body with its life forces; the cerebro-spinal system is under the dominant control of the desires and the selfish will of the ego. As the ego becomes "unselfed" and unites its will to the Will of Cosmic Good, it gains control of the sympathetic nervous system, and its powers are greatly augmented. The individual then becomes aware of ethereal but mighty forces pouring through nature in great tides. Being aware of them, he is able to use them advantageously and thus to create a more perfect world and achieve illumination himself.

The alchemical mystery always involves the balancing or

harmonizing of the dual creative forces of the universe, in human experience termed masculine and feminine. We have said that the cerebro-spinal nerve system is termed positive, or masculine, the sympathetic negative, or feminine. A balance achieved between them means that neither one nor the other predominates, but both are equal and cooperative under the will of the ego, which is biune. Then love and reason function together as a unity, for reason is one aspect of Cosmic Wisdom as it operates at the human level. "These are the two anointed ones that stand by the Lord of the whole earth."

## Chapter XIII

## THE THIRD SEPTENARY OF ARCANA

### ARCANE XV–TYPHON

The eighth, the tenth and the thirteenth Arcanum enunciated the truth of the great law of cause and effect as clearly and explicitly as does the Bible when it states, "Whatsoever a man sows, that shall he also reap."

In the ninth Arcanum we have seen the light of Wisdom beginning to shine within.

In the eleventh Arcanum still greater progress was noted, as the force of the desire nature is transferred into the power of Spirit.

In the fourteenth Arcanum we observe the beginning of the preparatory work incidental to the building of the house (body) not made with hands but eternal in the heavens.

The fifteenth Arcanum places before the aspirant the reminder that "the higher we climb, the harder we fall." It pictures the spirit of evil which has been known by many names throughout world literature. Here he is represented with the body of a hippopotamus, head of a crocodile, great bat wings and the feet of a goat. A serpent is seen emerging from the lower part of the body, indicative of the fact that all of his works are dedicated to evil.

In one hand he holds aloft the scepter of destruction, in the other the scepter of division, confusion and hatred. Bound by chains to his feet are two human figures with goats' heads, suggesting the depravity into which man may descend when he allies himself consciously with the forces of destruction.

The hideous figure shown in this Arcanum typifies the spirit behind the dark forces which have sought to control and subjugate our planet since the beginning of human evolution and which are tremendously accelerated as the Age draws to its close, for with the end of the Piscean Age the spirits of evil is finished. Hebrew mystics spoke of the Piscean Age as the time of the "Agonies of the Messiah."

"If thou canst grasp it, that liberation consisteth in the breaking down and utter destruction of the hedge of protection which now encircleth thee and guardeth thee from the terror of the darkness which is without. Then shall the dreadful darkness be revealed to thy perfected vision as the flashing radiance of the Light Limitless, and from the field of sin and punishment thou shalt pass into the boundless freedom of my divine protection."

As we study contemporary history it is easy to see the dark forces seeking to perpetuate outmoded conditions, struggling against the armies of the light. Hatred, strife, wars and rumors of wars are characteristic of their influence. The dominant evil force is popularly given the name Devil. Sometimes he is called Lucifer, who is said to be the cause of the Fall of Angels and men; or again, Satan. In Hebrew mythology he is identified with the serpent in the Garden of Eden, and he is the world-engirdling serpent of many mythologies. (The Hebrew myths are actually far older than the Hebrew race; they contain elements belonging to the aboriginal Aryan race, which includes the *Original* Semites.)

It is this same serpent who appears once again in the Christian symbolism of the Book of Revelation as the great beast who will be bound for a thousand years. By whatever name he is known, however, he is the master who directs the work of the dark forces throughout the entire world, and it has been his aim to subjugate the earth and its humanity since the beginning of human evolution.

## ARCANE XVI

*The Thunderstruck Tower*

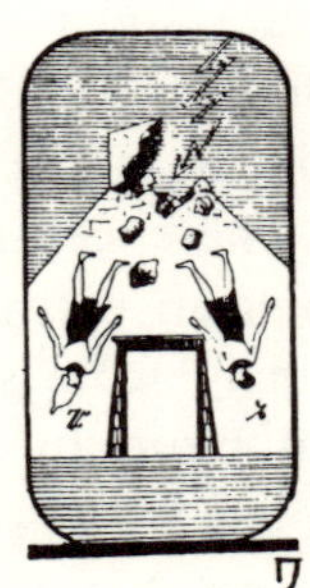

The sixteenth Arcanum portrays a great tower whose pinnacle has been destroyed by a stroke of lightning. In its fall it carries down with it two men, one of whom is wearing a crown. This tells us that the working of Cosmic Law is no respecter of position or rank. Every action is followed by its own reaction in which justice will eventually prevail. (Note that the concept of Justice is balance and harmony, not revenge.)

The thunderstruck tower represents a certain era in human evolution in which division, confusion and hatred prevail. This time is aptly described in the Book of Genesis in the story of the Tower of Babel.

The story of the Tower of Babel tells us in allegory of humanity's original state of unity, when all spoke a common language, and shows that as man journeyed "from the East" he gradually lost his perception of the Universal Light, descended to a lower "plain" of consciousness, of division and egoism, where such confusion of tongues ensued that people could no longer "understand one another's speech." They were beginning to live in terms of self-will instead of the divine will. Thus divided in interests and purposes, the Lord (Law) "did scatter them abroad upon the face of all the earth."

In the earlier stages of human development before the race consciousness had extended beyond the subjective state into the objective, it was easily amenable, as a unit, to a single directing will. That One Will operated through the twelve zodiacal Hierarchies in directing the destiny of the entire human race.

Later, embryonic humanity reached the stage of

individualization. It acquired mind and developed self-will. Humanity divided into separate races and nations. Consciousness was directed more and more to the external world. The many individualized minds and separated races were now no longer unitedly receptive to a synthesized hierarchical guidance In the divine order of things this was henceforth delegated to a number of lesser beings chosen from among the Archangels, working under the direction of the Lord Jehovah. Each race and nation received its immediate divine guidance from an archangelic Race Spirit. This is still the chief source of inner guidance in the life of nearly all the races and nations of the earth. The exceptions are the new pioneering peoples who are an amalgam of many races. These are emancipating themselves increasingly from such control, their destinies being directed more and more by the awakening god within themselves.

The Race Spirit broods over its people like a psychic cloud, impregnating them with the consciousness of the large racial ends they are intended to serve, and controlling them by means of the breath and the spoken word. Language and music are the principal mediums by which one may come into touch with the Race Spirit of a people.

The celestial language which was used by humanity before the division known biblically as the Tower of Babel, we are told, is still the language by which the angelic hosts communicate with one another.

It was only after man had lost the right to use this language that he became divided into tribes, races and nations. After this division came fear, suspicion, dread, animosity and, finally, the terrible scourge of war.

Literature holds many references to the power of the Lost Word. Each human being has within his throat a certain latent center which in ages to come will be awakened. Then it is that he will regain the use of this celestial language which he lost so long ago, and he will come to understand anew the meaning of the divine creative Word.

In that glad day the dream which has lived down through the ages in humanity's heart will have become a reality, and the glorious golden light of an eternal peace will lie upon the land and the Fatherhood of God and the Brotherhood of Man will be like a tangible benediction upon all the earth.

## ARCANE XVII

*The Star of the Magi*

Here we see a young maiden kneeling with one foot on the sea and one on land. In each hand she holds an urn from which she is pouring upon land and sea simultaneously the precious fluid of love and kindness. She typifies the New Age in which mercy and loving kindness will prevail in all the earth. Beside her stands a plant having three lotus blossoms, which represent three planes–physical, mental and spiritual–and also man's threefold personality wherein the physical and mental are being lifted and united with the spirit. Above the flowers hovers a beautiful butterfly–a perfect symbol of transmutation. Over the girl's head shines a great eight-pointed star, in the center of which is a double triangle, the upper one White, pointing toward heaven, the lower Black, pointing toward earth. The message of this double triangle is expressed in the occult maxim, "As above, so below," a promise that earth will one day reflect the glories of heaven.

The Wise Men of all ages have followed the Star of the Magi, the Star of the light of the golden Christ which suffuses heaven and earth. Previous to the Baptism, at which time He became the indwelling Planetary Spirit, this great Being worked with the earth from the outside. His was the glorious Star that guided the Wise Men to the little town of Bethlehem where they paid allegiance to the Holy Child and to his saintly Mother.

# ARCANE XVIII

*The Twilight*

This Arcanum shows us two pyramids–one white, the other black–standing beside a road. Before them are seated two dogs, one black the other white, both baying at the moon which is partially concealed by clouds. The white and black pyramids represent the teachings of that wisdom which leads to the light and the subtle force of evil which turns the teaching into darkness. The white pyramid shows an open door leading into its interior, above which is the symbol of Aquarius and of Venus, indicative of the fact that true wisdom will lead men into the New Age of the Son of Man, the keynote of which is Love, which is also the keynote of the planet Venus.

The dark pyramid shows no opening, indicating that its knowledge must be gained in devious ways.

The position of these two pyramids teaches in symbol that the aspirant must be prepared to encounter the temptations of the dark forces which follow him even to the very doorway of the Temple of Light. At the same time there is no place, no state of consciousness, exclusively dark; Light penetrates the darkness and is always at hand to lead the penitent one upward and outward. "Though I make my bed in hell, Thou art there," is the biblical statement of this truth.

We have observed in an earlier Arcanum that one of the first lessons given to the aspirant is that of Discrimination, the ability to distinguish between the True and the False in all their subtle phases. Temptation should never be feared by the disciple, for it is one of the greatest helps in spiritual development.

## ARCANE XIX

*The Dazzling Light*

We have here a youth and maiden standing hand in hand within a circle of everblooming flowers. In Arcanum XIV we saw the picture of a youth who typifies a pioneer of the New or Aquarian Age.

In Arcanum XVII we found a representation of a maiden who typifies a pioneer of the Aquarian Age also. In Arcanum XIX we see the the youth and maiden united in the glory of the bright day when all sorrow, poverty, pain and death have passed away, and life eternal prevails. Here man and woman–the new Adam and the new Eve–stand triumphant, hand in hand, knowing perfect equality and perfect spiritual equilibrium on every plane of manifestation. Above their heads shines a vast luminous sun that bears within its heart the symbol of universal regeneration. As we meditate upon this glorious golden Light we hear the voice of the supreme Master saying, "I am the Light of the World"; and the voices of the youth and the maiden respond in the words of St. John, "If we walk in the Light as He is in the Light, we have fellowship one with another."

## ARCANE XX

*The Rising of the Dead*

The twentieth Arcanum depicts a celestial being blowing a great trumpet, whereupon a sarcophagus opens and the mummies of a man, woman and child emerge. In Christian tradition it is the Angel Gabriel who is the Angel with the Trumpet who calls the dead from the grave in the day of the Great Judgment. The time is the end of this world when all must stand before the Judgment Seat of God. To the esotericist, however, this Arcanum has a far more wonderful meaning. It is concerned with a marvelous expansion of consciousness with which the pioneer will be endowed. For him there will be no interval of unconsciousness between sleeping and waking. He will be able to pass easily from inner-plane awareness in his work as an Invisible Helper during the hours of sleep to outer-plane awareness in which he is a Helper Visible to all. He will know from first-hand knowledge that there is no death and that that which is mistakenly termed death is but a passing into larger and wider spheres of service and creative activity. It has been truly said that "the dead help us to live."

John the Beloved tells us that we shall not die but that we shall be changed, and St. Paul told his disciples to put off the old man and put on the new. As these truths became his own, Paul gave to the world his song of triumph:

*O grave, where is thy victory?*
*O death, where is thy sting?*

## ARCANE XXI

*The Crown of the Magi*

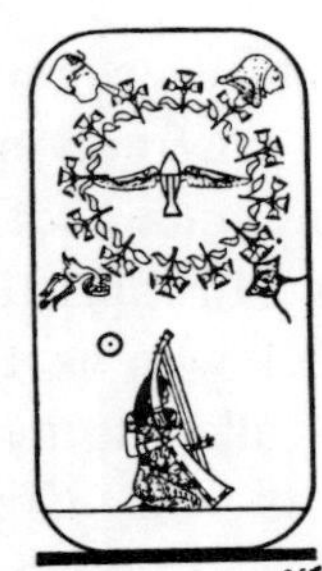

At the top of this picture a wreath of lotus blossoms encloses an occult symbol. Both the symbol and the wreath represent the great spirit of oneness, of unification, which draws together all created beings–persons, places, things–all nations, races, castes, creeds and cults.

In the lower part of the Arcanum is the figure of a girl, seated and playing upon a three-stringed harp. The three-stringed harp typifies the drawing together of physical body and mind and their linking up with spirit. Each human spirit sounds forth a unique keynote, which together add to the music of the spheres. When man learns to bring the physical body into harmony with the mind and both with the individual keynote of the ego itself, which is the human spirit, he will be able to cast out all disease, poverty and old age, and even death will be no more.

Grouped about the lotus wreath are the Four Beasts of Ezekiel's vision, the Bull, the Lion, the Eagle and the Man. The work of the Old Testament prophets may be divided mainly into two classes: first, the terrible prophecies enunciated which concerns all men who refuse to walk in the Path of Light; and second, the glorious prophecies of the incoming New Age, the Christ Age, which foreseen more than two thousand years ago, is now dawning over our planet.

Isaiah writes of the time when man shall beat his swords into plowshares, his spears into pruning-hooks, and when he shall not learn war anymore, when every man shall sit under his own vine and fig tree, and none shall make him afraid. Of that glad new day he adds that the knowledge of the Lord (spiritual Law) shall cover the earth as the waters cover the sea. He also wrote of the coming of the World Redeemer, "A virgin shall bring forth a son and shall call His name Immanuel." Malachi foresaw the rising of the Winged Sun, and John revealed the ultimate fulfilment of the ancient prophecies.

*Isaiah* 11:1-10

And there shall come forth a rod out of the stem of Jesse, and a Branch shall grow out of his roots:

And the spirit of the Lord shall rest upon him, the spirit of wisdom and understanding, the spirit of counsel and might, the spirit of knowledge and fear of the Lord;

And shall make him of quick understanding in the fear of the Lord; and he shall not judge after the sight of his eyes, neither reprove after the hearing of his ears:

But with righteousness shall he judge the poor, and reprove with equity for the meek of the earth, and he shall smite the earth with the rod of his mouth, and with the breath of his lips shall he slay the wicked.

And righteousness shall be the girdle of his loins, and faithfulness shall be the girdle of his reins.

The wolf also shall dwell with the lamb, and the leopard shall lie down with the kid; and the calf and the young lion and the fatling together; and a little child shall lead them . . .

They shall not hurt nor destroy in all my holy mountain; for the earth shall be full of the knowledge of the Lord, as the waters cover the sea.

*Malachi* 4:2

But unto you that fear my Name shall the sun of righteousness arise with healing in his wings.

*Revelation* 14:16

And I looked, and lo, a Lamb stood on the mount Zion, and with him an hundred forty and four thousand, having his Father's name written in their foreheads.

And I heard a voice from heaven, as the voice of many waters and as the voice of a great thunder: and I heard the voice of harpers harping with their harps:

And they sung as it were a new song before the throne, and before the four beasts, and the elders; and no man could learn that song but the hundred and forty and four thousand, which were redeemed from the earth.

These are they which were not defiled with women; for they are they which follow the Lamb whithersoever he goeth. These were redeemed from among men, being the first-fruits unto God and the Lamb.

And in their mouth was found no guile; for they are without fault before the throne of God.

And I saw another angel fly in the midst of heaven, having the everlasting gospel to preach unto them that dwell on the earth, and to every nation, and kindred, and tongue, and people.

144,000 digits 9, which is the number of humanity. This beautiful vision refers to the glorious destiny awaiting all mankind when they have made themselves worthy to receive it. The mark of God upon the forehead refers to the awakening of the spiritual organs in the head.

When awake and functioning, these organs, by reason of their luminosity, cast a golden halo about the head of one so illumined. This is the crown of the Magi as described in the ancient Wisdom Books, and it is the mark of the Lord in the Revelation of St. John.

Summing up: In the fifteenth and sixteenth Arcana are to be noted the terrible power of evil and the frightful destruction and devastation it causes.

In the eighteenth Arcanum the aspirant is subjected to his final subtle temptation and when this is successfully passed, then, clothed in all the glory of his New Race body, he is ready to enter into the New Heaven and the New Earth which are described in Arcana twenty and twenty-one.

## Chapter XIV

## THE TWENTY-SECOND ARCANUM: THE FOOL

## SUMMARY OF ARCANA

### ARCANE XXII

*The Fool*

This Arcanum has been variously named the Atheist, the Fool, the Crocodile. We see a man without eyes walking along the edge of a precipice, carrying a bag flung across his shoulder, guiding himself by means of a frail walking stick. In the abyss below the precipice a crocodile lies in wait with open jaws. A broken and fallen column, or obelisk, lies immediately at his feet, covered with many mystic inscriptions.

The meaning of this glyph is by no means readable at first sight. Its simplest interpretation refers to the worldly man without knowledge of spiritual realities, who may fancy himself wise and powerful. The staff of worldly wisdom upon which he leans is frail, and the double bag in which he carries his worldly wealth is of no avail to save him from the crocodile which he does not see. His eyes are blind to the light of the spirit and its truth which, represented by a sun partially obscured by clouds, is nevertheless shining in the sky, visible to those who have eyes. The picture may be taken as representing the Epicurean materialist who lives but to "eat, drink and be merry, for tomorrow we die." In some Tarot systems, this man is not blind but only blindfolded, suggesting that he chooses to walk in the darkness rather than the light, regardless of consequences.

To such heedless ones are directed the terrible denunciations of the Old Testament prophets. We have "fools" amongst us today as in past centuries, and the words of the prophets apply now as of yore. Many of the Old Testament prophecies, the entire twenty-first chapter of Matthew, and many pages of the Book of Revelation, read like excerpts from a modern-day periodical. The poor (in spirit) ye have always with you, and these "poor" are the "Fool" of the Tarot.

### *Summary of Arcana*

As stated at the outset of our exploration of the Tarot mysteries, the Tarot, like the Bible and other Wisdom Books, outlines in symbol the steps and stages of the Path of Initiation or Illumination, forewarning of trials and temptations, foreshowing triumphs and delights. They represent for the modern neophyte an ideographic approach to the inner worlds, and their ideograms reach back into nameless epochs of past evolution, back to the dawn of human consciousness when the germ of mind was given to primitive man by cosmic Hierophants. The first Temples of Initiation were built for man when he became a "thinking animal," and there were as many of these Temples built, in various parts of the world, as there were kinds of people who needed them. Yet the basic Teaching was always and everywhere the same, though adapted to varying conditions in human life—both external and internal—to the outward conditions of space and time, to the inward conditions of heredity and the spirit's urge toward perfection.

The first three Arcanes give the cosmic pattern of the perfect man and the perfect woman. The first septenary of the Arcana outlines the path of instruction for the disciple.

From the seventh to the fourteenth Arcana, the second septenary, deeper aspects of the divine work are symbolically presented. In the fourteenth Arcanum we note the inception of the alchemical processes by means of which the new or "celestial body" of the New Age is to be fashioned.

In the septenary, from the fifteenth to the twenty-first Arcana, these alchemical processes are raised to a higher plane; the nineteenth, twentieth and twenty-first Arcana show the completion of the Great Work.

The twenty-second Arcanum voices a final warning that the day of accounting is at hand, and no time is to be lost in idleness and procrastination. "Now is the day of salvation."

## Chapter XV

## SAYINGS OF CHRIST

## CORRELATED WITH THE TAROT

### I

*The Magician or Magus–Divine Purpose*

John 6:39

*And this is the Father's will which has sent me, that of all which he hath given me, I shall lose nothing, but shall raise it up again at the last day.*

### II

*The High Priestess–Divine Feminine*

Matthew 16:19

*And I will give unto thee the keys of the kingdom of heaven, and whatsoever thou shalt loose on earth shall be loosed in heaven.*

### III

*The Empress–Divine Activity*

Matthew 13:33

*The kingdom of heaven is like unto leaven, which a woman took and hid in three measures of meal till the whole is leavened.*

## IV

### *The Emperor–Divine Overcoming*

John 16:33

*These things have I spoken unto you that in me ye might have peace. In the world ye shall have tribulation, but be of good cheer for I have overcome the world.*

Mark 12:10

*And have ye not read this scripture, the stone which the builders rejected is become the head of the corner.*

## V

### *The Hierophant–Divine Voice*

Matthew 28:20

*Teaching them to observe all things whatsoever I have commanded you; and lo, I am with you always, even unto the end of the world.*

Matthew 13:16

*Blessed are your eyes for they see: and your ears for they hear.*

## VI

### *The Lovers–Divine Path*

Matthew 7:14

*Enter ye in at the strait gate, because strait is the gate and narrow is the way which leadeth unto life, and few there be that find it.*

Matthew 26:41

*Watch and pray that ye enter not into temptation: the spirit indeed is willing but the flesh is weak.*

John 13:34

*And a new commandment give I unto you, that ye love one another as I have loved you.*

VII

*The Chariot–Divine Victory*

Matthew 6:48

*Be ye also perfect as your Father in heaven is perfect.*

Luke 6:40

*The disciple is not above his master: but every one that is perfect shall be as his master.*

VIII

*Justice–Divine Balance*

John 8:15,16

*Ye judge after the flesh: I judge no man–and yet if I judge, my judgment is true: for I am not alone, but I and the Father that sent me.*

Luke 6:37,38

*Judge not and ye shall not be judged. Condemn not and ye shall not be condemned. Forgive and ye shall be forgiven. For with the same measure ye mete it shall be measured to you again.*

IX

*The Hermit–Divine Light*

Matt. 5:14,16; Luke 12:35

*Ye are the light of the world. A city that is set on a hill cannot be hid. Let your light so shine before men that they may see your good works and glorify your Father which is in heaven.*

X

*The Wheel of Life Divine Unfoldment*

Luke 19:13,17

*He called his ten servants and delivered unto them ten pounds and said, "Occupy till I come."*

*Well done, thou good servant, because thou hast been faithful over a very little, have thou authority over ten cities.*

Matthew 15:8

*Eitner what woman having ten pieces of silver, if she lose one piece, doth not light a candle and sweep the house and seek diligently till she find it.*

XI

*Strength–Divine Strength*

Luke 10:3,19

*Go your ways: behold, I send you out as lambs among wolves.*

*Behold, I give unto you power to tread on serpents and scorpions, and over all the enemy, and nothing shall by any means hurt you.*

XII

*The Hanged Man–Divine Sacrifice*

Luke 9:23,24

*And he said unto them all, If any man will come after me let him deny himself, take up his cross daily, and follow me. Whosoever shall save his life shall lose it, but whosoever will lose his life for my sake, the same shall save it.*

## XIII

*Death–Divine Transformation*

John 5:21

*For as the Father raiseth up the dead and quickeneth them: even so the Son quickeneth whom he will.*

Mark 18, 27

*He is not the God of the dead, but the God of the living.*

John 5:25

*Verily I say unto you, the hour is coming and now is, when the dead shall hear the voice of the Son of God, and they that hear shall live.*

## XIV

*Temperance–Divine Baptism*

John 4:14

*Whosoever shall drink of the water that I shall give him shall never thirst, but the water shall be in him a well of water springing up unto everlasting life.*

John 5:4

*For an angel went down at a certain season into the pool and troubled the water. Whosoever then first after the troubling of the waters stepped in, was made whole.*

## XV

*The Devil–Divine Reversal*

Mark 3:26

*If Satan rise up against himself and be divided he cannot stand but hath an end.*

Matthew 12:28

*If I cast out devils by the Spirit of God, then the kingdom of God is come to you.*

XVI

*The Lightning-Struck Tower—Divine Fire*

Luke 12:49,50

*I am come to send fire on the earth: and what will I if it be already kindled? But I have a baptism to be baptized with, and how am I straitened till it be accomplished.*

Matthew 23:38,39

*Behold, your house is left unto you desolate. For I say unto you, ye shall not see me henceforth till ye shall say, Blessed is he that cometh in the name of the Lord.*

Luke 10:18

*I beheld Satan as lightning fell from heaven.*

XVII

*The Star—Divine Truth*

John 8:32

*Ye shall know the truth and the truth shall make you free.*

John 14:17

*Even the spirit of truth whom the world cannot receive because it seeth him not neither knoweth him: but ye know him: for he dwelleth with you and shall be in you.*

XVIII

*The Moon—Divine Shadow*

Acts 2:20

*The sun shall be turned into darkness and the moon into blood before that great and notable day of the Lord come.*

Luke 13:4

*Or those eighteen upon whom the tower in Siloam fell and slew them, think ye they were sinners above all men that dwell in Jerusalem? I tell you Nay: but except ye repent ye shall all likewise perish.*

## XIX

### *The Sun–Divine Light and Love*

John 15:11

*These things have I spoken unto you that my joy might remain in you and that your joy might be full.*

Luke 18:17

*Verily I say unto you, Whosoever shall not receive the kingdom of heaven as a little child shall in no wise enter therein.*

Luke 10:21

*I thank thee, O Father, Lord of heaven and earth, that thou hast hid these things from the wise and prudent and hast revealed them unto babes.*

## XX

### *The Judgment–Divine Resurrection*

John 11:25

*I am the resurrection and the life: he that believeth in me, though he were dead, yet shall he live.*

Luke 20:36

*Neither can they die any more, for they are equal unto the angels and are the children of God, being the children of the resurrection.*

## XXI

*The World–Divine Attainment*

John 17:4,5

*I have glorified thee on the earth: I have finished the work which thou gavest me to do. And now, O Father, glorify me with thine own self, with the glory which I had with thee before the world was.*

## XXII

*The Fool–Mortal Blindness–Ignorance*

Luke 12:20

*Thou fool, this night shall thy soul be required of thee; then whose shall those things be which thou hast provided? So is he that layeth up treasures for himself and is not rich toward God.*

Matthew 23:17

*Ye fools and blind, for whether is greater, the gift or the altar that sanctifieth the gift?*

Matthew 23:26

*Thou blind Pharisee, cleanse first that which is in the cup and the platter, that the outside of them may be clean also.*

# PART IV

# OUTLINE OF THE PATH
# AS SYMBOLIZED IN THE HEBREW LETTERS
# OF THE 119TH PSALM
# AND THE TAROT

## Chapter XVI

# SONGS OF INITIATION AND THEIR ALPHABETICAL KEYS

hen we say that the Psalms are true hymns of Initiation, this does not mean that they were all written by Initiates. They were assembled from every period of Hebrew history and from all classes and types of people, though most of them came from the Levitical class of Temple servitors; and as the divine purpose in Israel was more and more clearly revealed, these dedicated singers chanted with ever greater freedom of the divine glories. Beginning with simple songs of faith and moral instruction, much of it designed for a primitive society, they rise to a crescendo of triumph in the songs of illumination wherein the soul's union with God is known and declared.

The processes of Initiation do not remain the same throughout all times and cultures. Initiation is the scientific–consciously knowing and designed–method for unfolding the innate powers of the human spirit during incarnation. It therefore must change from age to age, as it is adapted to changing needs of the human ego by the great teachers and leaders of human evolution.

We may say that the Initiate recapitulates the history of his race and then steps forward beyond it. The Initiate is not a miraculous phenomenon set apart from his people and his time, but he is the apotheosis of civilization. He is the flowering of the race–plant and shows all men what it is their destiny to be. For this reason every part of his life has universal significance, and the experiences of all men are gathered up in him.

The work of the Bible did not cease with the closing of the orthodox canon of Scripture. Books are but the outward sign of an interior unfoldment of consciousness. The esotericism of Hebrew Scripture continued to develop right through the inter-testamental period when the apocryphal Books were written, the New Testament came into being and the Gnostic Scriptures added. The growth continued in both Christianity and Judaism under the name of Kabbalah, which means not merely "received" in the sense of instruction from a teacher, but "received" in the sense of Illumination from Spirit, or Initiation in the Mystery School tradition.

In the thirteenth century of our era Moses de Leon, the great kabbalist of Moorish Spain where the Arabs had established a brilliant civilization, gathered together the esoteric teachings of the Hebrew people in the book Zohar, which means Brilliance or Splendor. It is not an original work but a compendium from every source. Kabbalism had begun to flower in Spain in the tenth and eleventh centuries, and one great teacher succeeded another until the time when Moses de Leon assembled the kabbalistic lore in his encyclopedia of esotericism which survives as the great source book of modern kabbalism. Moses de Leon passed into the higher life in 1305, a few years before Christian Rosenkreutz founded the Order or School ("Academy") of the Rose Cross in 1313.

Thus the esoteric teaching from the "Celestial Academy" descended through Church and Synagogue, incorporating the basic principles, the inmost divine essence as it were, of the Mystery Schools of antiquity, Babylonian, Egyptian, Persian, Greek and Roman; to which were added elements from the teachings of other lands and peoples during the centuries of the Piscean Age.

The Moslem civilization had already rediscovered the Greek wisdom, and so the Kabbalah which flowered in Moorish Spain incorporated these new elements along with that which they had retained from the earliest times when their nation had been under the rule of the hellenistic Pharaohs of Egypt and Kings of Syria. Hence the references to the "Celestial Academy," recalling memories of Plato and his Academy in Athens. It was at Alexandria in Egypt that these Platonic teachings took on a new and advanced form.

The great esoteric Teacher of the Zohar is the Prophet Elijah, or Elias as he is called in the New Testament. It was he who instructed Simon ben Yohai, the central figure of the Zohar, and to whom Moses de Leon ascribes the teachings. We need not follow the example of modern critics who term Moses de Leon a fraud but must understand that the Hebrew mystics and seers did truly believe that the great Masters came to them in ethereal bodies and taught them and led them through the gates of Initiation.

Thus we find in the Zohar the many spiritual adventures which in ancient times belonged to the Mysteries. Moses de Leon discusses the "Mansions and Abodes" of the inner world—Heaven, Paradise and Hell—the Creative Intelligences or Sephiroth which collectively are God, the Faithful Shepherd (Simon or Simeon in conversation with Moses), and many other things of profound interest, such as the ability of the soul to leave the body at night during sleep and attend the "Celestial Academy"; the brilliant color emanations of the angelic choirs; the diamond Glory of Deity; healing by the laying on of hands; the unfoldment of spiritual vision; the Mystic Marriage of the soul with God, and much more. The doctrine of reincarnation is taught but has been misunderstood by modern commentators. The Zohar mentions three rebirths, but this is not to be taken as meaning that the ego has only three reincarnations on earth. The reference is to the Platonic teaching that before the ego can be liberated from the wheel of birth and death it must have had three lifetimes, both before death and in the interval after death when it is awaiting rebirth, during which it has committed no sin either of thought, word or deed. When the human spirit has reached this condition, then it is ready for immortality. It is interesting to note that the three final lives of perfection are not restricted to lives on the physical earth but include the life of the spirit in the psychospiritual planes which follow death, for the occultist knows that the spirit may commit evil even after the death of the body, while in the lower planes of the soul world, which includes the purgatory and hell of orthodox believers.

In modern speech this would mean that the human being must have lived three lifetimes on earth so pure and holy that he has no purgatory or "hell" in the soul world after death before he is ready for Liberation from the wheel of death and rebirth.

The Zohar pivots about the Mystery of the Divine Balance, or spiritual Equilibrium, which is the secret of all esoteric revelation and of all creative activity whatsoever, for it resolves the problem of polarity. Hence the supreme Mystery is always the Mystic Marriage of the soul with God, under the similitude of the love of the Bride and Bridegroom.

These esoteric Mysteries the author draws out of the Pentateuch–the first five books of the Bible, which are attributed to Moses–by an intricate process of interpreting by letters, numbers and names, in the manner handed down from earliest times.

Similar codes are to be discovered throughout the entire Bible; none of its divisions are without them. There are no less than nine psalms in which the first letters of each stanza, in the Hebrew, are taken in alphabetical order. Most important of these is the 119th Psalm, in which all eight lines of each stanza begin with the same letter, proceeding successively through the twenty-two letters of the Hebrew alphabet. Hebrew scholars know of others, such as the first four poems of the Book of Lamentations, and verses ten through thirty-one of Proverbs 31, extolling the perfect wife. These are examples of the way in which "mysteries" have been encoded in the scriptural texts, a great many never having been discovered by the orthodox who have lost the mystical key to their recovery and interpretation. Similar codes are incorporated in every great Scripture of the world, for there has always been "milk for babes" and "meat for strong men" in all religions.

Turning now to the 119th Psalm, the kabbalistic psalm *par excellence*, we discover that the mystical meaning of each stanza accords with the symbolical and kabbalistic interpretation of the letter which leads the line, as we have learned of them in Part II of this volume. This is not immediately apparent in the English translation where the English alphabet is used, and yet there is a correspondence, since the Hebrew, Greek, Latin and English alphabets are related; but there is a mystical song for each of the twenty-two letters of the Hebrew alphabet, each song consisting of eight verses, as in the original Hebrew, although leading letters cannot be the same.

The kabbalists say that the number eight is a channel for the inflow and outflow of the spiritual power and light. It is the symbol of the world of the Ogdoad, the Eighth Spiritual Sphere of the Gnosis, which is called the World of the Christ.

Macrobius, the famous Pythagorean philosopher, wrote of the number eight that it signifies justice, for the reason that when equally divided into fours, these indicate the equilibrium of the inner and outer worlds. The symbol for eight which comes by way of the Arabs, 8, pictures clearly the flow of spiritual forces.

In the Eleusinian Mysteries the Initiates were the Wise Men, whose number was eight. On the eighth day of these Mysteries the Feast of Aesculapius was celebrated, dedicated to the physician who was canonized and became a "god," or "saint" as referred to today. It was said that he had raised a man from the dead and had also himself entered the ranks of the immortal gods.

Inasmuch as the twenty-two letters of the Hebrew alphabet represent spiritual qualities to be developed on the Path of Attainment, they may be described as marking steps or degrees in unfoldment as the aspirant cultivates the inner powers that lead to Initiation.

Like the Psalms generally, which were not all composed by the same person, the 119th Psalm consists of a collection of songs composed by various poets and singers. Some are the utterances of the young neophyte making his dedication to the Path. Others are composed by those who have gone farther on the Way of Holiness and express their joy in the larger vistas of

Truth that open up before them. Still others voice lamentation over failures and errors, set over against songs of thanksgiving for spiritual illumination and songs invoking protection in times of trial and suffering.

The Psalm as such contains only the praises, the prayers and the lamentations uttered by the aspirant struggling on the straight and narrow way which leads to Initiation and the ultimate Liberation. Other meanings must be deciphered kabbalistically.

A careful and meditative study of the Hebrew letter, together with the twenty-two Major Arcana of the Tarot and the songs which comprise the 119th Psalm, will prove deeply rewarding. To facilitate this comparative study we give here a diagram showing the twenty-two letters, their keywords, and their numbers. Remember that in this study we are dealing with what the Magi of Palestine termed "letters of light." Each letter has its own unique meaning and quality, its own spiritual keynote or tonal pattern—for every verse of the sacred texts was formed for chanting—and when the keynote is sounded it calls forth the vibration of a mighty spiritual Hierarch. In meditation the neophyte experiences these keynotes of cosmic vibration one by one, moment by moment, in terms of time and space; but one day, as he learns to rise into the higher spheres of meditation, he will experience them collectively and simultaneously, the Music of the Spheres known to the Cosmic Consciousness wherein man is One with God, and where God is All and in all.

Thus Christian Ginsberg comments that "some of the most distinguished Jewish doctors in the days of Christ, and afterwards, claimed an attainment of superhuman knowledge, communicated to them by a voice from heaven or by Elias (Elijah) the prophet."

In the 119th Psalm we find the corresponding brief key statements:

*Aleph,* as stated previously, denotes the power of self-control, the first lesson to be learned by an aspirant. The Psalm indicates that self-control is the law of the Lord, "Blessed are they that keep his testimonies and that seek him with the whole heart."

*Beth* stands for the purification and exaltation of love, "Thy word have I hid in mine heart, that I might not sin against thee."

In *Gimel* is heard the prayer of the newly awakened one, "Open thou mine eyes, that I may behold wondrous things out of thy law."

*Daleth* sings the song of true humility, "My soul cleaveth unto the dust; quicken thou me according to thy word."

*He,* as the force of regeneration, inspires the prayer that every neophyte learns to voice, "Turn thou my reproach (causation) which I fear, for thy judgments are good."

*Vau,* symbolizing balance or equilibirum (harmony with cosmic law), has its prayer, "So shall I keep thy law continually for ever and ever. And I will walk at liberty (the body no longer a prison house), for I seek thy precepts."

*Zain* represents victory which is the power attained by mastery of the lower self, "Thy statutes have been my song in the house of my pilgrimage."

*Cheth* or *Heth*, indicative of oneness with spirit after the new birth, is fulfilled in the prayer, "I thought on my ways, and turned my feet unto thy testimonies."

*Teth,* denoting wisdom, sounds forth in the prayer, "It is food for me that I have been afflicted; that I might learn thy statues."

*Yod,* transmutation of generation into regeneration, lifts the Psalmist voice in song of rejoicing, "They that fear thee will be glad when they see me because I have hoped in thy word."

*Kaph* signifies strength through spiritual developments, "For I am become like a bottle in the smoke; yet I do not forget thy statues."

*Lamed* signifies sacrifice, of which prayer is made, "They continue this day according to thine ordinances; for all are thy servants."

*Mem* reaches the place of mastery or Adeptship, where it lifts its voice in exhaltation, "Oh how I love thy law! It is my meditation all the day."

For *Nun* the psalmist sings of individualization, "Thy testimonies have I taken for an heritage for ever, for they are the rejoicing of my heart."

*Samekh* stands for the Path leading to Initiation by overcoming temptation, whereon the aspirant prays, "Thou art my hiding-place and my shield; I hope in thy word."

*Ayin* or *Oin* is the beginning of spiritualized consciousness, when the neophyte can say, "Therefore I love thy commandments above gold; yea, above fine gold."

*Pe* is intuitive knowing that heralds immortality. When the seeker unfolds this faculty he declares, "Thy testimonies are wonderful; therefore doth my soul keep them."

*Tzaddi* is indicative of elevation, and the prayer for this attainment is, "The righteousness of thy testimonies is everlasting; therefore doth my soul keep them."

*Quoph* or *Koph* is the prodigal son after his return unto his Father's house. He can then pray in all earnestness, "Thou art near, O Lord; and all thy commandments are truth."

*Resh* ends the struggle for self-mastery when, from the heights of transfiguration, the illumined one cries, "Thy word is true from the beginning; and every one of thy righteous judgments endureth forever."

*Schin* is the bearer of glad tidings, voiced in the words, "Great peace have they which love thy law: and nothing shall offend them."

In *Tav* or *Tau* the seeker is still bound to the cross of matter but is uttering unceasingly, "Let my cry come near before thee, O Lord; give me understanding according to thy words."

## THE TWENTY-TWO HEBREW LETTERS, NUMBERS AND KEYWORDS

| | | | |
|---|---|---|---|
| 1 | א | Aleph (A or silent) . . . | The Christed Man: the Magus |
| 2 | ב | Beth (B) . . . . . . | Purity: the High Priestess of Isis |
| 3 | ג | Gimel (G) . . . . . . . | Wisdom of Nature: the Empress |
| 4 | ד | Daleth (D) . . . | Dedication to the Path: the Emperor |
| 5 | ה | He (H, E) . . . . | Self-Conquest: the High Priest of Isis, Master of the Arcanes, the Double Feminine |
| 6 | ו | Vau (V, W) . . . . . . | Discrimination: the Two Ways |
| 7 | ז | Zain (Z) . | Victorious Attainment: the Chariot of Osiris |
| 8 | ח | Cheth (H, CH) . . . . . . | Detachment: Divine Justice, the Balance and the Sword |
| 9 | ט | Teth (T, TH) . | Wisdom: the Veiled Lamp, the Teacher |
| 10 | י | Yod (Y, J, I) . . . . . . . . . | The Conquest of Fate: the Sphinx and the Wheel |
| 20 | כ | Kaph (K, KH) (final K, 500) . . | The Strength of Love: Self-Control, the Virgin and the Lion |
| 30 | ל | Lamed (L) . . . . | Selfless Sacrifice: the Hanged Man or the Just One |
| 40 | מ | Mem (M) (final M, 500) . . . . . | The Law and the Kingdom Within: the Reaping Skeleton |

50 נ Nun (N) . . . Man Know Thyself: the Angel with the
(final N, 700) Gold and Silver Urns: Polarity

60 ס Samekh (S, X) . . . . . . . . . . . . The Conquest of
the Spirit of Evil: Typhon

70 ע Ayin or Oin (O or silent) . . . Chaos and Confusion:
the Aftermath of Wrong-Doing:
the Lightening-Struck Pyramid

80 פ Pe or Phe (P, F) . . Lemniscate Currents, Stabilized:
(final P, 800) the Star of the Magi, Truth

90 צ Tzaddi (Tz, Ts) . . . . The Two Paths: the Black and
(Final Tz, 900) White Pyramids: the Enneads

100 ק Koph or Quoph (K, Q) . . . . . . . Polarity Attained:
the Mystic Marriage

200 ר Resh (R) . . . . . . Rebirth: the Raising of the Dead

300 שׁ Schin (S, SH) . . . . The Goal Supreme: the Crown of
the Magi, the Lotus Wreath and Harp of God

400 ת Tau or Tav (T, TH)Consummation and New Beginnings:
the Crocodile and the Fool

1000 "Many" . . . . . . . . . . A tribe, a people, a Myriad

We have seen that the twenty-two letters of the Hebrew alphabet were used to denote numbers, 1 to 10 being signified by the letters Aleph to Yod; while beginning with Kaph, the eleventh letter, the numbers were taken by decans, with K as 20, L as 30, M as 40, N as 50, Samekh as 60, Ayin or Oin as 70, Pe or Phe as 80, Tzaddi as 90, Koph or Quoph as 100; after which the numeration continues in hundreds with Resh as 200, Schin as 300, and Tau as 400.

Esotericists discerned special mysteries in each new form which the letter-number took, and these meanings were included in the kabbalistic ciphers.

Note that although Kaph and Koph are both pronounced with a K sound, Koph (Q) is the number 100 whereas Kaph (K) is 20. The name Kabbalah is usually spelled in English with a K, but this K is not Kaph but Koph or Quoph, and to make this plain some kabbalists spell the word with a Q instead of a K–Qabbalah.

For still higher numbers the signification returns to the five letters which have a separate picture when they come last in a word. These are the "finals"–K, or Kaph, whose first number is 20, has a final form which denotes 500. M,Mem, whose first number is 40, has a final form which signifies 800. And Tz, or Tzaddi, whose first number is 90, as a final, signifies 900.

We find in the Old Testament a word which signifies "Many," and which is also synonymous for "tribe" and "family," which was used numerically to mean 1000. Both Babylonians and Phoenicians, who bestowed on the West its numberical system, used symbols for numbers long in advance of the Hebrews, who in early times wrote out the name of the number. The Egyptians used the lotus as a symbol for thousand, and it is said that the Egyptian lotus bears upon its stamen the interlaced triangles which are the sign of the Royal Family of David, hence of the Messiah, thus pointing to the millennial kingdom. Since in the Hebrew the word often read "many" may signify tribe or family, or a thousand, this again reveals a mystery concerning the Lily of Israel and the Messianic Kingdom.

Of the primary cycles the number 7, in all its varied relationships, refer to cycles of time and cycles of accomplishment. The human being reincarnates in cycles of seven; there are Seven Cosmic Planes, and the Seventh Cosmic Plane is divided into Seven Worlds, and these again into seven regions of subplanes. Any reference to 7 hints of a cycle or period of growth and development. The letters of the Hebrew alphabet are divided, on this symbolism, into three septenaries, with Tau added; but in any of these cycles, when the number 7 reveals itself, we know that we are viewing a culminating phase of a cycle. On the Sabbath God rests, having completed, in the six previous Days, the Plan of Creation. The number 70 has a special significance as a cycle number because it associates with eclipse cycles.

Another kabbalistic system counts by tens. The first cycle is from Aleph to Yod, 1 to 10; the second from Kah to Resh, 20-200; with Schin and Tau, 300 and 400, added. Sometimes it is said that Tau is really a supernumerary, or that Ayin or Oin is to be taken as Zero.

In the cycles of ten each number of the decad repeats on a higher cycle the power of the corresponding number of the first or basic decad. These again return upon the centennial cycle, named in hundreds, and these in the millennial cycles, named in thousands as dealing with cosmic and world periods.

A pyramidal arrangement yields a first series of letters, Aleph to Yod (ten letters), showing forth the beginning of the Path. A second series, Kaph to Pe (seven letters), indicate further steps on the Way. A third series, Tzaddi to Schin (four letters), shadow forth the supreme attainment. In Tau, the twenty-second and last step, the aspirant is tried and proved steadfast.

## Chapter XVII

## THE FIRST SEPTENARY, ALEPH–ZAIN

### Verses 1 – 56

### ARCANE I

ALEPH A = 1

*The 119th Psalm*

Verses 1 – 8

*Blessed are the undefiled in the way, who walk in the law of the Lord.*

*Blessed are they that keep his testimonies, and that seek him with the whole heart. They also do no iniquity: they walk in his ways.*

*Thou hast commanded me to keep thy precepts diligently. O that my ways were directed to keep thy statutes! Then shall I not be ashamed, when I have respect unto all thy commandments.*

*I will praise thee with uprightness of heart, when I shall have learned thy righteous judgments. I will keep thy statutes: O forsake me not utterly!*

Aleph is the first letter of the Hebrew alphabet, and the number 1; it is representative of the secret God-power manifesting in man, and correlates with the first Tarot card of the Major Arcana. This card shows the Master or Magus, the Wise One, who is described in the early chapters of Genesis as man made in the image and likeness of God–the supreme ideal toward which all the spiritual philosophers of the world have ever aspired.

We have stated previously that the Path of Initiation is divided into three parts, the parts denoting the three classes of disciples–first, the Neophytes; second, the Disciples; third, those who have been found worthy to part the veil and enter the Holy of Holies, the Initiates. In many schools the threefold divisions are named Studentship, Probationship and Discipleship; Initiation being the full flowering of the third degree.

In the 119th Psalm, the opening invocation to the Divine Principle represented by Aleph, the first letter of the Hebrew alphabet, we hear the voice of the Neophyte making supplication as he dedicates his life to God, "Blessed are the undefiled who walk in the law of the Lord . . . Blessed are they which keep his testimonies and seek him with the whole heart . . . I will keep thy statues; O forsake me not."

*Meditation for Aleph*

I AM the Light that permeates all creation. I AM Life Universal. I AM Love Eternal. I AM all the Power that is, both manifest and unmanifest.

Aleph speaks of the First Commandment, "I am the Lord which have brought thee out of the house of bondage. Thou shalt have no other gods before me."

## ARCANE II

BETH B = 2

Verses 9 – 16

*Wherewithal shall a young man cleanse his way? By taking heed thereto according to thy word.*

*With my whole heart have I sought thee; O let me not wander from thy commandments. Thy word have I hid in my heart, that I might not sin against thee.*

*Blessed art thou, O Lord, teach me thy statutes.*

*With my lips have I declared all the judgments of thy mouth. I have rejoiced in the way of thy testimonies, as much as in all riches. I will meditate in thy precepts, and have respect unto thy ways. I will delight myself in thy statutes? I will not forget thy Word.*

Beth is the second letter of the Hebrew alphabet. The number two signifies balance and equilibrium. Beth correlates with the second Tarot card of the major Arcanes. Perfect balance is represented by the High Priestess who sits upon a throne between two perfectly proportioned columns—one white, the other black. She is partially veiled, which suggests the mystery surrounding the high feminine principle, both in man and nature. It is something of this divine mystery which always radiates from the Divine Feminine that is felt as a strange fascination, on the spiritual planes as well as on the physical. The Divine Feminine is the wisdom Principle, hid behind a veil. In the invocation of Beth we hear the voice of the neophyte who stands before the veil and prays that he may behold Truth face to face.

The two columns, one black and one white, are those which stood before the portals of every Mystery Temple the world has ever known. To the esotericist they reveal the true meaning of polarity—that the two cosmic principles are equal throughout the universe, on all planes of manifestation. These are the Jachin and Boaz of Masonry; but the majority of the Jachin disciples do not as yet understand this divine truth. There can never be a New Age on this planet until equality between man and woman has been fully demonstrated upon all planes, for Truth—the sacred Glory which hides behind the veil—is no respecter of persons. "With my whole heart have I sought thee—O let me not wander from thy commandments . . . I will meditate in thy precepts and have respect unto thy ways."

David, the Initiate, knew well the truth of the words: "Wherewithal shall a young man cleanse his way? By taking heed thereto according to thy Word." The *power* of *love* is vested in *self-control*—Aleph and Beth—the two columns of the Temple gate. "Thy *Word* which *I hide in my heart that I might not sin against thee.*" A supreme dedication of the life lies in his words: "I will delight myself in thy statutes. I will not forget thy Word."

*Meditation for Beth*

I AM the great harmonizer, the unifying Force which underlies all creation. In the house not made with hands I hold the cosmic pattern of all forms on earth.

Beth relates to the Second Commandment: "Thou shalt not make thyself any graven image."

**ARCANE III**

GIMEL G = 3

Verses 17 – 24

*Deal bountifully with thy servant, that I may live and keep thy Word. Open thou mine eyes, that I may behold wondrous things out of thy law.*

*I am a stranger in the earth: hide not thy commandments from me. My soul breaketh for the longing that it hath unto thy judgments at all times.*

*Thou hast rebuked the proud that are cursed, which do err from thy commandments. Remove from me reproach and contempt: for I have kept thy testimonies.*

*Princes also did sit and speak against me: but thy servant did meditate in thy statutes. Thy testimonies also are my delight and my counsellors.*

Gimel and the third Tarot card represent the Empress. The symbolism shows that "the Mother of the Universe" means Mother Nature and the laws which bring order out of chaos in the created universe. The symbol of the planet Venus nearby shows that she is also called Venus-Urania, or Iris-Urania. There is a harmony of natures between the planets Venus and Uranus; but the full force of Uranus will not be felt until the Aquarian Age dawns, although its energizing and revolutionary influence is already apparent. Mankind stands on the threshold of the Aquarian Age; when the threshold is crossed, mysteries of space yet undreamed of will be revealed, and secrets of life for which there are as yet no words adequate to describe them.

The Empress sits upon a throne in the glow of a great sun and with the crescent moon under her feet; near her is the symbol of Venus. She wears a crown of twelve stars, which conveys the promise of conscious and uninterrupted communion with the Divine Hierarchies, the twelve signs of the zodiac. Upon her right hand is the eagle, the king of birds, which flies closer to the sun than any other bird. This Tarot conveys the message that Truth knows no limits, has no circumference, is all-powerful.

The Empress is the Woman Clothed with the Sun of the Book of Revelation. Gimel, or Three, signifies the Triad of Divine Force which is the basis of creation, the Trinity of the West and the Trimurti of the East, the Three First Sephiroth of the Kabballah; the three Principles known as Will, Wisdom and Activity as they manifest throughout the universe and also in the human spirit.

All of this is exemplified in the eight stanzas led by Gimel "Thy testimonies also are my delight and my counselors." "Thou hast rebuked the proud that are cursed, which do err from Thy commandments." "Open Thou mine eyes that I may behold wonderful things out of Thy Law."

*Meditation for Gimel*

Mine is the power that ensouls all forms with Light. The secret of this Light no man may know until the coming of the Perfect Day when the Face of Truth is unveiled.

Gimel reminds us of the Third Commandment, "Thou shalt

not take the name of the Lord in vain."

## ARCANE IV

DALETH D = 4

Verses 25 – 32

*My soul cleaveth unto the dust: quicken thou me according to thy word. I have declared may ways, and thou heardst me: teach me thy statutes. Make me to understand the way of thy precepts: so shall I talk of thy wondrous works.*

*My soul melteth for heaviness: strengthen thou me according to thy word. Remove from me the way of lying: and grant me thy law graciously.*

*I have chosen the way of truth; thy judgments have I laid before me. I have stuck unto thy testimonies: O Lord, put me not to shame. I will run the way of thy commandments, when thou shalt enlarge my heart.*

In these eight stanzas, led by Daleth, we see that a door is before the neophyte, and he waits for it to open, "My soul cleaveth to the dust: quicken thou me according to thy word. Make me understand the way of thy precepts; so shall I talk of thy wondrous works . . . I have chosen the Way of Truth . . . I will run the way of thy commandements when thou shalt enlarge my heart."

Four is the number of the Cubic Stone, which is the title of the fourth Tarot. The cube occurs often in the Tarot series, and it is of the profoundest importance in Mystic Masonry. The cube upon which the Mystic Mason works is himself. When it is opened out it is a Cross, and the Cross is the Doorway to Life Eternal.

Therefore the youthful Pharaoh on his cubic throne wears the White Crown and holds the Scepter of Life. One leg is crossed over the other. On his breast is a snow-white dove, showing that he has attained through self-immolation and purity. He has conquered materiality toward which his left hand points. Sometimes he is called the Emperor. He images forth the words of St. Paul, "Now abideth Faith, Hope and Love; but the greatest of these is Love." Self-conquest has transformed the emotion of Love into a Power of Love in the hands of the Spirit. The Uraeus serpent on the front of the crown signifies the great wisdom attained when the spinal spirit fire force is raised up.

In the psalmist's supplication for Daleth, the dedication is made for all time to the spiritual life. A high point on the Path is reached when one is ready to make this dedication which applies not merely to the current life but to all lives that are to come. It is the strong soul that can make this dedication, this ultimate dedication, to the things of Spirit.

*Meditation for Daleth*

"I have chosen the Way of Truth."

Daleth reminds us of the Fourth Commandment, "Remember the Sabbath day and keep it holy."

## ARCANE V

HE E = 5

Verses 33 – 40

*Teach me, O Lord, the way of thy statutes; and I shall keep it unto the end. Give me understanding, and I shall keep thy law; yea, I shall observe it with my whole heart.*

*Make me to go in the path of thy commandments; for therein do I delight. Incline my heart unto thy testimonies, and not to covetousness.*

*Turn away mine eyes from beholding vanity; and quicken*

*thou me in thy way. Stablish thy word unto thy servant, who is devoted to thy fear.*

*Turn away my reproach which I fear: for thy judgments are good. Behold, I have longed after thy precepts: quicken me in thy righteousness.*

The letter He–E or H–though only the fifth letter of the Hebrew alphabet, is one of the supremely important letters because it occurs twice in the Sacred Tetragrammaton, as we have seen. It represents the Cosmic Feminine in two phases or aspects, The Double Shekinah Glory, which is close to the human spirit and is in a real sense its Mother, and the Exalted Feminine which is the Shekinah Glory on the highest cosmic planes, Theo-Sophia of the Greeks.

The fifth Tarot shows the Initiate-Priest, Master of the Arcanes, sometimes called the Pope, seated on his throne between the two columns, holding in his left hand the long cross with three cross-bars and upon his head the white Uraeus headdress which symbolizes the raising up of the fire-force and achievement of at-one-ment with the Deity within. He makes the sign known as the papal blessing with the right hand, which is a sign of true esoteric knowledge and power. At his feet kneel two devotees, garbed in red and in white, symbol of service and understanding, of the inner hidden mysteries. This show us that the true mission of the Initiate-Priest is to share the inner or esoteric secrets of his ministry with all who prove themselves ready and worthy to receive them, It is significant that for the first three centuries of our era none but an Initiate was deemed worthy to sit in the chair of St. Peter.

In the Egyptian Tarot the Initiate-Priest is the High Priest of Isis, but the symbology is similar to that of other systems.

The High Priest corresponds to Melchizedek of the Bible story. Melchizedek was the title of a dynasty of priest-kings whose ancestry went back to Atlantis. The last Melchizdek gave to Abram, the first leader of the present Fifth Root Race, the deeply mystic secrets of the Rite of the Eucharist. These secrets were passed in turn to Isaac, Jacob, and the Patriarchs; to Moses and Joshua; to David and Solomon for use in the Temple; and finally they descended into the hands of Christ Jesus, who taught them to the Disciples in the "Upper Room" just before the Crucifixion. The key to the right use of the Rite of the Holy Eucharist is the conservation of the life force, which is symbolized in the Bread. This life force, impregnating the Bread, enabled the Disciples to heal the sick and the erring when each evening they took portions of the sacred host to all in need, and legend has it that many were healed when they had but looked upon the Bread.

*Mediatation for He*

The Mystery of the Double Feminine was the central teaching of the ancient Priest-Kings of Atlantis. The Zohar says that the Shekinah Glory abode in the tent of Sarah, and when Abraham saw it there he knew that God was with him in his battles and trials.

The words of the Fifth Commandment, "Thou shalt honor thy father and thy mother," when taken mystically refer to honoring the dual principles of Godhead within oneself. The great work of Initiation is to bring the dual forces into equilibrium or perfect harmony. When this has been achieved the Initiate has become the Adept, able to create for himself deathless bodies in which he may live as an immortal, a god among gods.

"Teach me, O Lord, the way of thy statutes, and I shall keep it unto the end."

## ARCANE VI

VAU U-V = 6

Verses 41 – 48

*Let thy mercies come also unto me, O Lord, even thy*

*salvation , according to thy word. So shall I have wherewith to answer him that reproacheth me: for I trust in thy word. And take not the word of truth utterly out of my mouth; for I have hoped in thy judgments.*

*So shall I keep thy law continually for ever and ever. And I will walk at liberty: for I seek thy precepts. I will speak of thy testimonies also before kings, and will not be ashamed.*

*And I will delight myself in thy commandments, which I have loved. My hands also will I lift up unto thy commandments, which I have loved; and I will meditate in thy statutes.*

Vau or Vav is the sixth letter of the Hebrew alphabet. Six is a Venusian number and it expresses Love, Harmony and Light. It is also a number of attainment through action inspired by love. Although it is one of the even or "feminine" numbers in order of procession, it is considered by kabbalists to be a supremely masculine number, and the love which it expresses is the Love of God. The two Hs in the Tetragrammaton (JHVH) show forth the Double Feminine, the Higher and Lower Shekinah, but the Vau is the second masculine letter, Jod being the first.

The sixth of the Tarot cards represents the Two Ways. A youth stands between two maidens. Each has a hand on his shoulder, urging him to go her way. The maiden on his right wears a Uraeus crown; the one on his left a crown made of the leaves of the grapevine. They typify what is known as the Way of Virtue and the Way of Vice.

To this place upon the highroad of destiny every man must come, time after time and life after life, until spirit is supreme.

In one Tarot series the sixth card shows Adam and Eve in the Garden of Eden. Adam stands before the Tree of Life and Eve before the Tree of Good and Evil, round the trunk of which a serpent twines.

Over the human figures of the sixth card hovers a great being. Sometimes it is Hermes or Mercury. In the Egyptian series it is a Genii—or Genius—but always this figure represents the immutable and unalterable law of retributive justice. He carries a bow and arrow which is pointed toward the maiden at the left, implying that if her path is chosen the ultimate consequences may well be seen in the sixteenth card known as the Tower of Destruction, where there is only confusion, upheaval, destruction and final annihilation. If the right-hand Path be chosen, its consequences may be traced in the nineteenth card, which is known as The Sun or the Dazzling Light. There we see a youth and maiden in a beautiful garden–but now there is no Tree of Good and Evil. The young couple are enfolded in a glow of golden light from the great sun which illumines all the heavens and the surrounding landscape It is here that the lower man has been completely subjugated and the higher powers reign supreme.

Temptation is a tremendous factor in soul growth. One never realizes his own strength until he has been tempted and tried. It is for this reason that the Temptation is so powerfully portrayed in the initiatory ritual which we know as the life-story of Christ Jesus. The Bible states, "Although He was tempted, He remained without sin." This is the ideal which He left for the emulation of all mankind.

In Wagner's glorious opera *Parsifal* we find the nearest modern version of this story. Parsifal came as a youth to the Grail Castle, there to study the immortal precepts of Truth from the wise Guernemanz, teacher of the Grail Knights. After a period of training he was sent forth to be tempted and tried in the outer world. There he met the beautiful flower maidens, but true to the ideals given by the Lord Christ, though tempted, he remained without sin. Later he was found worthy to return to the Grail Castle to become the Teacher of the Knights and Guardian of the Holy Grail.

### *Meditation for Vau*

In the 119th Psalm the prayer for the letter Vau is the high and beautiful affirmation of those who have attained first-hand knowledge, for whom there is now no faltering and whose dedication is secure for all time to come.

"So shall I keep thy precepts for ever and ever. And I shall walk at liberty; for I seek thy precepts. I will speak of thy testimonies before kings, and will not be ashamed."

Vau speaks of the Sixth Commandment, "Thou shalt not kill," for V is the letter of Life.

## ARCANE VII

ZAIN    Z = 7

Verses 49 – 56

*Remember the word unto thy servant, upon which thou hast caused me to hope. This is my comfort in my affliction: for thy Word hath quickened me.*

*The proud have had me greatly in derision: yet have I not declined thy law. I remembered thy judgments of old, O Lord; and have comforted myself.*

*Horror hath taken hold upon me because of the wicked that forsake thy law.*

*Thy statutes have been my songs in the house of my pilgrimage. I have remembered thy name, O Lord, in the night, and have kept thy law. This I had, because I kept thy precepts.*

The Hebrew letter Zain implies Victory.

Seven is the number which represents an interval of rest after a long period of difficult and arduous work and accomplishment. The Lord God created the heavens and the earth and He rested on the seventh day. However, rest in its highest sense does not mean inaction but rather a complete at-one-ment with that which has been produced or made manifest.

The seventh Tarot card of the Egyptian series shows us the cubic chariot, in which the Victor rides. It is called the Chariot of Osiris. Here is one who has attained to mastership, standing in his cube-shaped chariot, which is attached to two sphinxes, one black and one white, which crouch at rest. The cube always denotes successful accomplishment after long and difficult labor.

The sphinxes rest in perfect relaxation, indicating that the evil forces both in man and in nature have been completely subjugated and that the Initiate now lives, moves and has his being in perfect at-one-ment with the powers of All-Good.

Upon the chest of the charioteer we see the three symbolic T-squares, representing Strength, Discrimination and Self-Control or spiritualized Will. The cuirass is again reminiscent of the breastplate of the Hebrew High Priest. On his head he wears the familiar Uraeus Crown of Egypt. The lotuses adorning the chariot show the balanced masculine and feminine powers of the Master. In moderm terminology this represents the Christing of the Mind. The sword which he holds shows that he is the Victorious One. He holds the scepter of Initiate Power. Upon the scepter is a square surmounted by a circle surmounted by a triangle, emblematic of Matter, Eternity and Divinity—the World. Spirit and God.

The star-decked canopy over the chariot and charioteer is supported on four columns, which are the Four Elements. This shows us the Initiate's power to pass through Earth. Air. Water and Fire unharmed, and to enter at will into the very heart of the planet as he gives himself in service for all God's living creatures.

Upon the front of the chariot is one of the most meaningful of the symbols belonging to ancient Egypt. This is the Winged Sphere, whose deep significance belongs to the Man of the Aquarian Age who will investigate the wonders of trackless space and become, in literal fact, rover among the farthest stars.

### *Meditation for Zain*

This brings us to the end of the first septenary. The ideal of man "made in the image and likeness of God" was given by means of the first Tarot card, the Magus, and the first Hebrew letter, Aleph, while in the seventh Tarot card, the Chariot, and the seventh Hebrew letter, Zain, we find the victorious mankind in whom this ideal has become real, or, in familiar terminology, the pioneers of the New Aquarian Age, so soon to dawn.

"Number Seven is the festival day of all the earth, the birthday of the world. I know not whether anyone would be able to celebrate the number Seven in adequate terms" (*The Secret Doctrine*).

The prayer of the Hebrew letter Zain sounds the same high spiritual keynote as does the number seven, "Thy statutes have been my songs in the house of my pilgrimage. I have remembered thy name O Lord, in the night and have kept thy law."

Zain represents the power which is attained by the mastery of the four elements, Fire, Air, Water and Earth. The development of the fourfold power within himself gives the disciple mastery over all important earth processes, and he becomes known as a miracle worker. The letter Zain means, in deed and in truth, the Victorious One.

Zain teaches the lesson of purity in selfless love. The Seventh Commandment reads, "Thou shalt not commit adultery." The defilement of the love potencies of the body, soul and mind are a sin not only against the Holy Spirit of God but against that holy spirit which we call the spirit of man, the true or Virgin Spirit which is man in the likeness of God.

## Chapter XVIII

## THE SECOND SEPTENARY, CHETH--NUN

### Verses 57 – 112

### ARCANE VIII

CHETH or HETH C-H, H = 8

Verses 57 – 62

*Thou art my portion, O Lord: I have said that I would keep thy words. I entreated thy favour with my whole heart: be merciful unto me according to thy word.*

*I thought on my ways, and turned my feet unto thy testimonies. I made haste, and delayed not to keep thy commandments.*

*The bands of the wicked have robbed me: but I have not forgotten thy law. At midnight I will rise to give thanks unto thee because of thy righteous judgments.*

*I am a companion of all them that fear thee, and of them that keep thy precepts. The earth, O Lord, is full of thy mercy: teach me thy statutes.*

Cheth or Heth, like He, has a resemblance to the English H. The name of this letter may also be written Chet or Het. Its pronunciation is shown by an H with a dot below it. He, on the other hand, actually represents, in English translation, the initial E of the word Elohim. Cheth or Heth is sometimes compared with the German "ch," as in "doch," rather than H or K. "Zechariel" (Archangel of Jupiter) may also be pronounced Zaharied ("a" as in father).

Cheth or Heth, like H in the English alphabet, is the eighth letter in the series.

The letter H is important in the story of Abram and Sarai, who adopted the letter H into their names when they entered Canaan, Abram becoming Abraham and Sarai becoming Sarah.

Abraham bought the Field of Machpelah from the Sons of Heth (Hittites), as a burial place for Sarah and himself and their descendants. Thenceforward Machpelah was sacred to the memory of Sarah and Abraham, and it was believed that the souls of the faithful ones would return and pass through the Cave "to the bosom of Abraham," or to Paradise and the underworld. The eighth sign of the zodiac is the Scorpion, and the eighth house of the horoscopical wheel is called the House of Death.

Eight is the number of forever becoming, the endless chain of life, the lemniscate currents of spiritual life force represented in the double square or double cube, of evolution under the laws of nature. The Cave was in the field belonging to the Sons of Heth. The field represents the labor of planting, sowing and reaping, and therefore also the cycles of renewal, of death and rebirth of the human spirit.

The Eighth Tarot card, called Justice, shows a female figure seated on a throne. Three steps lead up to the throne. They typify the three worlds in which man's evolution currently proceeds. Her Law governs all life in the three worlds, both during physical incarnation and after death, between incarnations. Upon her head she wears an iron crown. Her eyes are bandaged, showing that Divine Law is impartial and impersonal. In one hand she holds an uplifted sword, the weapon of retribution, in the other the balance or scales, by which justice is meted out with accuracy. This Tarot signifies the Twin Laws of Rebirth and Causation.

It is only in the understanding of the Twin Laws that a reasonable answer is found to all the inequalities and apparent injustices which we see about us; the good things of life heaped upon one who has seemingly done nothing to deserve them, while another who to all appearances is noble and deserving of the best spends an entire life time in a fruitless quest for the good things of life which seem always to elude him. But as St. Paul says, "We see in part, we know in part—but when that which is perfect is come (meaning a full understanding truth), then that which is in part shall be done away. For now we see through a glass, darkly; but then, face to face."

In the Book of the Dead it is related that the great god Thoth meets each person who is newly deceased. The heart of this person is placed in one side of a balance, a feather in the other. If the heart outweighs the feather the deceased must spend some time in purgatory before he is permitted to enter Paradise.

The lion which rests near the feet of the figure of Justice represents the spiritual power which enforces the Law.

*Meditation for Cheth*

The Eighth Commandment is, "Thou shalt not steal." This entails infinitely more than the misappropriation of material goods. Under the Twin Laws of Rebirth and Causation, each person is held responsible not only for his deeds but equally for his thoughts of envy, jealousy, hatred, malice and revenge is, through telepathic influence, depriving another of his self-confidence and self-esteem, thus doing him incalculable injury, while for himself he is amassing a heavy karmic debt, to be paid in suffering, sorrow and humiliation.

The prayer for Cheth refers to the working of the great Twin Laws toward the transformation of society in accordance with its edicts. "The bands of the wicked have robbed me, but I have not forgotten Thy Law . . . I am a companion of all them that fear thee and that keep thy precepts."

## ARCANE IX

TETH T or TH = 9

Verses 65 – 72

*Thou hast dealt well with thy servant, O Lord, according unto thy word. Teach me good judgment and knowledge: for I have believed thy commandments. Before I was afflicted I went astray: but now have I kept thy word.*

*Thou art good, and doest good; teach me thy statutes. The proud have forged a lie against me: but I will keep thy precepts with my whole heart. Their heart is as fat as grease; but I delight in thy law.*

*It is good for me that I have been afflicted; that I might learn thy statutes. The law of thy mouth is better unto me than thousands of gold and silver.*

Nine we have seen as the number of humanity. Nine is also the number of Initiation. Nine represents the Son of Wisdom, the high Initiate. "Thou hast done well with thy servant, O Lord, according to thy word."

The name TETH means a roof. The word brings to mind a place of shelter or protection and refers to a "tent" which the Initiate learns to build. This "tent" is sometimes termed "The Illumined Heart" and sometimes the "Sacred Heart". It is to this tabernacle that one retires to be protected from the onslaughts of the world, and it was from the protection of this place that St. Paul declared, "None of these things (of the outer world) move me."

The ninth card of the Tarot is the Hermit or Sage. He is old in wisdom and experience. He conceals a Lamp under his large square mantle. All of the mystical meanings of Light are concerned in this Tarot symbolism. First of all, the Initiate learns to commune with the Light Center in the heart, and the key to that communion is found in the words, "Be still and know that I Am God."

The Bible contains many fascinating statements relative to the power of Light. We read there that God is Light, and the Lord Christ declared, "I am the Light of the World." St. John adds, "If we walk in the Light as He is in the light we have Fellowship one with another." Also, "The Light shineth in darkness and the darkness comprehendeth it not."

The staff upon which the Sage leans is the Rod of Power of the Initiate, representing the uplifted creative fires. In the Bible we read that when Moses lifted up his rod the land blossomed and the people were happy, healed of all their diseases and problems; but when he laid down his rod, famine, disease and death swept through the land.

This means, in part, that when the people obeyed the precepts which Moses gave them, all was well; but when they departed from them, suffering and sorrow came as the fruit of their errors and wrong-doing.

The Sage's Lamp, half-hidden by his cloak, teaches us the lesson of Discrimination. Christ Jesus said, "Cast not your pearls before swine." The Sage is Teacher of the Mysteries. His care for the Light shows his love and reverence for Truth, which is more to him than wealth or power. He wanders through the world seeking those worthy of the Light. "When the pupil is ready, the Master appears." When Master and pupil have found each other, the pupil cries, "Thou art good and doeth good. Teach me thy statutes!"

### *Meditation for Teth*

Mind is the most precious of all gifts. It is in My power to bestow or withhold it. There are a few in the world today who are able and worthy to understand and to rightly use this most precious gift. I Am the spirit of Wisdom. I Am Nine, the number of Initiation.

"I AM the hedge of protection, enclosing the field of existence. In this field thou dwellest and I AM thy defence against the darkness that is without. Yet is this hedge of protection also a wall of limitation—and the darkness against which it defendeth thee is the radiant darkness of the LIMITLESS LIGHT too brilliant for thine eyes."

The prayer for Teth is the supplication of those in whom this inner life has been awakened; as St. Paul described it, "Christ in You, the hope of glory."

Cheth speaks of the Ninth Commandment, "Thou shalt not bear false witness against thy neighbor." Every human being is the Son of God the Father, and to this the neophyte must bear witness at all times. The wise teachers of India instructed their pupils to greet one another with the words, "I salute the divinity in you!" This is bearing witness to the truth, and the neophyte in the West will do well to follow their example, making the salutation in the quiet of his mind and heart since the custom of the land does not permit that it be done openly.

## ARCANE X

YOD I, J, or Y = 10

Verses 73 – 80

*Thy hands have made me and fashioned me: give me understanding, that I may learn thy commandments. They that fear thee will be glad when they see me; because I have hoped in thy Word.*

*I know, O Lord, that thy judgments are right, and that thou in faithfulness hast afflicted me. Let, I pray thee, thy merciful kindness be for my comfort, according to thy word unto thy servant. Let thy tender mercies come unto me, that I may live: for thy law is my delight.*

*Let the proud be ashamed; for they dealt perversely with me without a cause: but I will meditate on thy precepts.*

*Let those that fear thee turn unto me, and those that have known thy testimonies. Let my heart be sound in thy statutes; that I be not ashamed.*

"Ten is the number both of Creation and Manifestation. One (1) is the positive or Father principle which manifests in creation. Zero (0) is the Feminine or Mother Principle which shows forth in manifestation. For this reason the 10 is sometimes referred to as the Hand of God." –**Papus**.

The hieroglyphic for Yod is the finger of man; the forefinger extended as a sign of command. This letter has therefore become the image of potential manifestation, of spiritual duration, and lastly of the eternity which swallows up time, with all the ideas referring to it. As in the other stanzas of the 119th Psalm, the same letter leads each line. Here it is the flame of Yod which is eight times repeated.

Among the twenty-two letters of the Hebrew alphabet which, mystically understood, outline first the general path of evolution for the many but also the straight and narrow initiatory path for the few, the letter Yod is one of the most important and most powerful. It forms an essential part of each and every one of the other letters of the Hebrew alphabet. It is therefore a symbol of the omnipresence of Deity.

The tenth Arcanum of the Tarot is the Wheel, shown as a great wheel with eight spokes, known to Buddhists as the Wheel of the Law. In other words, it is the power of God, which overshadows, underlies and surrounds our world and all that belongs to it. As St. Paul says, "In Him we live and move and have our being." All spiritual teachings are interpretations of God's Law as applied to humanity. The Psalmist sings, "Underneath are the everlasting arms."

On one side of the wheel Anubis, the Egyptian god, is ascending; on the other, Typhon is descending. This shows us that throughout the world the power of Good is positive, the power of evil negative. Evil is continually destroying itself; therefore the power of Good is always in the Ascendency.

The Wheel of the Tarot is variously termed the Wheel of Life, the Wheel of Fate or Destiny, the Wheel of Fortune, and, as the same Tarot would suggest, the Wheel of Law as described above.

With the beginning of the new century this destiny-work will pass largely under the control of Aquarius, whose keynote is brotherhood, and Leo, whose keynote is love—for at this time a definite beginning will be made to prepare the planet and the life upon it for the New Aquarian-Leo Age. Thus we may be sure that the twenty-first century will bring a fairer sky, a brighter day and a new and harmonious way of life for the entire earth planet.

Seated upon the top of the Wheel of Fortune is a winged sphinx who holds upright a sword, symbol of victory through Truth. He (or she) remains calm and unperturbed despite the rapid whirling of the wheel, for he represents the Law of God operative throughout nature and brings to mind the words of Pascal, "God is a circle; His center is everywhere, His circumference is nowhere."

Yod is the "Workman of Deity," symbol of the High Masculine and its cooperation with the Divine Feminine in the work of creation. His is the Tenth Commandment, "Thou shalt not covet." Yod possesses the glories of all creation. Each man has his own place in God's work, and a reward which no other can ever take away.

The tenth Arcanum is sometimes called the Sphinx, or the Seal of Destiny. It might be termed equally well the Mystery of God, for this Tarot emphasizes the mercy and loving kindness of universal Law, the divine compassion which is the highest expression of justice and includes it. Robert Browning described this Mystery well when he wrote:

*God is Love*
*But God is Law.*

The Ten Commandments are repeated in another form for the second decan of Hebrew letters, Kaph to Resh. These may be correlated with Christ's Sermon on the Mount, as they will form the basis for the new Commandments which will be given in the New Aquarian Age. The two final letters, Schin and Tau, represent the consummation of both series, symbolized in the well known glyph of the Serpent raised up upon the cross.

*Meditation for Yod*

The prayer for Yod is that one may live aright in harmony with the great laws of life, "Let thy tender mercies come unto me that I may live: for thy law is my delight. Let the proud be ashamed, for they have dealt perversely with me without a cause: but I will meditate upon thy precepts. Let my heart be sound in thy statutes."

Yod is Creative Power. Therefore we meditate, I AM the God Presence which is latent in every individual, which, when awakened to full functioning, makes each man a god-man. My divine power within, rightly used, leads to celestial heights. Misused, it leads to the uttermost depths.

## ARCANE XI

KAPH K = 20, K-final = 500

Verses 81 – 88

*My soul fainteth for thy salvation: but I hope in thy Word. Mine eyes fail for thy word, saying, When wilt thou comfort me? For I am become like a bottle in the smoke; yet do I not forget thy statutes.*

*How many are the days of thy servant? when wilt thou execute judgment on them that persecute me? The proud have digged pits for me, which are not after thy law.*

*All thy commandments are faithful: they persecute me wrongfully; help thou me. They had almost consumed me upon earth; but I forsook not thy precepts.*

*Quicken me after thy loving-kindness; so shall I keep the testimony of thy mouth.*

Kaph, the eleventh letter of the Hebrew alphabet, is represented by a man's right hand half closed, which implies bodily strength and power.

The eleventh Tarot Arcanum is a young girl standing beside a lion, closing its mouth with her hand. This card also implies strength, not only physical strength but an inner spiritual force which few persons are even aware they possess and still fewer know how to awaken and use aright. This instruction forms one of the most interesting phases of advanced Discipleship.

In the Egyptian Series The Uraeus headdress denotes power and authority. On top of her head rest two eagles with outstretched wings. These symbolize the profound spiritual wisdom and high idealism which the awakening of the inner force or power bestows.

In other Tarot series the young woman wears a large hat, the top of which is interwoven with the lemniscate which belongs to the Path of Discipleship. There are three very important psychospiritual force centers in man's body. One is focused at the base of the spine. Here the life force sleeps until it is awakened. In the head, near the forehead, is another important center. Here the life force is raised by means of spiritual living. The third center is the heart, which is the balance-wheel between the two.

Medieval alchemists stated that "many talk about the Lion, but few really know him." The lion represents the fire element throughout all nature. In man this fire element is centered in the desire body. Closing the mouth of the lion symbolizes the subjugation of the desire nature and its transmutation into the Light Body, which is the composite "wedding garment" of the purified life-forces of both desire and vital bodies.

In the story of Samson, the word meaning the Sun Man or Strong Man, Samson also subdued the lion. When he had rent it in twain he found within the carcass bees and honey of which he partook. This refers to the exhilaration and spiritual joy which accompany the ever-deepening understanding and revelations attendant upon the great transmutation.

Later the sons of the Philistines (the lowest forces of the material nature) speak to the beautiful young maiden Delilah and tell her that if she will seduce Samson so they may gain control over him, they will reward her with eleven hundred pieces of silver.

The feminine principle operates on the highest spiritual plane in the case of the young maiden who closes the lion's mouth, when it is known esoterically as the Feminine in Liberation.

In the case of Delilah the feminine is operating on the lowest sensual plane. Here it is known esoterically as the feminine in bondage.

It is significant that eleven is termed a feminine number and that silver is a feminine metal.

In Masonic symbolism we are shown a female figure, but she is not closing the mouth of the lion; she is, instead, holding in her arms a broken pillar.

The prayer for Kaph is for those who have glimpsed the

Vision but have not yet made the Transmutation. Our enemies are most often within ourselves rather than in the outer world about us, hence the admonition of St. Paul to "put off the old man and put on the new."

"All thy commandments are faithful; they persecute me wrongfully; help thou me. They had almost consumed me upon earth; but I forsook not thy precepts. Quicken me after Thy loving kindness; so shall I keep the testimony of thy mouth."

### *Meditation for Kaph*

Love is a magical power. It can work miracles. The aspirant realizes how true this is as he meditates upon what is perhaps the most beautiful love song every given to the world, the thirteenth chapter of First Corinthians. This song carries with it an aura of protection against all evil. It is a rhapsody of bliss which expresses the heart beat of life itself.

> Though I speak with the tongues of men and of angels, and have not charity (love), I am become as sounding brass, or a tinkling cymbal.
>
> And though I have the gift of prophecy, and understand all mysteries, and all knowledge; and though I have all faith, so that I could remove mountains, and have not charity, I am nothing.
>
> And though I bestow all my goods to feed the poor, and though I give my body to be burned, and have not charity, it profiteth me nothing. Charity suffereth long, and is kind; charity envieth not; charity vaunteth not itself, is not puffed up,
>
> Doth not behave itself unseemly, seeketh not her own, is not easily provoked, thinketh no evil;
>
> Rejoiceth not in iniquity, but rejoiceth in the truth;
>
> Beareth all things, believeth all things, hopeth all things, endureth all things.
>
> Charity never faileth.

## ARCANE XII

LAMED L = 30

Verses 89 – 96

*For ever, O Lord, thy word is settled in heaven. Thy faithfulness is unto all generations: thou hast established the earth, and it abideth. They continue this day according to Thine ordinances: for all are thy servants.*

*Unless thy law had been by delights, I should then have perished in mine affliction. I will never forget thy precepts: for with them thou hast quickened me. I am thine, save me; for I have sought thy precepts.*

*The wicked have waited for me to destroy me: but I will consider thy testimonies. I have seen an end of all perfection: but thy commandment is exceedingly broad.*

Lamed, the twelfth letter of the Hebrew Alphabet, is represented by an outstretched arm which implies both Protection and Expansion. The twelfth Tarot card, the Hanged Man, refers not to physical death but to the total subjugation of the personal man or personality to the force or power of spirit. It is significant that one of the titles given to this card is the Great Work. Eliphaz Levi writes, "The great work is, before all things, the creation of man by himself, that is to say, the full and entire conquest of his faculties and his future."

In the Bible there are many references to the Path of Initiation. In the New Testament, "Broad is the way and wide the gate that leadeth to destruction; but straight is the gate and narrow the way that leadeth to eternal life, and few there be that find it." And in Job, "There is a path which no fowl knoweth and which the vulture's eye hath not seen." Again the Supreme Master said, "Whosoever doth not bear his cross and come after Me, cannot be my disciple." Lamed cries, "I am thine–save me!"

The lessons which prepare the disciple for the Great Overcoming (the conquest of the personal man) are difficult and varied in accordance with the development and temperament, but are concerned always more or less with the relinquishment of the person, place or thing which is best beloved.

Abraham's greatest treasure was his son Isaac. In the end he was required to renounce the lad as test of his willingness to adhere to divine will. When his worthiness was proved, a lamb was substituted for the child and Abraham was companioned by Angels.

The rich young man who came to Christ set great store by his worldly possessions. Christ said, "Go sell all that thou hast and give to the poor; then come and follow me." The young man turned sorrowfully away and followed the Christ no more. This is the common reaction. Many start upon the Path and walk a little way but soon become tired and disillusioned and return to the ways of the world. Some few will journey to the very foot of Golgotha and there turn back. Fewer still will ascend the slope; but few and far between are those who will consent to be bound to the cross. The Bible states that even His disciples followed the Christ afar off, and the legends say that only the Blessed Virgin, St. John and the Magdalene stood at the foot of the cross and saw the consummation of the Great Work.

Because of its increasing materiality, the world has long since discarded the truths of Initiation, which have been abandoned even by the Churches; and yet it is Initiation that will form the cornerstone of the New Aquarian Age religion. To those who would become pioneers of the New Age we say, "Dedicate yourselves anew to follow the Illumined Way, and do not falter or turn back until you have completed the Great Work. As you reach the final step which means liberation from the cross, you will hear the clear, sustaining voice of the blessed Lord Christ saying, 'I Am the Good Shepherd and all my sheep know my voice.' "

The prayer for Lamed is the supplication of those who have

passed through the Great Overcoming. They now know no barriers—no limitations. They live only to love and to serve. The universe is their home and all mankind their brothers.

The high message of all true Schools of Initiation has always been, "Man must learn to die to self before he can be born into Eternal Life."

"I have seen an end of all perfection; but thy commandments are exceeding broad."

### *Meditation for Lamed*

The Hebrew letter L or Lamed means sacrifice. The ancients referred to this letter as the ox-goad. Self-sacrifice is of tremendous importance in spiritual development, and no aspirant will go far on the Path until he learns to practice this virtue. The following maxim is recommended for frequent meditation, "Loving self-forgetting service is the surest, the safest and the most joyful road to God."

"Until you empty yourself of self you can never escape from it."

An apocryphal tradition states that when the Messiah should come, he would make the sacrifices to cease. This the Christ did, for His self-sacrifice made all other sacrifices unnecessary. His blood was shed for all living things. Therefore those who hear His voice know fellowship with the lower orders of life on this planet, with beasts and birds, with flowers and trees and even with the elements. The New Age Man is the elder brother of the world, the guardian and protector of his younger brethren of the evolutionary kingdom. He will establish concord among all forms of life. Ferocity will no more exist between man and animal or between animal and animal, and the biblical prophecy will be realized, "The lion and the lamb shall lie down together, and a little child (one possessing Initiate powers) shall lead them."

Lamed is the Just Man made perfect in the Christ sacrifice.

Lamed is the divine Martyr, the Sacrifice on the altar of Good, whose blood is shed for the salvation of many.

## ARCANE XIII

MEM M = 40, M-Final = 600

*O how I love thy law! it is my meditation all the day. Thou through thy commandments hast made me wiser than mine enemies. I have more understanding than all my teachers: for thy testimonies are my meditation.*

*I understand more than the ancients, because I keep thy precepts. I have refrained my feet from every evil way, that I might keep thy word. I have not departed from thy judgments: for thou hast taught me.*

*How sweet are thy words unto my taste! yea, sweeter than honey to my mouth. Through thy precepts I get understanding: therefore I hate every false way.*

*Mem* is the thirteenth letter of the Hebrew Alphabet. It is one of three great Mother Letters and is correlated with the feminine element of Water. We know that *Mem* corresponds with the English letter M, and again it is interesting to note that the mothers of almost all of the great world saviors had names beginning with the letter M, which signifies all the brooding, hovering, protective tenderness which is associated with the Mother Principle.

The number 13 belongs to both mysticism and magic. One (1) in its highest significance represents the divine ego, and 12 is the number of high attainment or perfection. The higher the attainment, the greater the revelations of mysteries inherent in the number 13. It is only to the uninformed and superstitious that 13 is a portent of misfortune.

Thirteen is an important number throughout the Bible.

In the Old Testament we have the story of Jacob who, like a central sun, is surrounded by his twelve sons. Upon each son he bestows his spiritual blessing and its correlative material heritage. The life, deeds and teachings of the Twelve Patriarchs are the foundation of the Old Testament.

In the New Testament we find the Lord Christ as the Central Sun. Around this great Life are grouped the twelve Disciples, who become illumined with his power and his glory–and it is their lives, words and deeds that form the foundation of the New Testament.

There is within the body of man (who is a Christ in the making) twelve foci of spiritual force, but these are mostly latent in present-day humanity. The principal light of the body is the ego, centered in the head. When the ego becomes illumined, its light is diffused throughout the twelve body centers, and of such an Illumined One it is said that he walks in the Light as He (Christ) is in the Light.

The Tarot card for Mem is the Reaping Skeleton. Death reaps men, women and children; but behind and above him is the beautiful rainbow promising that beyond death is life.

Other Tarot Series yield slightly different interpretations. One of the most interesting is that of a horseman astride a white horse. He holds aloft in one hand a banner upon which is emblazoned a large, luminous white Rose, which is the universal symbol of Transmutation. –"Behold a white horse; and he that sat on him had a bow; and a crown was given unto him, and he went forth conquering and to conquer." (Rev. 6:2).

### *Meditation for Mem*

The prayer for Mem is a petition of all those illumined ones who have come to realize through first-hand knowledge that there is no death.

Through eons of time the Angels have sought to teach this transcendent lesson to mankind. They surround the earth, particularly at the seasons of Christmas and Easter, with the music of their insistent song: "There is no death–All God's universe is Life! There is no death!" Handel caught the inspired rhythms of their glorious chanting and translated them into his Hallelujah Chorus. The Angels will continue pouring out upon us their beautiful music until mankind has become renewed and awakened and united with them in the heavenly Song, "There is no death–All God's universe is Life! There is no death!"

"How sweet are thy words to my taste! yea, sweeter than honey to my mouth! Through thy precepts I get understanding, therefore I hate every false way."

## ARCANE XIV

NUN N = 50, N-Final = 700

Verses 105 – 112

*Thy word is a lamp unto my feet, and a light unto my path. I have sworn, and I will perform it, that I will keep thy righteous judgments.*

*I am afflicted very much: quicken me, O Lord, according unto thy word. Accept, I beseech thee the farewell offerings of my mouth, O Lord, and teach me thy judgments. My soul is continually in my hand: yet I do not forget thy law.*

*The wicked have laid a snare for me: yet I erred not from thy precepts. Thy testimonies have I taken as an heritage for ever: for they are the rejoicing of my heart. I have inclined my heart to perform thy statutes always, even unto the end.*

In esoteric symbology the *fish* always refers to something hidden or secret. Nun, which is the 14th or "fish" letter of the Hebrew alphabet, has many profound and far-reaching implications. We note how frequently the word *fish* is used during the ministry of Christ. For example, his Disciples were not fishermen in the ordinary acceptance of the term. The majority of them had for some time been followers of John the Baptist and so were prepared to receive the teachings of the Great Master. Nor did He partake of fish in the ordinary manner with His disciples. The meal of fish refers to the profound truths which they partook of together. It was their understanding and practice of these truths which gave them their great spiritual power.

One (1), in the number 14, refers to the illumined or awakened ego, and 4 has reference to the pure white stone which the builders rejected but which will some day become the chief corner stone of the body temple. Upon the four corners of this pure white stone are engraved in letters of light the four mantramic sayings which have been familiar to all true disciples of all ages, To Know, To Do, To Dare, To Be Silent.

The fourteenth Tarot card depicts an angelic being who is sometimes termed the Genius of the Sun. He bears upon his forehead a symbol of the sun from which emanates a golden nimbus encircling his head and radiating out about his body in a luminous aureole.

Mention has been made earlier that the ego has its seat (focus of power) in the head. It is the awakened and illumined ego which is signified by the radiance of the sun upon the forehead of the Angel of the fourteenth card. In his hands he holds two urns–one gold, the other silver. From the golden urn (masculine) he is pouring life fluid into the silver urn (feminine), careful that never a drop is spilled. This Arcanum is sometimes known as Temperance. Creative force is spent in all human activities whatsoever, whether thinking, feeling or acting. The ancient Initiates had come to understand that in all his activities, whether mental, emotional or physical, the ego must exert control and see that nothing of his divine power was wasted either by "too little" or "too much."

In its cosmic interpretation we note the blending throughout all nature of the electric or fire forces (masculine) with the magnetic or water forces (feminine). It is this blending which produces all the magnificent phenomena of the changing seasons. In the Spring it is the uniting of the forces of Aries (April, masculine) and Taurus (May, feminine), which produces the glorious Summertide which is spread before us in the month of June (Gemini).

The angelic figure of the fourteenth Tarot wears on its breast a square in which a triangle is enclosed. The square represents the number 4, the triangle represents the number 3, which together are 7, the number of growth cycles, and half of the 14 which represents a period of perfected work. This figure in its entirety represents the New Age body of which we have spoken. Man must continue to use a body of flesh so long as he lives in a physical world, but the New Age body will be constructed of finer etheric substance, having all the capacities of today's gross body but none of its incapacities. It will be sensitive to spiritual influences, and super-physical senses (clairvoyance, clairaudience, telepathy, etc.) will take the place of the physical senses of the common body today.

The N-final, signifying 700, associates this Tarot with the 7 of Victory, and, as the last letter of the second septenary N, is again the symbol of the completion of a cycle.

In the ancient Egyptian legends we read that when the god of evil, Set, through envy slew his brother, the great leader, Osiris, he cut the body up into fourteen pieces and distributed them over the land of Egypt. Then Isis, the sister-wife of Osiris, began her search to recover the scattered pieces of his body. Some say this work lasted fourteen years, others say fourteen days–the cycle of the moon from new to full or from full to new. When at last she had found all of the parts of the sacred body, one part was missing which had been destroyed by a fish, and this part she replaced by creating a replica. She then assembled the parts together, purified them and chanted over them the words of life; and into the beautiful and immortal body of light which she had created, Osiris descended again and took possession. The time came when he left the earth to ascend into heaven, and there he reigned forever as the guardian deity of Egypt and her people, but also the savior-god of all peoples everywhere who called upon his name.

This legend hints of the high transmutative power of the number 14.

One of the beautiful romances of the Bible illustrates the kabbalistic significance of the powers of 7 and 14. Jacob saw and loved the beautiful maiden Rachel and desired her for his wife, but he was told by her father, Laban, that he must first prove himself worthy through seven years of faithful service. His love for her was so great that he worked and served as required, and the seven years seemed but as a few days. When the seven years were ended Laban told him that he was still not worthy of Rachel and was given her sister Leah instead, Leah whose eyes were tender. Jacob worked another seven years for Rachael, and again so great was his love that the seven years seemed but as a few days. At last then, after proving his love through fourteen long years, Jacob received Rachel to be his wife.

This is a story of the Path of Discipleship. Many attempt to walk the spiritual highway, but few continue to its end with unabated ardor and enthusiasm. The end of the Path is the Mystic Marriage. The disciple must be willing to serve seven years, and again seven years, while he fashions by his labor the vesture of golden light in which to celebrate the Mystic Marriage.

The prayer for the letter Nun is a prayer of triumph, for it is the song of those who have gone so far on the illumined way that they are ready to pioneer for the New Age. It is significant that this letter, whose number is 50, was important in the esoteric mathematics of the Essenes.

"Thy testimonies have I taken as an heritage forever, for they are the rejoicing of my heart."

### *Meditation for Nun*

The letter N, or Nun, means "fish" and is the token of all hidden or profound truths. The sign of the fish was used by early Christians as a means of identification or countersign. When ever a Christian came upon this sign he knew that Christians had passed that way. The fish, cosmically, refers to the constellation Pisces, called by the ancient Hebrew esotericists "the sign of the Messiah." Hence Christ was the Great Fish, and all who followed Him were little fishes swimming together in the great ocean of God, "And the knowledge of God shall cover the earth as the waters cover the sea."

## Chapter XIX

## THE THIRD SEPTENARY, SAMEKH–SCHIN

Verses 113 – 168

## ARCANE XV

SAMEKH S = 60

Verses 113 – 120

*I hate vain thoughts: but thy law do I love. Thou art my hiding place and my shield: I hope in thy Word.*

*Depart from me, ye evil-doers: for I will keep the commandments of my God. Uphold me according unto thy word, that I may live: and let me not be ashamed of my hope. Hold thou me up, and I shall be safe: and I will have respect unto thy statutes continually.*

*Thou hast trodden down all them that err from thy statutes: for their deceit is falsehood. Thou puttest away all the wicked of the earth like dross: therefore I love thy testimonies. My flesh trembleth for fear of thee; and I am afraid of thy judgments.*

The fifteenth Hebrew letter, Samekh, the number 15 and the fifteenth Tarot card are alike in one important respect, their transmutative power. Samekh is not the letter S of the English alphabet, but it has the sound of S, and the name of the letter is sometimes written Xmekh, as we have shown earlier. It is not be confused with Schin, the twenty-first letter, which does correspond more closely with the English S.

The letter Samekh relates to Sagittarius, which in its low phases tends toward worldliness but in its high phases produces the priest, the prophet and the seer.

The fifteenth Tarot Arcanum shows the spirit of evil–generally termed the devil or Typhon, which has been described elsewhere in these pages. In some of the Tarot series it is represented as sitting in the ruins of a temple which has been destroyed by fire, the torch which he holds in his hand having been the cause of this destruction. In other series he is represented as wearing an inverted pentagram upon his forehead–the sign of black magic. The two male and female figures previously described as being bound to his feet with chains are connected with the inverted pentagram.

An important point for study and meditation just here is the fact that evil cannot forge the chain by which it is bound to any individual. Only man himself can do this. Evil may entice and seduce, but only man himself can forge the links which bind him to evil ways, and only he himself has the power to break the chain and free himself. Others may advise and point the way, but the individual himself must do the work.

The most important point of all to be considered in connection with the fifteenth Arcanum is the fact that there is not and never has been a personal devil; nor is there a burning hell to which hapless persons may be consigned for everlasting punishment. These hideous images are the product of false concepts and diseased imaginations.

Comparatively few persons even in this modern day understand the tremendous power of thought and the need that it be used constructively. The Bible says, "As a man thinketh in his heart, so is he." And so he will certainly become. It is possible to think one's self into health and prosperity. Young children should be taught these things and be led into habits of constructive mental image-making.

The occult scientist knows that the physical body, seen by physical vision, is not the only "body" which the ego possesses. He has finer vehicles–etheric, astral, mental and spiritual–which can only be studied by means of higher or extended vision. He understands that this earth planet also has similar envelopes, or shields, in addition to the physical sphere upon which humanity lives. It is in the mental envelope or body of the planet that we plant our thought seed. If planted by a strong will and powerful, vivid imagination, these seeds grow and influence not only those who have planted them but others who are thinking on the same subjects. Thus we may note the great blessings wrought through the lives of such souls as St. Francis of Assisi, whose thought seems to have inspired and influenced all generations since his time. A modern example is Mahatma Gandhi. An opposite picture is shown by dictators and war lords. Any individual who dreams of world domination can be powerfully influenced by the seed-thoughts planted in the mental realm by such characters.

### *Meditation for Samekh*

As we meditate upon these far-reaching truths we realize anew the deep importance of the poet's words, "Thoughts are things."

The hideous symbolic figure of evil has sometimes been confused in the mind of the occult student with the Dweller on the Threshold. This is not always correct, for unless a person is consciously vicious or evil (which is certainly not true of the majority of mankind), the Dweller is not necessarily evil. It is a wraith-like figure which has been formed from the mistaken or negative thoughts and deeds of the individual to whom it may appear as an apparition, not always evil in appearance, but sometimes bearing an aspect of deep sadness which affects the soul with profound melancholy. This figure bars the gates of Initiation until the disciple has dissolved it by means of love, understanding, forgiveness and compassion.

The Bible prayer for Samekh is the petition sent forth by those devotees who are seeking to eradicate every form of fear from their lives and to replace it by the great and wondrous healing power of Love. This is a most difficult task, but it can be accomplished if one possesses sufficient faith and perseverance.

"Thou art my hiding place and my shield; I hope in thy word. Hold thou me up and I shall be safe; and I will have respect unto thy statutes continually. Thou puttest away all the wicked of the earth like dross: therefore I love thy testimonies."

It is only when fear has been cast out of the life that the aspirant may know the sublime bliss of being cradled in "the Everlasting Arms."

## ARCANE XVI

AYIN or OIN    O = 70

Verses 121 – 128

*I have done judgment and justice: leave me not to mine oppressors. Be surety to thy servant for good: let not the proud oppress me.*

*Mine eyes fail for thy salvation, and for the word of thy righteousness. Deal with thy servant according to thy mercy, and teach me thy statutes. I am thy servant; give me understanding, that I may know thy testimonies.*

*It is time for thee, Lord, to work: for they have made void thy law. Therefore I love thy commandments above gold; yea, above fine gold. Therefore I esteem all thy precepts concerning all things to be right; and I hate every false way.*

Ayin, or Oin, the sixteenth letter of the Hebrew alphabet, relates to the cleansing and purifying of desire and emotion. Its virtue is to tear down and eliminate all that does not contribute to the highest phases of the Love power. Again, 1 + 6 = 7 represents a certain *time cycle* (ruled by the seven planets) in which a specific work is to be accomplished.

The sixteenth Arcanum is the Lightning-struck Tower or Pyramid from which the two figures are seen falling as the tower crumbles, the one with a crown and the other without, showing that Cosmic Law is no respecter of persons. There is ONE COSMIC LAW FOR ALL, and its commandment is the same for all, *Do unto others as ye would that they should do unto you*; but unfortunately the majority of mankind have not accepted this message, being wholly absorbed in narrowly selfish interests and paying little heed to the welfare of others. This has divided society into two classes, the "haves" and the "have nots" and has filled the world with restless discontent, causing wars and rumors of wars.

It must be understood that we, and we alone, are responsible for everything that happens to us. Nothing can come to us that is not of our own making. When we realize this and cease to blame outside agencies for trials and misfortunes, we shall the sooner be able to remedy conditions and make for ourselves a new and better life.

Do we send forth to others thoughts of hatred, envy, jealousy or vengeance? Then sometime, somewhere, these same things will return to us. Just when we think our dreams are about to be realized they will turn to ashes in our hands, like Dead Sea fruit. The person who places his confidence solely in material gain builds upon a crumbling foundation and may at any time be bereft of all that seemed to him secure. Any individual or nation whose foundation is not laid in God is impermanent and is eventually swept away.

The way in which Nature aids in bringing about the right causation in the life of man is most interestingly described in Max Heindel's *Rosicrucian Cosmo-Conception*, from which we quote:

"Refracting Stratum: This part of the Earth corresponds to the World of Divine Spirit. There are, in occult science, what are known as 'The Seven Unspeakable Secrets.' For those who are not acquainted with these secrets, or have not at least an inkling of their import, the properties of this stratum must seem particularly absurd and grotesque. In it all the forces which are known to us as the 'Laws of Nature' exist as moral or, rather, immoral forces. In the beginning of the conscious career of man they were much worse than at present. But it appears that as humanity progresses in morals, these forces improve correspondingly; also that any lapse in morals has a tendency to unleash these Nature forces and causes them to create havoc upon the Earth, while the striving for high ideals makes them less inimical to man.

"The forces in this stratum are thus, at any time, an exact reflection of the existing moral status of mankind. From the occult point of view the 'hand of God' which smites a Sodom or a Gomorrah is not a foolish superstition, for as surely as there is individual responsibility to the Law of Consequence which brings to each person the just results of his deeds, whether for good or evil, so is there also community and national responsibility, which brings upon groups of men corresponding results for their collective acts. Nature forces are the general agents for such retributive justice, causing floods or earthquakes or the beneficent formation of oil or coal for various groups, according to their desserts."

A man's self-created destiny may send him across the world that he may be present where some catastrophe is to take place. There he may be required to yield up his life or, again, to be the instrument of salvation for many others. It is only in the light of the Twin Laws of Rebirth and Causation that a solution is found to problems such as these. The Twin Laws are eternal, ever-enduring, and unerring. All that we send forth must return to us sooner or later. Nowhere are these two laws enunciated more clearly and precisely than in the Bible and in the Tarot. Troward, the English metaphysician, rightly said, "There are three gates to the Mysteries–the Bible, the Tarot and the Pyramid."

The disciples exemplified in the supplication of Ayin are those who are learning, despite all outer trials, and inharmonious circumstances, to *put God first*. "It is time for thee, Lord, to work: for they have made void thy Law."

### *Meditation for Ayin*

The letter Ayin, termed "silent" but sometimes correlated with the sound O, having something of the force of a vowel, refers kabbalistically to the Eye of God, which in esoteric symbology is sometimes enclosed in a triangle representing the Triune Godhead. This is the Great Eye or All-Seeing Eye which ranges over the universe, seeing all and knowing all and rendering judgment. It proclaims God's omnipresence. It is the Eye which is seen in the triangular capstone of the perfect pyramid. The lightning-struck pyramid, like the Great Pyramid of Gizeh in Egypt, has no summit stone.

The slogan of the white forces, or forces of Good, is, *Harmonize and unify*. The slogan of the dark forces, those of evil is, *Divide and destroy*. It is not difficult to see on which side most of the nations of the world have placed themselves today.

Inharmonious conditions which now hold the world captive are already showing signs of dissolution, are already melting away like the troubled dreams of the night, to be remembered no more.

King Solomon, wisest of kings, was once asked what was the greatest comfort he could give to those in trouble, and he replied, "And these things, too, shall pass away."

## ARCANE XVII

PE or PHE PE = 80, PE-Final = 800

Verses 129 – 136

*Thy testimonies are wonderful: therefore doth my soul keep them. The entrance of thy words giveth light; it giveth understanding unto the simple.*

*I opened by mouth, and panted: for I longed for thy commandments. Look thou upon me, and be merciful unto me, as thou usest to do unto those that love thy name.*

*Order my steps in thy word: and let not any iniquity have dominion over me. Deliver me from the oppression of man: so will I keep thy precepts.*

*Make thy face to shine upon thy servant; and teach me thy statutes. Rivers of waters run down mine eyes, because they keep not thy law.*

The seventeenth Arcanum, termed The Star, is one of the most beautiful and inspiring of the entire Tarot series. There is a close connection between Arcane 14 and Arcane 17. In the fourteenth Arcanum the young maiden is holding in her hands two urns, one golden and one silver. She is pouring the contents of the golden urn into the silver urn, taking care that not a drop shall be spilled. The seventeenth shows the same maiden, save that this time she is pouring from the silver urn into the sea and from the golden urn upon the land.

We noted in the fourteenth card that preparatory work was begun upon the building of the New Age body, the two urns representing the two masculine and feminine force-centers of head and heart. Not a drop of the precious life fluid is spilled, indicating that perfect equilibrium or balance has been established between these two centers. In the seventeenth Arcanum this work has been completed, the maiden is now pouring its extracted essence in love and blessing upon the world.

At the beginning of the Great Work the disciple spends much time alone studying, praying and meditating. Later, as he begins to walk in the Light and to see in that Light many glorious revelations, he is filled with eagerness to share them with the world, for truly "out of the abundance of the heart the mouth speaketh."

Above the head of the maiden shines a great luminous eight-pointed star, surrounded by seven smaller eight-pointed stars. Herein is depicted the future development of mankind. Within every human body are seven important centers awaiting development, for they are latent in the vast majority. One of these centers is located at the base of the spine; one near the spleen, one in the solar plexus, another in the heart, one in the throat and two in the head. All Mystic Schools have taught their students how to awaken these centers, and various philosophies have given them different names. Some have called them stars, others, blossoms. They are the Lotus blossoms of the Orient and the Roses of the Western Wisdom schools. The beautiful salutation of the Rosicrucians, "May the Roses bloom upon your Cross," is a prayer that these blossoms may unfold in all their radiant beauty; and it is this attainment which is figured in the luminous Star over the head of the maiden, for when these centers become alive in all their sparkling, swirling beauty, one does literally walk in Light and become a Christed individual.

In Revelation the soul body with its seven centers is referred to as the Book of the Seven Seals, and there is great lamentation because no man is found worthy to open the book except the lamb of God, which means that this attainment belongs to the coming Christed Dispensation. "And no man in heaven, nor in earth, neither under the earth, was able to open the book, neither to look thereon." (Rev. 5:3)

Christ, the Lamb, whose advent marked the beginning of the Great Sidereal Year of Aries (and the Piscean Age within that Great Year), opened the Way of Initiation to all. Previously this high spiritual prerogative had belonged only to the priestly class. Through Initiation the seals (centers) are awakened and become as scintillant flowers of light blossoming upon the cross of the human body. Hence the origin in early Masonry of the Roses upon the Cross and the term *Rosicrucian*

The beautiful maiden in this Arcanum represents the great Cosmic Mother or the Exalted Feminine who holds in her possession, and bestows upon those worthy to receive it, the highest phases of spiritual Truth.

St. John, the most advanced of Christ's Disciples, had attained to this exalted experience when he proclaimed exultantly, "You shall know the truth and the truth shall make you free."

The number 17 is one of great strength and power. Seven is a number of completeness, accomplishment and perfection. 7 + 1 = 8, the *Christed* number, and points to the coming *Christed* Dispensation in 80 and 800.

The Hebrew letter *Pe* is also correlated with great spiritual strength and power. It is significant to note that it is sometimes called the "letter of the Star" and sometimes "the letter of the Rose." Because of the beauty and harmony with which this letter is associated, some writers have placed it under the direction of the planet Venus, but because of the great wisdom with which it is also endowed, other writers have placed it under the direction of the planet Mercury.

To quote the Sepher Yetzirah, "He produced *Pe* and referred it to Power; He crowned it, combined and formed with it Mercury in the universe, the fifth day of the week, and left ear of man."

The prayer for Pe is for the few who are seriously working to cultivate the high state of consciousness wherein they may say with the psalmist, "The entrance of thy words giveth light; it giveth understanding to the simple. I opened my mouth and panted, for I longed for thy commandments. Thy testimonies are wonderful; therefore doth my soul keep them."

### *Meditation for Pe*

The Cosmic Christ is the Star which has guided the Magi or Wise Men all down the ages, both before and during the Christ

Ministry on earth as well as afterward. It is this same Christ Star which shines on the threshold of the New Age of Aquarius, and the Voice of the Master is heard, "Behold, I stand at the door and knock. If any man hear my voice and open the door, I will come in to him."

The Christing of mankind is the work of the Aquarian Age. This does not mean that every individual in the world must accept the Christian religion as it is presently known in the West. It does mean that he must follow the example set by the Christ and attune his life to the Golden Rule, for the Christ Life and the Christ Rule are universal in scope and applicable to every creed, cult and civilization. It is not what one believes but how one lives that is of first importance.

For all men everywhere St. Paul's word still holds, "Let the Christ be formed in you."

The aspirant who follows the Christ Star has set his feet in the Path of the Wise, and he will have the companioning of Angels to the ultimate destination.

## ARCANE XVIII

TZADDI  TZ = 90, TZ-Final = 900

Verses 137 – 144

*Righteous art thou, O Lord, and upright are thy judgments. Thy testimonies that thou hast commanded are righteous and very faithful.*

*My zeal hath consumed me because mine enemies have forgotten thy words. Thy word is very pure: therefore thy servant loveth it.*

*I am small and despised: yet do not I forget thy precepts. Thy righteousness is an everlasting righteousness, and thy law is the truth.*

*Trouble and anguish have taken hold on me: Yet thy commandments are my delights. The righteousness of thy testimonies is everlasting: give me understanding, and I shall live.*

"He produced Tzaddi, predominant in taste, crowned it, combined and formed with it Aquarius in the Year and the gullet of man."–*Sepher Yetzirah*

Tzaddi is a letter of power and authority. The word means a fish-hook, which is an instrument used to draw an object up out of the depths of darkness and bring it forth into the light. This was the chief work of the Master's disciples and the reason they were called fishers of men. It has nothing to do with the catching of fish in the ordinary sense of the term.

Tzaddi placed at or near the beginning of a word indicates that some new object or concept is in process of formation. If placed near or at the ending of a word, it indicated that the project of concept has been successfully accomplished.

The number 18, 90 and 900 may be read as 9 in the esoteric code. This is of far-reaching importance, for 9 is the number of humanity and also the number of Initiation.

The eighteenth Tarot Arcanum is one of the most interesting and important of the entire series, well worth the study and prayerful meditation of the most serious student. In this Arcanum a large Full Moon hangs in the sky, but its light is largely veiled by a mass of dark clouds; hence the two names by which the card is known, *The Twilight* and *The Moon*. There is an open road (the path of life) which winds away and is lost amid distant hills. On each side of this road stands a pyramid–one white, one black–and before each pyramid sits a dog baying at the moon, and one dog is white, the other black. The black dog sits before the white pyramid and the white dog sits before the black pyramid. This tells us that evil and sinister forces will follow the aspirant to the very door of the Temple; and again it tells us that the love of God is all-encompassing and will follow the errant soul into the darkest pits of hell, and an Angel of mercy attends us all the way.

Upon the winding path between the two dogs lies a large scorpion, which represents the sign Scorpio in the heavens, this being one of the most powerful of the zodiacal signs. The Scorpio native can reach the depths of depravity, as illustrated by the scorpion with the sting of death in his tail. He can also attain to the heights of transfiguration, as expressed by the eagle which flies closer to the Sun than does any other bird.

In the Book of Revelation these two paths are plainly outlined. The way of the dark pyramid may be noted in the Mark of the Beast whose number is 666,–which denotes 18 or 9; and, in the 144 which denotes 9 also–the number of humanity–all humanity–who stand on the sea of glass and bear upon their forehead the sign of Christ (the awakening of the spiritual centers in the head).

We recall that in Arcane six where the neophyte first enters the Path, he stands between two maidens, one crowned with vine leaves, the other with stars; and we saw that this represented a place of decision, where the soul must choose one way or the other. He cannot follow both. If he has chosen the positive path, then we have followed his progress through the successive cards of the Tarot up to this point; and we have seen the varied gifts of the spirit bestowed upon him as he slowly but surely climbed the Path of Life Eternal.

In Arcane Eighteen he has now reached the place of the last great decision. Here the path rises abruptly, becoming steep and narrow. We have said that life is itself the great Initiator and that the most important trials come in the course of daily living. Here man is tested by the Higher Powers who attend him every step of the way.

If now he chooses the way of the dark pyramid, it will not seem to him to be dark, because he is subjected to every sort of flattery, the object being to increase his sense of self-importance, to make him proud, arrogant, inflated with self-conceit. Nothing more effectually closes the door to spiritual fulfillment than this subtle failing, which is all too prevalent among aspirants to the higher life.

If he chooses the way of the white pyramid, this does not mean that his path is all sunshine and flowers. On the contrary, the way becomes more difficult than before. He stands alone and must learn to put self in the background, to live only to serve, and to be a lamp for the darkness of the world, guiding and uplifting all who come within the radius of his light. He must learn to say with the Blessed Christ, "Of myself I can do nothing–the Father within me doeth the works."

Nowhere is this more beautifully evidenced than in the Eighteenth or Rose Croix Degree of Masonry. This has been depicted by the Swan or Pelican (always a symbol of Initiation) wherein we see the mother bird surrounded by her seven little ones, tearing her breast to nourish them with her life-blood.

Albert Pike, the great Masonic genius, in writing of the beauty of this Degree, quotes, "Whomsoever God loveth, him He chasteneth," an expression that formulates a whole dogma. The trials of life are the blessings of life to the individual or the nation, if either has a soul that is worthy of salvation. "Light and darkness," said Zoroaster, "are the world's eternal ways." The Light and the Shadow are everywhere and always in proportion; the Light occasions the Shadow and also obliterates it. It is by trials only, by the agonies of sorrow and the sharp discipline of adversity, that men and nations attain Initiation. The agonies in the Garden of Gethsemane and those of the Cross on Calvary preceded Resurrection and were the means of Redemption. "It is with prosperity that God afflicts humanity."

As one studies the great wisdom concealed and revealed in the Tarot, one is filled with awe and reverence for the profound wisdom of the great sages who gave these truths to humanity, for they have been given in some form to every race and nation the planet has ever known.

"Then I saw that wisdom excelleth folly as far as light excelleth darkness." (Eccle. 2.1)

"The wisdom of the prudent is to understand His way; but the folly of fools is deceit." (Prov. 14:8)

The prayer for Tzaddi belongs to those brave, strong souls who are cultivating discrimination and discernment, so that they may serve as chief cornerstones of the Temple not made with hands, which is eternal in the heavens.

### *Meditation for Tzaddi*

The fishhook is something with which an object is drawn up out of the darkness into the light. The letter Tzaddi is indicative of that force within man which, when awakened, enables him to exchange darkness for light and error for truth. This does not mean that the darkness must be assailed but that it must be filled with light, which is the real formula of transmutation. Transmutation is the high peak of the Initiate life, where he learns to *become the light* which makes darkness impossible. The Initiate has the power to lift the life force and convert it into light force, thus greatly enhancing his inner spiritual power. An ancient Wise One said that in the blending of light and darkness is constituted the supreme mystery of all mysteries, but the secret of that blending is that Light is the sole reality.

## ARCANE XIX

QUOPH or KOPH    Q = 100

Verses 145 – 152

*I cried with my whole heart; hear me, O Lord: I will keep thy statutes. I cried unto thee; save me, and I shall keep thy testimonies.*

*I prevented the dawning of the morning, and cried: I hoped in thy word. Mine eyes prevent the night watches, that I might meditate in thy word.*

*Hear my voice according to thy judgment. They draw nigh that follow after mischief: they are far from thy law.*

*Thou art near, O Lord; and all thy commandments are truth. Concerning thy testimonies, I have known of old that thou hast founded them for ever.*

The nineteenth letter of the Hebrew alphabet is Quoph, signifying the back of the head, the cerebellum or "feminine" brain, the medulla, where the keynote of the archetype is heard in sounding flame, the pons Varolii, the Tree of Life or Holy of Holies within the human skull.

Quoph or Koph is the higher octave of Kaph wherein the work of illumining this holy place is first begun. In Quoph the "Great White Work" is consummated. One who reaches this high place knows the truth of the statement, "Thou art near, O Lord, and all thy commandments are truth."

The nineteenth Tarot card has been called The House of the Sun, and these words well describe this Arcanum, for the Sun is its main feature, shedding its golden glory over the landscape. The two human figures are a youth and a maiden standing hand in hand, enclosed in a wreath of eternal green. This card depicts the Edenic realm, but here there is no sign of the Tree of Good and Evil or of the serpent. All dark shadows have disappeared, and peace, harmony and beauty reign in their stead.

Man lost the celestial realms through his own misdeeds. Now he is undergoing sorrow, pain and suffering in the long pilgrimage through materiality. The day will come, however, when he will be worthy once more to live in the celestial realms. This is God's divine plan for His earth children, and it will some day know a glorious consummation.

The youth and the maiden standing together hand in hand typify the union of the masculine and feminine poles within the human body. 1 + 9 = 10—which is the number of this perfect blending. 1 is masculine, O is feminine; their union forms the number 10, which means spiritual consummation. In the union of these two forces the love power of the awakened heart is united harmoniously with the Will power of the illumined mind in the Mystic Marriage Rite of all Temple teachings. The 10 x 10 or 100 of Quoph shows the power of ten raised to the cosmic level. The prayer for Quoph is the petition of those who are striving to know the glories of the Mystic Marriage Rite, "Thou art near, O Lord; and all thy commandments are truth. Concerning thy testimonies, I have known of old that thou hast founded them forever."

*Meditation for Koph (Quoph)*

The Wedding Song of Wisdom

Among the treasures of ancient Gnosis which have come down to modern times is a "wedding song of Wisdom" which illustrates most beautifully the meaning of Quoph and the nineteenth Tarot Arcanum.

*The Maiden is a daughter of the Light in whom is set*
*. . . . the radiance of the Kings;*
*And delightful is the sight of her shining with*
*luminous beauty,*
*Whose garments are like spring flowers, and from them*
*a breath of fragrance is wafted*

*While on her head the King is found feeding on His Nectar*
*there before Him.*
*Now Truth reposes on her head, while with her feet she*
*rays out joy;*
*Her mouth is gracefully open—thirty and two are those*
*who sing her praises.*
*Her tongue is like a curtain of the door which is shaken*
*for those who enter;*
*Her neck rises like a flight of stairs which the*
*First Creator has fashioned.*
*Now her two hands make signs and suggest that the*
*choir of the happy Aeons are preaching,*
*While her ten fingers suggest the gates of the City.*
*Her bridechamber is brightly lit, breathing an odor*
*of balsam and spice,*
*And giving out sweet scent of myrrh and foliage,*
*while myrtle branches are spread within*
*And heaps of sweet-breathed flowers; the folding-doors*
*are beautiful with reeds.*
*Her bridesmen have closely surrounded her, whose*
*number is seven, whom she herself selected;*
*While her bridesmaids too are seven, who lead the dance*
*before her.*
*But twelve is the number of those who serve before her*
*and under her have watch and gaze on the*
*Bridegroom,*
*That at the sight of Him they may be filled with light,*
*And forevermore they will be with Him for that eternal*
*joy;*
*And they shall remain in that Wedding whereto the*
*Nobles are gathered together,*
*And stay in the Feast whereof the Eternals are held worthy;*
*And they shall be clad in Royal Robes of Light, and*
*in both joy and ecstasy.*
*Then they shall glorify the universal Father whose*
*superabundant Light they have received,*
*For they have been filled with Light at the very sight*

*of their Master,*
*Whose Nectar they have obtained which has no waste at all,*
*And they have also drunk of the Wine that gives*
*them no thirst and bodily desire.*
*And so they glorified and hymned, together with*
*the Living Spirit,*
*The Father of the Truth and the Mother of the Wisdom.*

–*Gnostic Hymn* in "The Gospel of the Gnostics," *Duncan Greenlees.* *

The words of this hymn reveal that it was both sung and danced. The dancer, and the chorus of dancers attending her, "dance out the Mystery," to use the ancient term. Singers chant the narrative and text, the dancers with mime and gesture illustrate the meaning. Musicians accompany the singers and dancers. The dance portrays the descent of the soul into the outer universe, and its ascension therefrom, led by the Light of Wisdom. "Her two hands make signs" to show that "the happy Aeons (Hierarchies) are preaching." "Her ten fingers" show that the Gates of the Heavenly City are raised up so that the glorified soul, the King, may come in. Within the City is the palace and the bridal chamber brightly lighted, odorous with the incense of sacred branches from the Tree of Life, gay with the beauty and sweet with the perfume of celestial flowers. The Bridegroom is God or the Cosmic Christ.

## ARCANE XX

RESH R = 200

Verses 153 – 160

*Consider mine affliction, and deliver me: for I do not forget thy law. Plead my cause, and deliver me: quicken me according to thy word.*

*Salvation is far from the wicked: for they seek not thy statutes. Great are thy tender mercies, O Lord: quicken me according to thy judgments.*

*Many are my persecutors and mine enemies; yet do I not decline from thy testimonies. I beheld the transgressors and was grieved; because they kept not thy word.*

*Consider how I love thy precepts: quicken me, O Lord, according to thy loving kindness. Thy word is true from the beginning: and every one of thy righteous judgments endureth forever.*

*Twenty* is a number of power. It is formed of two cycles of 10, the first meaning successful accomplishment upon a high plane of attainment and the second cycle meaning successful accomplishment upon a still higher plane. 20 is a feminine number, both 2 and 0 are feminine, and 200 implies that power, mysticism and beauty which is contained in the High Feminine.

The Hebrew letter Resh also denotes great power. It represents Freedom, Independence, Originality and Intuitiveness, in fact, all the characteristics of the New Aquarian Age toward which its powers tend.

The twentieth Tarot Arcanum depicts, as previously observed a mighty Angel hovering above the earth, his magnificent aura extending in all directions about him. When he blows a mighty blast upon his trumpet a grave opens on the earth, and from it arise a man, a woman and a child. The Angel is Gabriel, who blows the trumpet of the Resurrection.

For the occultist this Arcanum holds a profound significance, far other than the superficial reading of its outer symbolism.

In one of the Tarot series number 20 is represented by a man, a woman and a child standing knee-deep in a stream of running water. This typifies cleansing, purifying, renewal and regeneration, the spiritual Baptism.

Saturn is the planet most closely related to this Arcanum. So long as man lives for material things alone, Saturn is his sternest and ofttimes his most cruel taskmaster. But when one enters upon the initiatory path, Saturn is transformed into his wisest Counsellor and most loving Guardian.

Initiation has always been the foundation-stone of Temple teachings, both ancient and modern; and the processes by which the candidate is initiated have not been too different. In ancient times the body of the candidate was put to rest in an open crypt or casket and left in charge of two guardians, usually a man and a woman who had been through a similar experience. Then under the care of a competent Teacher the spirit of the candidate was taken into the inner realms, and at sunrise on the morning of the third day he returned to his body, where he was greeted with much rejoicing as the "New-Born." For this reason the candidate in this Arcanum is represented as a child. "You must be born again (become as a little child) before you can enter the Kingdom of Heaven," said the Christ.

Singularly beautiful is the account in the Torah of the passing of Moses at the end of his mission to the people of Israel, "One Angel after another sought to take his life but in vain. First came the Angel who had been his instructor, but whose courage failed when he essayed to destroy the fabric on which he had spent so much time. Then came the Angel of Death. He approached eagerly, but when he saw the wonderful luster of that face shining like the sun, he, too, shrank back, abashed. At last came Jehovah Himself, and in one long and tender kiss He drew away the soul of His faithful disciple. Michael, Gabriel and all the heavenly host assembled in rejoicing to welcome this exalted spirit into the heaven worlds." Thus was described the initiatory passing of Moses.

The kabbalists said that Moses was reborn as Elijah. The ascension of Elijah in the fiery chariot represents the highest phase of the Fire Initiation as known in the Old Testament Dispensation. It represents mastery over death. However, it does not mean that the imperfect body into which each soul is born will be rendered immortal and deathless but that the interval stretching between the death of this body and the soul's awakening into a new and larger life will be spanned by the fully awake Initiate consciousness and that this consciousness will extend into the succeeding incarnation. This attainment is the high spiritual meaning of the Fire Initiation in ancient times and for the majority of disciples today. The New Testament equivalent is the blessing of St. John by the Christ. Jesus saith unto him, "If I will that he tarry till I come, what is that to thee? Follow thou me." Occult tradition has long held that St. John is the Initiate name of Lazarus.

The processes of death are processes of crystallization. The fiery life force which keeps the atoms of the body tingling with life is withdrawn little by little, or suddenly, as the case may be. The increasingly inert atoms then gradually separate from one another, and the body disintegrates in chemical processes. The life forces are of the Spirit in man, and every sensitive has felt that the atoms of his body are accelerated when he passes through an exalting spiritual experience, which tends to lift the consciousness far above and beyond the ordinary daily living. It was in this exaltation of consciousness that St. John lived, hence it was that his vibratory rhythm was so high that death was powerless to touch him. This is the glorious ideal set before all mankind, and it is the meaning of St. Paul's statement, "The last enemy to be overcome is death."

Our Blessed Lord the Christ, Way shower for all mankind, has outlined for us the process by which death may be transformed into Eternal Life.

On that first Easter morning when the disciples approached the empty tomb they were met by angels who said, "He is not here, He has risen."

Again we read in Revelation 20:6, "Blessed and holy is he that hath part in the first resurrection; on such the second death hath no power, but they shall be priests of God and of Christ, and shall reign with him a thousand years."

The spirit of this most wonderful twentieth Arcanum may be summed up in the words, "Mortality has been swallowed up in Immortality."

The prayer of Resh is the petition of those who are endeavoring to learn by means of the expansion of consciousness to build the bridge between Waking and Sleeping and between Life and Death.

"Great are thy tender mercies, O Lord; quicken me according to thy precepts: quicken me, O Lord, according to thy loving-kindness. Thy word is true from the beginning: and every one of thy righteous judgments endureth forever."

*Meditation for Resh*

The letter R or Resh refers to the process of Transmutation. We noted in the study of the letter Yod the beginning of the process, and in the letter Resh we may observe its consummation. The last enemy to be overcome is death. The time will come when all mankind will know from actual firsthand knowledge that there is no death and that life is continuous and eternal, for the darkness of death will have been transmuted into Light Eternal.

In this high state of consciousness the Resurrection will become a Cosmic Event, and the entire earth will be filled with the triumphant chorale of the Angels as they sing of the glories of Eternal Life.

*I AM Aleph and Tau.*
*I AM Alpha and Omega.*
*I AM the Beginning and the End, for I AM Life Eternal.*

## ARCANE XXI

SCHIN    S = 300

Verses 161 – 168

*Princes have persecuted me without a cause: but my heart standeth in awe of thy word. I rejoice at thy word, as one that findeth great spoil.*

*I hate and abhor lying: but thy law do I love. Seven times a day do I praise thee because of thy righteous judgments. Great peace have they which love thy law: and nothing shall offend them.*

*Lord, I have hoped for thy salvation, and done thy commandments. My soul hath kept thy testimonies; and I love them exceedingly. I have kept thy precepts and thy testimonies: for all my ways are before thee.*

The number 21 is formed of three cycles of seven, which typifies successful accomplishment on all three planes of manifestation – physical, mental and spiritual.

It is also a divine number because it equals 3 in the esoteric code (2+1), the number of the Trinity. It is the threefold God-power which manifests as the Father or Divine Will-principle, the Son or Cosmic Love principle, and the Holy Ghost or spiritualized Activity principle, through which all creation on this earth takes place. By means of this threefold God-power all creation is formed through Love and sustained by Love, for God is Love. Hence it is that all creation in its original concept is perfect. Both the Bible and the Tarot verify this Truth. "And God saw what He had made and pronounced it Good."

The twenty-first Arcanum is termed "The World." Here is shown a young girl kneeling in adoration as she plays upon a three-stringed harp. Above her head is a wreath formed of twelve stalks of Lotus blossoms, each stalk bearing three blossoms, full-blown. These twelve flower-stalks symbolize the twelve zodiacal Hierarchies which surround this solar system and supervise its working. The three blossoms on each stalk and the three-stringed harp typify the perfect functioning of the threefold body, physical, mental and spiritual, of the coming Sixth Root Race – for which this beautiful New World will be the home.

St. John saw the vision of this new World and its glorified inhabitants, which he described in the Book of Revelation, saying, "I saw a new Heaven and a new Earth coming down like a bride adorned for her bridegroom."

The young maiden playing the harp indicates the marked importance of music in the life of the New World. Every human body has its archetype or pattern that emits a musical keynote which sustains the body. This keynote sounds continually from the moment of birth to the time when the heart is stilled in death.

Every great tree in the forest is also continually sounding its own keynote – every flower that blows in the wind; every star that shines in the heavens has its musical tone. Birds in the forest often catch echoes of this sublime music in their enchanting songs, but with rare exceptions the earth-dulled ears of mankind cannot hear the heavenly melodies.

We are told that in the second heaven the glorious music is a source of amazement and delight, for in this realm one literally lives, moves and has his being in music. Even the very means of communication of one with another is through melody. Much of the miracle-life contained in archetypal music will be transplanted into the lives of the Sixth Root Race in the New World which they will inhabit.

In the four corners of the twenty-first Arcanum are placed the four beasts of the Ezekiel vision – the Bull (Taurus), the Eagle (Scorpio), the Man (Aquarius) and the Lion (Leo), which we also saw on the tenth Tarot card. There we beheld the Hierarchies of Taurus and Scorpio holding the whiplash of dire necessity over man and nations until the last karmic debt has been paid with Aquarius and Leo holding forth the beautiful ideals of the incoming Aquarian Age.

Now, however, in this new World of the twenty-first Arcanum all karmic debts have been paid, and peace, harmony and beauty reign supreme. The Hierarchy of Taurus holds the cosmic pattern of form for all the earth, and under the supervision of its opposite sign, Scorpio, the Lords of Form, all forms upon the earth are builded. Under Aquarius each man will meet every other man as his brother, and under Leo all Law will be motivated by Love. Every thought, word and deed will be centered in Love, which, as St. Paul states, is truly the greatest virtue of them all.

In the second septenary we noted the number 14 in which preparatory work was begun for the building of the New Age body. This work was tremendously increased in the seventeenth Arcanum and was brought to high degree of perfection in the nineteenth.

In the eighteenth Arcanum man passed his last subtle testing and proved his worthiness to enter into and inhabit the New World of Arcanum Twenty-One.

The first three cards of the Tarot and the Book of Genesis describe early man as being made in the image and likeness of God. The Book of Revelation and the last three cards in the Tarot series – 19, 20, 21 – depict the new, regenerated and redeemed race who are worthy to return again to the Father's House.

Sometimes the four Hebrew letters Yod, He, Vav, He which take the place of the sacred unpronounceable Name, are included beside the four Sacred Beasts, for they imply the Name of One who was, who is and who ever shall be.

Papus, the French Tarot scholar, puts it admirably in stating that the first septenary, the Absolute, manifests through God. In the second, the Absolute, manifests through man; in the third septenary the Absolute manifests through the universe.

The prayer of the 119th Psalm for Schin is the supplication of those Illumined Ones who are learning to "walk in the Light as He is in the Light." "My heart standeth in awe of thy word. I rejoice at thy word as one that findeth great spoil. Seven times a day do I praise thee because of thy righteous judgments. Great peace have they who love thy law, and nothing shall offend thee. My soul hath kept thy testimonies, and I love them exceedingly."

*Meditation for Schin*

Schin, S or SH, as the twenty-first letter of the Hebrew alphabet concludes the septenaries. It represents the highest stage of regeneration, lifting to cosmic consciousness. We know that every human spirit sounds forth its own unique keynote and that this keynote sustains life in the threefold body which we call the personality (physical, astral and mental) and brings them into attunement with itself.

This is true also of the planets belonging to our solar system, each of which has its own keynote. The keynote of the planet Earth sustains the physical globe and its permeating envelopes of etheric, astral and mental stuff, together with all that lives upon it and within its spiritual atmosphere, attuning all with God.

The musical note of our planet sounds in the keynote of the threefold song which the Angels sang on the first Christmas night:

*Glory to God in the highest,*
*Peace on Earth,*
*Good Will to men.*

## Chapter XX

## THE TWENTY-SECOND LETTER, TAU

Verses 169 – 176

## ARCANE XXII

TAU or TAV    T = 400

Verses 169 – 176

*Let my cry come near before thee, O Lord: give me understanding according to thy word. Let my supplication come before thee: deliver me according to thy word.*

*My lips shall utter praise, when thou hast taught me thy statutes. My tongue shall speak of thy word: for all thy commandments are righteous.*

*Let thine hand help me: for I have chosen thy precepts. I have longed for thy salvation, O Lord: and thy law is my delight. Let my soul live, and it shall praise thee: and let thy judgments help me.*

*I have gone astray like a lost sheep; seek thy servant: for I do not forget thy commandments.*

Once more we have arrived at the end of our pilgrimage, at the foot of the cross which is the letter Tau, or T in the Greek alphabet. From the twenty-second Psalm come the words which the Christ spoke on the Cross. The concluding verse of the 119th Psalm also sounds the key phrase of the Crucifixion and the Cross.

"I have gone astray like a lost sheep . . . I have longed for thy salvation. Let my cry come before thee."

In Christian esotericism the Path of Initiation is called the Way of the Cross. It has a meaning which is close to that of

Lamed, the Hanged Man, yet there are differences. Lamed hangs head downward. Tau is the elevated cross upon which the Just Man is raised aloft. "If I be lifted up, I will draw all men unto me."

The Hanged Man of Lamed is also the symbol of the holy martyr, personified in the New Testament record in St. Peter, who was crucified head downward at his own request. There is an ancient teaching that God will accept the martyrdom of certain holy ones in order that a remnant may escape the retribution demanded by cosmic law. Moses was not willing that even one of his Israelites should be blotted from the book of life and offered himself to die in their place, even though he knew that they had been disobedient and faithless. This is the doctrine of the Faithful Shepherd, most beautifully fulfilled in the Birth, Crucifixion and Resurrection of our Lord Christ Jesus.

Whether in the fashion of Lamed with head downward, the martyr with calm visage whose blood drops like gold upon the earth, or the fashion of the cross elevated on Golgotha where the Son of God is raised against the sky for all men to behold, the Cruicufixion represents the ultimate and complete self-conquest – not defeat, but victory!

The final Tarot Arcanum holds a similar symbolism, though it is not on the surface. This Arcanum is The Fool, or The Divine Idiot. It has several meanings. Here we see the blind or the blindfolded youth walking unconcernedly toweard a precipice, where a crocodile waits to devour him; a dog barks at his heels, whether in play or warning connot be immediately discerned. It may typify the uncontrolled animal nature. An obelisk covered with mysterious hieraglyphs lies at his feet, but he cannot see it. A bag is flung across his shoulder in which he carries all his earthly possessions. These treasures will become heavier and heavier as he proceeds on his way, weighting him down.

This, however, does not mean that his name is blotted from the Book of Life, for every man is God's child, and God is Love; and when at last he calls upon his Father, like the Prodigal Son, an Angel of Mercy is at hand instantly to aid him in the struggle toward regeneration.

The number 22 is a Master Number, and miracles may be accomplished through its power. For this reason we hold that the twenty-second Tarot is rightly considered the culmination of the series and is not an un-numbered card as some kabbalists say. The Tarot ascribed to Ayin or Oin is likewise taken to be important in the spiritual series and is not a mere zero, except as the zero is ascribed to the deepest mysteries of the Absolute.

The prayer for Tau is the petition of those who know the meaning of bearing the Cross and who have learned to bear it alone, and who dedicate themselves to the ministry of crossbearers.

"Let my cry come near before thee, O Lord: give me understanding according to thy word . . . Deliver me according to thy word. Let my soul live and it shall praise thee, and let thy judgments help me. I have gone astray like a lost sheep; seek thy servant, for I do not forget thy commandments."

### *Meditation for Tau*

T, Tau or Tav is the final letter of the Hebrew alphabet; hence, Consummation. But every end of a cycle begins a new cycle, and therefore it is New Beginnings.

In the sixth Tarot Arcanum the neophyte stood between two divergent paths. His decision there affects his entire destiny, for all lives to come. The path of carnal pleasure, flower-strewn as it may appear to be, leads inevitably to the cross of sorrow. The straight and narrow way, which has so formidable an aspect and seems well-nigh impossible of ascent, leads with equal inevitability to the high and holy joys of spiritual illumination at-one with God.

In the twenty-second Aracanum, The Fool, we see one who had chosen the path of the senses, of pleasure and frivolity, in terms of the carnal man. He has followed this path, and it has led him to the extreme verge of destruction. Yet in the heavens above him a bright sun is just emerging from eclipse, or is half-hidden by a cloud, suggesting that no man ever reaches the place where he cannot save himself from destruction by means of repentance, reform and restitution and thus exchange the Cross of Sorrow for the Crown of Life Everlasting.

## BIBLE and TAROT — INDEX


Adam Kadmon . . . . . . . . . . . . . . . . . . . . . . . . . . . . . . 10, 13
Aleph . . . . 5, 9, 12, 13, 28, 29, 42, 53, 54, 55, 78, 90, 114, 124, 132, 190, 193, 197
Allbright, Dr. William . . . . . . . . . . . . . . . . . . . . . . . . . 32
Angels . . . . . . . . . . . . . . . . . . . . . . . . . . . . . . . 29, 33
Anabita . . . . . . . . . . . . . . . . . . . . . . . . . . . . . . . . 20
Aniel . . . . . . . . . . . . . . . . . . . . . . . . . . . . . . . . . 38
Appollonius of Tyana . . . . . . . . . . . . . . . . . . . . . . . . 96
Aquarius . . . .12, 30, 60, 95, 103, 151, 153, 158, 167, 168, 201, 209, 218, 224, 244, 253, 258, 259

Arcana or Tarot System
- Alpha I — The Magus . . . . . . . . . . . . . . . . . . 53, 132, 197
- Beth II — The High Priestess . . . . . . . . . . . . . . 56, 134, 198
- Gimel III — The Isis—Urania . . . . . . . . . . . . . . 58, 136, 200
- Daleth IV — The Cubic Stone . . . . . . . . . . . . . . 61, 138, 202
- He V — The Master of the Arcanes . . . . . . . . . . 62, 140, 203
- Vau VI — The Two Ways . . . . . . . . . . . . . . . . . 64, 141, 205
- Zain VII — The Chariot of Osiris . . . . . . . . . . . . 66, 142, 208
- Cheth VIII — The Balance and the Sword . . . . . . 69, 145, 211
- Teth IX — The Veiled Lamp . . . . . . . . . . . . . . . 71, 148, 214
- Yod X — The Sphinx . . . . . . . . . . . . . . . . . . . 77, 150, 217
- Kaph XI — The Maiden and the Lion . . . . . . . . . 81, 153, 220
- Lamed XII — The Sacrifice . . . . . . . . . . . . . . . 83, 155, 223
- Mem XIII — The Reaping Skeleton . . . . . . . . . . 85, 157, 226
- Nun XIV — The Two Urns . . . . . . . . . . . . . . . . 86, 158, 229
- Samekh XV — Typhon . . . . . . . . . . . . . . . . . . 89, 161, 233
- Ayin XVI — The Thunderstruck Tower . . . . . . . 91, 163, 237
- Phe XVII — The Star of the Magi . . . . . . . . . . . 92, 166, 241
- Tzaddi XVIII — The Twilight . . . . . . . . . . . . . . 94, 167, 245
- Koph XIX — The Dazzling Light . . . . . . . . . . . . 96, 168, 249
- Resch XX — The Rising of the Dead . . . . . . . . 101, 169, 253
- Schin XXI — The Crown of the Magi . . . . . . . . 102, 170, 257
- Tav XXII — The Fool . . . . . . . . . . . . . . . . . . 105, 173, 261

Archangels or Sephiroth . . . . . . . . .19, 21, 24, 25, 36, 37, 164
Ithuriel . . . . . . . . . . . . . . . . . . . . . . . . . . . . . 39
Michael . . . . . . . . . . . . . . . . . . . . . . . . 34, 36, 77
Sandalphon . . . . . . . . . . . . . . . . . . . . . . . . . . 28
Zechariel . . . . . . . . . . . . . . . . . . . . . . . . . . . 211
Aries . . . . . . . . . . . . . . . . . 12, 30, 63, 74, 110, 230, 242
Ark . . . . . . . . . . . . . . . . . . . . . . . . . . . . . . . . . 25
Askew, Dr. . . . . . . . . . . . . . . . . . . . . . . . . . . . . 128
Assiah . . . . . . . . . . . . . . . . . . . . . . . . . . . . . 17, 93
Atlantis . . . . . . . . . . . . . . . . . . . . . . . . 10, 204, 205
Atziluth . . . . . . . . . . . . . . . . . . . . . . . . . . . . 17, 93
Ayin . . . . . . . . . . . . . . . 5, 12, 13, 91, 122, 192, 194, 237
Babylon . . . . . . . . . . . . . . . . . . . . . . . . . . . . . . . . 3
Beth . . . . . 5, 11, 28, 29, 56, 57, 58, 81, 92, 124, 191, 193, 198
Binah . . . . . . . . . . . . . . . . . . . . . . . . . . . . . 28, 131
Boaz . . . . . . . . . . . . . . . . . . . . See Jachin and Boaz
Briah . . . . . . . . . . . . . . . . . . . . . . . . . . . . . 17, 93
Bruce . . . . . . . . . . . . . . . . . . . . . . . . . . . . . . . 128
Cadmus . . . . . . . . . . . . . . . . . . . . . . 15, 73, 105, 106
Caduceus . . . . . . . . . . . . . . . . . . . . . . . . . . . 19, 111
Cagliostro . . . . . . . . . . . . . . . . . . . . . . . . . . . . 129
Cancer . . . . . . . . . . . . . . . . . . . . . . . . . . 12, 30, 69
Caph . . . . . . . . . . . . . . . . . . . . . . . . . . . See Kaph
Capricorn . . . . . . . . . . . . . . . . . . . . . . . . . 12, 30, 92
Champollion . . . . . . . . . . . . . . . . . . . . . . . . . . . 129
Chariot of Fire . . . . . . . . . . . . . . . . . . . . . . . . 25, 44
Cheth or Heth . . . . . . . . . . . . . 5, 12, 69, 70, 71, 191, 193, 211
Chockmah or Hokmah . . . . . . . . . . . . . . . . . . . . 28, 131
Color . . . . . . . . . . . . . . . . . . . . . . . . . . . . . . 7, 8, 9
Daath . . . . . . . . . . . . . . . . . . . . . . . . . 16, 21, 28, 30
Daleth . . . . . . . . . . . 5, 11, 61, 62, 69, 92, 124, 191, 193, 202
Demetrius . . . . . . . . . . . . . . . . . . . . . . . . . . . . . . . 9
Double Letters . . . . . . . . . . . . . .5, 11, 30, 81, 92, 102, 105
Druid . . . . . . . . . . . . . . . . . . . . . . . . . . . . . 2, 131
Eleusinian Mysteries . . . . . . . . . . . . . . . . . . . . . . . 189
Essenes . . . . . . . . . . . . . . . . . . . . . . . . . . 27, 38, 39
Evolution . . . . . . . . . . . . . . . . . . . . . . . . . . . . . . . 54

Ezra . . . . . . . . . . . . . . . . . . . . . . . . . . . . . . 41, 45
Final Letters . . . . . . . . . . . . . . . . . . . . . . . . . . . 92, 195
Freemasonry . . . . . . . . . . . . . . . . . . . . . . . . See Masonry
Gabriel . . . . . . . . . . . . . . . . . . . 15, 37, 39, 169, 253, 254
de Gebelin, Count . . . . . . . . . . . . . . . . . . . . . . . . . 127
Gemini . . . . . . . . . . . . . . . . . . . 12, 30, 67, 97, 153, 230
St. Germain, Count . . . . . . . . . . . . . . . . . . . . . .129, 150
Gimel . . . . 5, 11, 28, 29, 58, 59, 60, 72, 92, 124, 191, 193, 200
Ginsberg, Christian . . . . . . . . . . . . . . . . . . . . . . . . 190
Gnostics . . . . . . . . . . . . . . . . . . . . . . . . . . . . . . . .83
Gnostic Hymn . . . . . . . . . . . . . . . . . . . . . . . . . . . 250
Greenlees, Duncan . . . . . . . . . . . . . . . . . . . . 250—252
Haniel . . . . . . . . . . . . . . . . . . . . . . . . . . . . . . . . .38
He . . . . . . 5, 12, 24, 62, 63, 64, 136, 137, 191, 193, 203, 259
Heindel, Max . . . . . . . . . . . . . 6, 29, 33, 74, 76, 84, 129, 238
Hermit . . . . . . . . . . . . . . . . . . . . . . . . . . . . . .148, 197
Hermes . . . . . . . . . . . . . . . . . . . . . . . . . . See Mercury
Heth . . . . . . . . . . . . . . . . . . . . . . . . . . . . . See Cheth
Hierophants . . . . . . . . . . . . . . . . . . . . . . . . . . . . . .54
Hiram Abiff . . . . . . . . . . . . 22, 24, 74, 75, 90, 106, 109, 113
Hokmah . . . . . . . . . . . . . . . . . . . . . . . . . .See Chockmah
Involution . . . . . . . . . . . . . . . . . . . . . . . . . . . . . . .54
Ishim . . . . . . . . . . . . . . . . . . . . . . . . . . . . . . . . .17
Isis . . . . . . . . . .58, 73, 79, 108, 111, 112, 134, 140, 204, 231
Ituriel . . . . . . . . . . . . . . . . . . . . . . . . . . . . . . . .39
Jachin and Boaz . . . . . . . . . . . . . . . . . . . 24, 70, 82, 199
Jochai . . . . . . . . . . . . . . . . . . . . See Simeon ben Jochai
Jod . . . . . . . . . . . . . . . . . . . . . . . . . . . . . . . See Yod
Jubilees, Book of . . . . . . . . . . . . . . . . . . . . . . . . . . .29
Jupiter . . . . . . . . . . . . . . . . . . . . . . . . . 28, 30, 37, 38
Kabbalah . . . . 12, 14—22, 25, 26, 28, 29, 33, 34, 35, 40, 42, 46, 65, 67, 79, 83, 89, 116, 117, 118, 129, 136, 149, 186, 188 189, 195, 196, 255
Kadmus . . . . . . . . . . . . . . . . . . . . . . . . . . .See Cadmus
Kaph . . . . .3, 5, 11, 81, 82, 83, 92, 101, 116, 122, 191, 193, 220
Kassiel . . . . . . . . . . . . . . . . . . . . . . . . . . . . . . . . .38
Kether . . . . . . . . . . . . . . . . . . . . . 22, 23, 27, 28, 29, 42

Koph . . . . . . . . . . . . . . . . . . . . . . . . . . . . See Quoph
Lamed . . . . . . . . . . . . . . . . 5, 12, 83, 84, 191, 193, 223, 262
Lazarus . . . . . . . . . . . . . . . . 24, 32, 76, 106, 112, 148, 255
Leo . . . . . . 3, 12, 30, 74, 97, 103, 110, 151, 153, 218, 258, 259
de Leon, Moses . . . . . . . . . . . . . .43, 44, 119, 127, 186, 187
Levi, Eliphas . . . . . . . . . . . . . . . . . . . . . . . . . .127, 223
Libra . . . . . . . . . . . . . . . . . . . . . . . . . . . . . .12, 30, 83
Life Spirit . . . . . . . . . . . . . . . . . . . . . . . . . . . . . . .56
Lucifer . . . . . . . . . . . . . . . . . . . . . . . . . . . . . 62, 162
Lucian . . . . . . . . . . . . . . . . . . . . . . . . . . . . .106, 120
Macrobius . . . . . . . . . . . . . . . . . . . . . . . . . . . . . 189
Maimonides . . . . . . . . . . . . . . . . . . . . . . . . . 34, 46, 127
Malkuth . . . . . . . . . . . . . . . . . . . . . . . . . . . .27, 28, 80
Mars . . . . . . . . . . . . . . . . . . . . . . . . .28, 30, 37, 92, 113
Masonry . . . . .5, 22, 23, 46, 58, 60, 72, 73, 74, 75, 76, 90, 106,
112, 113, 117, 128, 129, 138, 199, 202, 221, 247
Masoretes . . . . . . . . . . . . . . . . . . . . . . . . . . . . . 43, 46
Melchizedek . . . . . . . . . . . . . . . . . . . . . . . . 77, 109, 204
Mem . . . . . . . . . .5, 12, 30, 54, 85, 92, 116, 122, 192, 193, 226
Mercury . . . . . . . . . 19, 28, 30, 37, 39, 58, 60, 72, 76, 111, 206
Metatron . . . . . . . . . . . . . . . . . . . . . . . . . 17, 19, 29, 34
Michael . . . . . . . . . . . . . . . . . .15, 29, 34, 36, 39, 77, 254
Mocha, Rabbi . . . . . . . . . . . . . . . . . . . . . . . . . . . 42, 43
Moon . . . . . . . . . . . . . . . .28, 30, 37, 58, 86, 87, 99, 111, 112
Mother Letters . . . . . . . . . . . 5, 12, 28, 54, 85, 102, 115, 226
Music . . . . . . . . . . . . . . . . . . . . . . . . . . . . . . . . . . .7
Mystic Marriage . . . . . . . . . . . . 64, 97, 98, 99, 187, 232, 250
Neptune . . . . . . . . . . . . . . . . . . . . . . . . . . . . . . . .39
Nun . . . . . . 5, 12, 86, 87, 88, 92, 116, 121, 122, 192, 194, 229
Oin . . . . . . . . . . . . . . . . . . . . . . . . . . . . . . .See Ayin
Origen . . . . . . . . . . . . . . . . . . . . . . . . . . . . . . . . 130
Osiris . . . . 12, 64, 72, 73, 76, 94, 108, 110, 111, 112, 113, 142,
208, 231
Oxenham, John . . . . . . . . . . . . . . . . . . . . . . . . . . . . .66
Papus . . . . . . . . . . . . . . . . . . . . . . . . . . . . . .217, 259
Paracelsus . . . . . . . . . . . . . . . . . . . . . . . . . . . . . . .85
Parsifal . . . . . . . . . . . . . . . . . . . . . . . . . . . . . . . 207

Pascal . . . . . . . . . . . . . . . . . . . . . . . . . . . . . 218
Paths . . . . . . . . . . . . . . . . . . . . . . . . . . . . . . 28
Phe or Pe . . . . . . . . . . . 5, 11, 92, 93, 116, 121, 192, 194, 241
Philo Judeus . . . . . . . . . . . . . . . . . . . . . 17, 29, 32, 47
Phoenician . . . . . . . . . . . . . . . . . . . . . . . . . . . 14
Pisces . . . . . . . . . . . . . 12, 30, 95, 96, 162, 186, 232, 242
Pistis Sophia . . . . . . . . . . . . . . . . . . . . . . . 127, 128
Pluto . . . . . . . . . . . . . . . . . . . . . . . . . . . . . . 39
Pythogorus . . . . . . . . . . . . . . . . . 2, 3, 85, 107, 117, 189
Quoph . . . . . . . 5, 12, 96, 97, 101, 117, 121, 122, 192, 194, 249
Rab Hammuna . . . . . . . . . . . . . . . . . . . . . . . . . 120
Raphael . . . . . . . . . . . . . . . . . . . . . . . . . . . . 37
Recording Angels . . . . . . . . . . . . . . . . . . 103, 170, 258
Resh . . . . . . . . . . . 5, 11, 92, 101, 102, 117, 121, 192, 194, 253
Rosenkreutz, Christian . . . . . . . . . . . . . . . . . . . . 186
Rosicrucian . . . . . . . . . . . 84, 128, 129, 148, 186, 238, 243
Sacrum . . . . . . . . . . . . . . . . . . . . . . . . . . . . . 12
Sagittarius . . . . . . . . . . . . . . . . . . 12, 30, 89, 110, 233
Samael . . . . . . . . . . . . . . . . . . . . . . . . . . . 29, 37
Samekh . . . . . . . . . . . 5, 12, 89, 90, 103, 111, 192, 194, 233
Sandalphon . . . . . . . . . . . . . . . . . . . . . . . . . 27, 28
Satanael . . . . . . . . . . . . . . . . . . . . . . . . . . 29, 167
Saturn . . . . . . . . . . . . . . . . . . . . . . 28, 30, 38, 83, 254
Schin . . . . 5, 12, 30, 54, 94, 100, 102, 103, 104, 111, 117, 121, 192, 194, 257
Scorpio . . . . . . . . . . . . . . 12, 30, 87, 103, 212, 246, 258, 259
Secret Doctrine . . . . . . . . . . . . . . . . . . . . . . . . 210
Sepher Yetsirah . . . . . . . . . . . . . . . . 11, 29, 47, 243, 245
Sephiroth or Archangels . . . . . 16, 22, 28, 29, 30, 36, 41, 44, 56, 72, 92, 131, 187, 201
Shekinah Glory . . . . . . . . . . . . . 8, 9, 79, 112, 135, 204, 205
Simeon ben Jochai . . . . . . . . . . . . . . . . . 25, 29, 44, 45, 47
Solar Logos . . . . . . . . . . . . . . . . . . . . . . . . . . . 6
Sun . . . . . . . . . . . . . . . . . 6, 28, 30, 36, 99, 102, 112, 207
Tarot . . . . . . . . . . . . . . . . . 127, 129, 145, 157, 174, 239
Tau . . . . 4, 5, 11, 15, 68, 94, 100, 105, 112, 113, 115, 117, 120, 192, 194, 261

Taurus . . . . . . . . . . . . . . . . . . . . . 12, 30, 65, 103, 230, 258, 259
Tav . . . . . . . . . . . . . . . . . . . . . . . . . . . . . . . . . See Tau
Tennyson . . . . . . . . . . . . . . . . . . . . . . . . . . . . . 87, 95
Teth . . 5, 12, 71, 72, 73, 74, 75, 76, 77, 94, 105, 111, 123, 191, 193, 214
Tetragrammation . . . . . 9, 24, 31, 32, 33, 34, 62, 65, 73, 78, 114, 136, 204, 206, 259
Theo—Sophia . . . . . . . . . . . . . . . . . . . . . . . . . . . 204
Thoth—Hermes . . . . . . . . . . . . . . . . . . 2, 38, 72, 111, 213
Torah . . . . . . . . . . . . . . . . . . . . . . . . . . . . . . . . 254
Tree of Life . . . . . . . . . . . . . . . . . . . . . . . . . 18, 20, 26
Troward . . . . . . . . . . . . . . . . . . . . . . . . . . . . . . 239
Tzaddi . . . . . . . . . . . 5, 12, 92, 94, 95, 116, 121, 192, 194, 245
Tzadkiel . . . . . . . . . . . . . . . . . . . . . . . . . . . . . . . 37
Uranus . . . . . . . . . . . . . . . . . . . . . . . . . . . . . 39, 201
Uriel . . . . . . . . . . . . . . . . . . . . . . . . . . . . . . . . . . 38
Vau . . . 5, 12, 24, 40, 64, 65, 123, 136, 137, 191, 193, 205, 259
Venus . . . . . . . . . . . . 28, 30, 38, 112, 136, 141, 167, 201, 243
Virgin Spirit . . . . . . . . . . . . . . . . 54, 70, 104, 149, 151, 210
Virgo . . . . . . . . . . . . . . . . . . . . . . 3, 12, 30, 78, 153, 154
Vowels . . . . . . . . . . . . . . . . . . . . . 7, 9, 10, 13, 28, 42, 53
Waite, A.E. . . . . . . . . . . . . . . . . . . . . 127, 130, 131, 150
Yetsirah . . . . . . . . . . . . . . . . . . . . . . 17, 29, 47, 93, 243
Yod . . . . . 5, 12, 22, 24, 28, 32, 40, 41, 54, 77, 78, 79, 80, 100, 121, 123, 137, 191, 193, 217, 256, 259
Yohai, Simon ben . . . . . . . . . . . . . . . . . . . . . . . . . 187
Young, Thomas . . . . . . . . . . . . . . . . . . . . . . . . . . . 129
Zachariel . . . . . . . . . . . . . . . . . . . . . . . . . . . . . . . 37
Zain . . . . . . . . . . . . . . . 5, 12, 66, 67, 68, 123, 191, 193, 208
Zerubbabel . . . . . . . . . . . . . . . . . . . . . . . . . . . . . . 22
Zohar . . . . . 7, 8, 10, 12, 19, 40, 43, 44, 45, 53, 57, 59, 99, 101, 107, 119, 186, 188, 205
Zoroaster . . . . . . . . . . . . . . . . . . . . . . . . . . . . . . 247